W9-AOU-303

You Can't Plant Tomatoes In Central Park

YOU CAN'T PLANT TOMATOES IN CENTRAL PARK

The Urban Dropout's Guide to Rural Relocation

Frank Ruegg and
Paul Bianchina

NEW HORIZON PRESS
Far Hills, New Jersey

Copyright © 1990 by Frank Ruegg and Paul Bianchina

All rights reserved. No part of this book may be reproduced or transmitted in any form whatsoever, including electronic, mechanical, or any information storage or retrieval system, except as may be expressly permitted by the 1976 Copyright Act or in writing from the publisher. Requests for permission should be addressed to New Horizon Press, P.O. Box 669, Far Hills, New Jersey 07931.

Library of Congress Cataloging Card Number: 90-53281

Frank Ruegg and Paul Bianchina
You Can't Plant Tomatoes in Central Park

ISBN: 0-88282-060-5
New Horizon Press

To Rose and Sarah, for their support;
To Sandy, for her faith;
and
To urban dropouts everywhere, for their belief in something better.

Acknowledgments

No book is ever written alone, and that is especially true for YOU CAN'T PLANT TOMATOES IN CENTRAL PARK.

We would like to extend our heartfelt thanks to all of the hundreds of urban dropouts that have eagerly shared their stories with us over the years, and to all the patient people, friends and strangers alike, who answered our surveys and fielded all of our questions.

We also extend our gratitude to Rose Bianchina, for many hours of typing, editing, proofreading, and just plain listening, as well as for her many valuable suggestions.

One person stands out above all the rest in helping to make this book a reality—our agent, Sandy Watt. We thank her for believing in this project, for sharing our vision, for never losing hope, for offering suggestion after suggestion, and for two years of patient persistence.

Contents

Unless we take a chance or two in order to begin,
There's nothing we can hope to gain, no prize that we
can win.

We must accept uncertainty, must set our doubts aside,
Be brave enough to risk a loss or setback to our pride.

We should not be afraid of change, nor be afraid to dare,
If we just take a chance, life holds rewards beyond compare.

—Author Unknown

Introduction

The sun was setting slowly over the Pacific, seemingly reluctant to leave the coastline behind in the wake of another warm California day. A profusion of reds and oranges overlapped each other in a mute competition to catch the attention of the millions of eyes below. The colors falsely intensified as they were diffused through the stubborn layer of noxious chemicals that hung over the horizon.

The scene was not lost on commuter Wayne C.. Traveling home, he watched it through the windshield of his Volvo as it crawled along the freeway, a seemingly slowly-moving parking lot. He ignored the distracting voices of the four other carpoolers, pressed tightly together on the car's expensive imported leather seats. He'd seen this early-evening show on hundreds of previous occasions. When he had first arrived in Los Angeles, it had held a special fascination for him. Now, ten years later, the ever-present sun was about the only thing remaining in Southern California that he liked about the area. But even that was rapidly losing its charm.

"Too much of anything can numb you to its pleasure after awhile," he reflected wryly. Wayne had had too much of a lot of things in his decade-long tenure as senior programmer at PacCal Computers. Too many people and too much continual contact with them had clouded his mind to their individuality. Too much crime served up in massive daily doses had dropped a veil of suspicion over everyone he met. He himself was a victim; his car had been stolen the previous month—although subsequently recovered. Too many hours of his life had been spent encapsulated in this expensive four-door prison during the ninety-minute drive to work in the morning and the two hour drive back home—a drive measured in inches rather than miles.

He left for work with the sun just a promise of the coming day, and arrived home with scarcely enough time for a good-night kiss from each of his children. He had missed three parent-teacher conferences, one parents' night, and two school plays in the last year alone. His younger daughter's gala premiere as a pineapple in *Agriculture of the World* had gone unseen, lost to him forever, just the night before as he clock-watched his way through yet another "crucial" conference.

His mind drifted to the Oregon forests and meadows where he had camped and fished the previous summer. Vivid images of cool pines, open vistas, and the all-encompassing silence danced in mute invitation over the sea of taillights before him. In recent months, the mountains had become like a magnet. There never was a day when Wayne didn't reflect upon them. They evolved into an obsession—the promise of a safer, saner way of life—growing from a casual freeway fantasy into a persistent, inescapable call.

Only the past week, his preoccupation with what he half-jokingly thought of as his "escape route" was so intense that he had approached a colleague on the subject. He'd been met with a derisive laugh, and his friend's words were still fresh in his mind.

"You think you're alone with thoughts and dreams like those, Wayne? Hell, we all have them, some of us worse than you. And something's always happening to keep the dream of moving away alive—like Jack's heart attack last week, or your having your car stolen, or when the daily air pollution index goes higher than the Dow Jones. Then when Tammy's two kids got accosted in the park after school—yeah, it's a lousy lifestyle.

"But I'm surprised that in ten years you haven't figured

out yet the reason you're still here with all the rest of us. Look around you this evening. Look at the home, the car, the boat, the balance in your savings account. You're shackled to this life and this town, and to the inescapable fact that you need the city to generate the big bucks. Keep the dream alive, my friend, but accept it for what it is: just a dream."

And Wayne did look around him—at all the expensive trappings, all the *things* that had always been so important to him and his family. But he also really *looked* at his wife, the woman with whom he had promised eighteen years ago to share his life, the woman he now rarely even had time to take to dinner. And he looked at the two precious daughters growing up without him and at the silly paper pineapple lying crumpled in a corner of the bedroom.

And then he looked at himself. He was haggard, exhausted, living on the razor's edge of stress, at least twenty years away from retirement—if he lasted that long. He was striving for goals that had once burned crucially important, but which seemed to grow more insignificant with each passing year. More money? A bigger house? Maybe a partnership in five or ten years? Were those things worth trying to survive in this urban wasteland?

Keep it in its place? Keep it just a dream? No, not when it could be more than that. There were things in life more fulfilling than what he had, reasons for each day that reached far outside his narrow cycle of waking, driving, working, and dropping into numbed sleep.

There was something more worthwhile out there, something better waiting. It was time to step outside the comfortable circle of what was secure and familiar. It was time to reach for a better life.

It has been called "The Decentralization of America", and it is responsible for the most massive population shift this country has seen since the dawn of the Industrial Revolution. The trickle of 1950s city dwellers moving to the green lawns of suburbia has grown into a torrent of people escaping the urban environment for a simpler, saner life in rural communities.

There are statistics and theories by the score to back this up; they will be examined in detail. There is a new school of deep physiological thinking designed to explain the dissatisfaction and the underlying need of urbanites to escape their environment; this will be discussed in depth.

But for you, the person with individual problems and unique dreams, moving is much more than statistics and theories and maps and predictions. It is bigger and more important; it is smaller and more focused. It's you, just you, trying to decide whether or not to make a move that seems at first glance impossible.

The issue of rural relocation for the authors was just as personal, and just as hard. We left the city and we know it's tough. Big and crowded and impersonal though it was, it was still home. We left businesses, friends and family behind, and gambled our futures on the conviction that something better awaited us ahead—and it did.

This book can be your guide to a better and richer life. From self-assessment to selecting a town, from hiring a mover to figuring out how to make a living, it's all included. We've interviewed other urban dropouts and compiled the experiences of hundreds of people dissatisfied with urban life. For information and inspiration, their stories are all here, too.

Yes, we've made it. Thousands of others before us have made it, too. But the important thing is that *you* can make it. If the time is right for you and you have a vision of a more worthwhile life, we are here to show you how to achieve it.

1

The Urban Society Into the 21st Century

Time and space—time to be alone, space to move about—these may well be the greatest scarcities of tomorrow.

—Edwin Way Teale,
Autumn Across America

From its very inception, America was a rural society. Towns and hamlets were small and isolated. Agriculture was the mainstay of the economy. Communities, by necessity and common goal, worked together. People knew each other and had concern for the safety and well-being of their neighbors.

But America was also a progressive nation, born from fearlessness and hard work. The country possessed a tremendous wealth of talent, open space, and natural resources. The fires of the War of Independence had barely cooled when the

Industrial Revolution began in Great Britain, a harbinger of the great changes our fledgling nation would soon encompass.

CENTRALIZATION

By the mid-19th century, the American Industrial Revolution was fully underway. Labor became less involved with the production of raw materials and primary products at home or on the farm, and became more concerned with the manufacture of finished goods and providing related services. Initially on a small scale, workers and equipment began to be brought together in common buildings at a common site. Through this concentration of effort, efficiency increased, and the production of finished goods increased with it. The centralization of industry and the labor force that supported it had begun.

With the dramatic rise in the production of finished goods and the attendant growth of domestic and world trade, considerable revenue was being generated. This money was quickly made available for industrial expansion. As manufacturing facilities were infused with this new capital, their capacities increased and a growing emphasis was placed on speed and efficiency. The standardization of parts and processes gave rise to the development of assembly lines.

Industry became even more centralized, interconnected, and concentrated, giving rise to the development of the great factories, mills, and foundries that dotted the country by the late 1800s and early 1900s. Factories rose side by side, and their related support industries—housing, food distribution, transportation and many other endeavors—expanded at a phenomenal rate.

Growth of the Urban Environment

With the growth of manufacturing capacity came a voracious appetite for workers. In trickles, and then in torrents, ever increasing numbers of men, women, and even children left the family farms to follow the golden road of opportunity to the city. More workers meant more production, more sales, and more working capital for the factories. This led to still more expansion, greater centralization, and the need for still more labor. The cycle established itself. The urbanization of America had begun.

Another new concept in the American industrial community was the need for specialization. As the manufacturing process became larger and more productive, it also became more complex. It was no longer possible for one man alone to take the raw wood and steel, work through each of the manufacturing steps and processes, and create a finished product. Once completely self-sufficient, workers now learned only one trade, then only one phase of a trade, and, finally, the operation of one single tool or machine. Great skill and craftsmanship were no longer needed. Soon, these abilities actually became something of a hindrance to the factory owners. Intelligence, education, and independence were not things an employer looked for at that time. The ideal factory worker possessed only a strong back and the ability to conform and follow orders.

New social classes began to emerge. The dividing lines were being drawn by those who possessed the capital for expansion and the physical plants for manufacturing. The labor force, the thousands of factory workers and those who worked within the infrastructure of the support industries that kept the factories humming, fell to the bottom of the ladder. Cities grew, and living conditions began to deteriorate.

As complexity had created specialization, specialization also created complexity. No one person possessed the knowledge or skill to perform all of the operations. Armies of people were needed to staff all phases of industry, each with particular positions and particular specialties that were known to increasingly fewer people within the firm.

With time, "middle" industries were created. No longer did most men earn their livings with their hands. In fact, fewer and fewer did each year. Whole platoons of salesmen were needed, along with advertisers and financial planners, commodities traders and labor liaisons, and a whole strata of middle managers at various levels with increasingly vague duties.

Legal issues became cloudy as understanding between the various trades and industries decreased, and more laws and more lawyers to interpret those laws further muddied the waters. By the middle of this century, consultants were actually needed to tie the various specialties together and provide corporate owners with some sort of overview of the entire process.

Labor unions grew in power. Initially formed to protect workers' rights and improve wages and working conditions, their growing stranglehold on industry led to spirals of inflation as wages skyrocketed, often with little regard for skill or ability. Buying power decreased as prices for manufactured goods rose. Living conditions in many parts of the urban environment began to deteriorate further as land became more valuable and housing costs increased.

Urbanization was at its peak, but production and efficiency were slipping. Economic conditions for those at the bottom of the ladder were worsening. Class distinctions were increasing as the gap between the haves and the have-nots went from a crack to a canyon.

Industry had shot itself in the foot.

DECENTRALIZATION

Within a scant one hundred and fifty years, the face of America changed dramatically. The cities and their industries were about as centralized as they could be and were beginning to bulge at the seams. Traffic increased, but city streets and outside support roads were limited by the size of the city itself. Land became increasingly valuable as it became more scarce, buildings went up instead of out, air and water quality declined due to the unchecked industrial growth, and crime rose dramatically in the close quarters of urban neighborhoods.

Suburbia

The golden road of the city had become tarnished as housing became increasingly less affordable and the simple amenities of the "good life" vanished for an increasing number of city residents. Suburban communities, on the outskirts of the city and boasting affordable housing, trees and fresh air, began to prosper after World War II, and the move away from the core city had begun.

But the rings of green belts and houses with yards also had only so much room in which to grow. Land prices for those areas within easy reach of the city began increasing at a fever pitch. Affordable housing for most people came to mean commutes of one, two, or even three hours from home to office. Suburban communities, once pastoral outposts away from the grime of the city, began to merge together with their urban host to become ever-larger cities in their own right.

Fed up with the increasingly stressful demands on time and income that the city and even the suburbs demanded, people began to look for alternatives. A "back to the land" movement began, further fueled by the social unrest and divisive currents of the 1960s.

Beyond Suburbia

Beyond suburbia, beyond back to the land, a whole new generation of American pioneer is being born. These are not office workers content to live in a bedroom community that is simply a greener extension of the city, nor are they cultural dropouts reverting to a primitive existence where an outhouse with a door is the height of sophistication.

Executives have given up high-stress jobs for quieter positions outside the fast track. Smaller companies are springing up in unlikely places, staffed by MBAs and Ph.D.'s who have willingly taken cuts in their personal bottom line in order to seek out and thrive on a saner existence.

Quantum leaps in the improvement of communications in recent years, plus continually improving methods of shipping and transportation, have made it possible for established companies to move away from the urban chaos and to seek out cheaper land and a variety of desirable amenities for their workers. Electronic marvels like the computer, the modem, and the FAX machine have made the interchange of communication and written materials even easier. These conveniences have made it possible for executives, small business owners, and even office staff to work at home.

In what anthropologists will probably research and write volumes upon in future years, a new revolution is underway—decentralization. It is the age of the urban escapee. Perhaps, for the first time in history, people seeking a better way of life outside the city environment are willing to trade a reduced income for a little bit of peace.

As quoted in a recent article in *USA Today,* "These spiritual descendants of Thoreau aren't part of the back-to-the-land movement of the 1960s and '70s. They don't shun indoor plumbing. Often they carry stereos, microwave ovens and computers with them. But, like those earlier models, they're drawn to a life they believe can be lived without moral compromise."

THE EXIT BEGINS

A recent survey by the *Los Angeles Times* determined that 60% of those polled felt that the quality of their life has declined significantly over the last fifteen years. *Over half* said that they had thought about leaving the city over the past twelve months. According to Nancy Minter, a demographer with the Los Angeles Health Services Department, people are leaving in droves. 40,000 people in the age fifty-five and over category alone are leaving Los Angeles *every year* since 1980, and nearly the same number of young families with children are moving away annually.

This large-scale exodus is not only being felt on the west coast, but in almost every other major city in the country as well, as reflected by the figures from the 1980 census:

-Detroit showed a population decrease of almost 21%;

-Buffalo was down 23%;

-St. Louis lost a sizable 27% of its population.

"Decentralization away from the cities is a phenomenon that is reshaping the economic and social life of many communities across the U.S." said a spokesman for the Urban Land Institute. According to census figures, small town and rural areas grew 15.5% faster than cities, and some ninety-two million Americans, the equivalent of a surprising 42% of the United States population, now live in small towns and rural areas.

For example, some of the most talented and educated young people are leaving the San Francisco Bay Area due to the crises in housing affordability. According to an analysis by the *San Francisco Chronicle* of driver license changes between July, 1984 and June, 1987, Oregon and Washington were the leading destinations for residents leaving the Bay Area. Oregon received 12,423 of these disenchanted dropouts, Washington 11,775, Texas 9,524 and Arizona 8,908.

A recent survey by the University of California indicated

that new arrivals to small Northern California towns were increasingly college-educated and sophisticated. More than half said they had moved without having a job in their new location.

"The new rural residents are often society's rebels with creative business ideas, retirees who want to escape the problems of the city, and skilled workers seeking a dream life," according to Ted Bradshaw, who conducted the study. "Until recently, few people could live out their desire to move from the city to the country because rural areas lacked jobs and economic opportunity."

Tomorrow's big city will no longer be the office center, either. This change is already underway, with companies like Exxon leaving New York for a small town in Texas, Citibank's credit card center moving to North Dakota, and a large mutual fund group, Colonial Management Associates, packing up for Denver.

According to Peter Drucker, professor of social sciences at Claremont Graduate School, "the city of the future will be occupied by headquarters of major companies with much of the clerical, accounting and administration located in the suburbs or even thousands of miles away from major urban centers".

BABY BOOMERS

Of all the developing trends in America today, perhaps the most important thing that will impact migration from the larger urban centers is the maturing of that huge and significant portion of our society—the "Baby Boom" generation.

Baby Boomers, those people born in the wake of World War II, who are now thirty- and forty-something, currently represent one-third of our country's population.

More than any one group in our nation's history, the Baby Boom generation has shaped markets and created trends and demands on society that will have lasting results. Perhaps the most affluent and prosperous single generation our country has ever seen, this diverse collection of Yuppies (Young Urban Professionals), DINKs (Double Income, No Kids) and other quantified, qualified, and over-analyzed middle and pre-middle age citizens has been undergoing a gradual and important change. The shift has been away from quantity of possessions and toward an improved quality of life for themselves and their families.

In a growing number of cases, this has involved leaving the congestion of the traditional urban centers to seek a new and better way of life in the previously scorned townships that dot the American landscape. These towns offer a true sense of community, combined with affordable housing, a sound environment, and room in which to move. The "me" generation is growing up and moving out of the city.

Another crucial aspect of this exodus is what will happen in the years to come. What will be the impact of the so-called "graying of the Baby Boom generation?" Each year, given the down-turn of child births as more and more two-career, two-income couples postpone or decide against children, the over-65 portion of our society is increasing. By the year 2030, sixty-five million Americans will have reached senior citizenship, more than twice the number of Seniors in the country today. At that time, senior citizens will account for 21% of America's population, as compared with the 12% segment that they currently represent. These are numbers that have everyone from economists and Social Security advisors to clothing and food manufacturers scrambling to establish guidelines and adjust to changing needs and trends.

THE AMERICAN WORK FORCE

Another developing trend is the reduction of the American work force. Large companies are phasing out employees by the thousands due to advanced technology and the need for increased profits. According to a recent study conducted by the United States Department of Commerce, 4.7 million workers who had held their jobs for at least three years have been dismissed. General Motors has cut its work force by 150,000 since 1980. Since the beginning of the 1980s, nearly one third of all companies in the United States have used the incentive of early retirement plans to trim their work force. In large part, retiring workers are not being replaced.

This thinning of the national work force is having a variety of ramifications. For example, it is estimated that thirty-six million Americans—more than one fourth of all United States workers—are part-time or on-call employees. Of those still working traditional, full-time jobs, a *Time CNN* poll of five hundred and twenty workers found that 57% of them thought companies were less loyal to employees when compared to conditions ten years ago, while only 25% thought they were more loyal.

Another example is the creation of a whole new strata of entrepreneurs, whether by design or by simple economic necessity. The United States Department of Commerce reported that in 1970, 7% of the American work force was self-employed. By 1986 that number had risen to 11%, and is projected to top 15% by the end of 1990. In fact, the rate of self-employed people is growing four times faster than the rate of growth in the salaried work force.

The same report showed that in 1950 we created new businesses at the rate of 93,000 per year. In 1980, that figure had jumped to 600,000, and the projections show new businesses will be created at the whopping rate of one million a year by the start of this decade.

Furthermore, of the eleven million businesses in the United States today, 10.8 million of them are rated as "small businesses" by the Department of Commerce, and almost all of them—10.1 million or a surprising 94%—are being operated out of the home.

Further evidence of the job market shift in America is seen in the evidence of where the new jobs are being created. Between 1980 and 1986, of the thirteen million new jobs created, 10.5 million (81%) were created by small companies, as compared to only 2.5 million (19%) that were by the Fortune 500 companies—traditionally America's biggest employers.

Here are a few other interesting statistics about entrepreneurs and home businesses that are worth noting:

- As of early 1988, some 24.9 million Americans currently work at home, either full- or part-time;
- The number of at-home workers is increasing by a steady seven percent per year;
- The percentage of businesses owned by women increased by 47.4% between 1980 and 1985;
- The number of United States universities offering programs in entrepreneurship went from one hundred and sixty three in 1981 to two hundred and fifty in 1985;
- In 1982, there were 2.4 million computers in American homes—by 1988 there were 22.8 million;
- There were 70,000 fax machines sold in the United States in 1983; in 1988 1.5 million were sold.

THE CRUNCH IN AFFORDABLE HOUSING

For both individuals and companies, the prohibitively high cost of living and doing business in the city has become a key element in their relocation decisions, as has the escalating cost of real estate.

Consider this recent Associated Press article:

"The price of a house increased faster than buyers' incomes in 1989, the 14th straight year the gap between the American dream and its realization has widened, a new study concludes.

"The Chicago Title & Trust Co. said its annual survey of home buyers in eighteen urban areas also revealed that the vast majority of 1989 home buyers were two-income couples who saved for an average of 2.9 years—the longest period in the survey's 14-year history—to make a down payment."

The survey concluded:

". . . since the first Chicago Trust survey in 1976, the difference between income gains and home-price increases grew a total of 6.5 percent over fourteen years.

"Those buying houses today have noticeably fewer discretionary dollars to spend on things other than housing than their counterparts did thirteen years ago."

To make matters worse, there is no indication whatsoever that the 14-year widening of the gap between income and home prices is going to decrease, or even remain stable. Take for example the cost of the average house in the San Francisco Bay Area. According to a study by Population-Environment Balance, the cost of a new home in the year 2000 will be $750,000, up from the current price of $168,300. Since 1986 the median price of housing in the Los Angeles area has increased 40%, and for some homes in the $200,000 to

$400,000 range, prices rose 40% in the last year alone according to the California Association of Realtors.

This increase in values has created a whole generation of "equity dropouts," people who are cashing in on their windfall and moving to small towns. The proceeds from the sale of a $400,000 house in Connecticut can buy a lot of house in most small towns in Vermont or New Hampshire with enough capital left over to start up a small business or bankroll a comfortable retirement.

WHERE'S EVERYONE GOING?

According to a recent survey of relocation trends by Allied Van Lines, the following states were listed as the top 10 "magnet" states.

1. District of Columbia
2. Rhode Island
3. Hawaii
4. Nevada
5. Maine
6. Vermont
7. Oregon
8. Washington
9. Georgia
10. South Carolina

The survey also listed the most mobile states, including both inbound and outbound moves:

1. California
2. Florida
3. Texas
4. Illinois
5. New York
6. Pennsylvania
7. Virginia

8. Ohio
9. New Jersey
10. Georgia

For the second year in a row, California, a traditional high-attraction state, led the nation in the volume of both inbound and outbound moves. Other western states experiencing a continued growth of inbound moves were Oregon, Washington, Arizona and Nevada, all of which were classified as magnet states for the second year in a row.

In a study conducted by the Household Goods Carriers Bureau of Alexandria, Virginia, a moving industry trade group representing seven major moving van lines, there were 11,974 moves into Oregon in 1988 representing a 52% increase over moves into the state in 1987. Of those nearly 12,000 new Oregon households, 41% were transplanted from California. According to the *Oregonian,* a Portland, Oregon-based newspaper, the large influx of newcomers is also reflected in a 66% increase in Oregon housing starts over the previous year.

In the northeast, less populated states drew the most activity. Rhode Island trailed only the District of Columbia in terms of percentage of inbound moves. Sparsely-populated Maine and Vermont also maintained a high percentage of attraction for new residents.

In a recent *Newsweek* survey, this weekly newsmagazine described America's ten hottest cities as "places that have jobs, cheap houses and good fishing minutes from downtown." It claims these cities have it all:

• Portland, Oregon, population 353,931, median home price $64,800

• St. Paul, Minnesota, population 261,036, median home price $86,000

• Birmingham, Alabama, population 272,841, median home price $77,300

• Fort Worth, Texas, population 438,433, median home price $84,700

• Orlando, Florida, population 149,527, median home price $81,300

• Sacramento, California, population 331,211, median home price $100,200

• Providence, Rhode Island, population 157,002, median home price $131,900

• Charlotte, North Carolina, population 342,146, median home price $100,000

• Columbus, Ohio, population 566,915, median home price $74,500

• Albuquerque, New Mexico, population 374,106, median home price $83,400

Urbanologists, a whole new species of researchers, have coined a new term for these areas: "second tier" cities. While obviously not "small towns" in the traditionally-perceived sense of the term, they fall short of being fully urban, either. They offer most of the amenities of big-city living, but are still considered small enough to offer some sense of belonging.

According to a study done by the University of Wisconsin, "given their choice, most refugees will move to a second tier city or a smaller community rather than to another big city".

In a recent issue, the *Wall Street Journal* listed a few of the other predicted "boom towns" of the 1990s, based on predicted growth of employment:

Dallas/Richardson, Texas (59.9% growth);
Troy/Warren, Michigan (45.3% growth);
Scottsdale/Sun City, Arizona (58% growth);
Newport Beach/Laguna, California (34.8% growth);
Herndon/Manassas, Virginia (41% growth);

Santa Ana/Costa Mesa, California (21.5% growth);
Virginia Beach/Chesapeake, Virginia (41% growth);
East Brunswick, New Jersey (29.4% growth);
Orlando/Kissimmee, Florida (40.9% growth).

It Doesn't Hurt to Advertise

The rural relocation trend has been fueled even further by the willingness of small towns to promote themselves, sometimes out of economic necessity.

During the recession of the early 1980s, agriculture, ranching, and the timber industries—the mainstays of most rural communities—took a beating from which they have been slow to recover. Many small towns began to look for other industries to employ their people who suddenly found themselves out of work. Economic Development Councils were formed in many communities with the primary objective of promoting their area to new businesses.

Some communities have recently budgeted and spent as much as a million dollars a year in just advertising alone. Depending on the area, one might see a strong focus on the livability of the region, or perhaps the skilled and available workforce. Enterprise zones were established where companies could receive generous tax breaks as incentive for moving to the area.

All combined, these economic development activities have helped to increase people's awareness of rural communities and the many and varied amenities they have to offer. In this era of urban dropouts, it is not unusual to see many governors stumping for new business in their state, armed with catchy slogans and beautiful four-color brochures touting everything from skiing to a clean and safe environment.

A NEW SPIRIT

Labeled the urban dropout, the rat race escapee, even the new American pioneer—the names don't matter. What does matter is the spirit of these people and their willingness to make sacrifices and take risks in the hope of moving beyond the status quo. They are looking for something better, and, by the hundreds of thousands, they are finding it.

As the subsequent chapters unfold, you'll see how you can too.

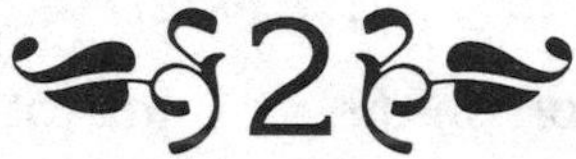

A Guide to Self-Assessment

by
JoAn Mann, M.B.A.

The question which one asks oneself begins, at last, to illuminate the world . . .

—James Baldwin
Nobody Knows My Name

Among the first questions potential urban transplants ask themselves are "Do *I* have what it takes to relocate? Could I make the move and actually survive and prosper?"

If you are like most people, confused and somewhat daunted by the thought of relocating to a rural or semi-rural setting, this chapter will help you assess and evaluate yourself. Hopefully, it will also ease some of your fears.

In addition to informally talking to hundreds of people who have been urban dropouts, we studied, in-depth, forty-two individuals in small, but growing, communities who have been identified by their local Chambers of Commerce as having "successfully" made the transition. Factors such as contribution to the new community, apparent financial success and overall satisfaction were used in the success definition.

Prior to the move, these dropouts were mostly in white collar occupations such as managers, physicians, lawyers, staff employees of large corporations, accountants, teachers, designers, sales persons, small business owners and several retirees. The study, although subjective and most applicable for business people, was nonetheless enlightening, and, surprisingly, did reveal strong trends that appear to predict some degree of success. It also indicated potential hazards.

In the process of conducting our in-depth study, we observed the participants' tremendous level of interest in the subject. Ordinarily, mailed-survey return rates are low. 25% is considered good in mass mailings of moderate personal interest topics. In our case, there was a 44% return rate. Of the ninety-five surveys originally mailed, forty-two were returned. Many people wrote extensive personal comments to assist us in the project.

By analyzing the demographics, questions, personality survey responses and extra comments, a general profile of a successful urban transplant was generated. This chapter will discuss the urban transplant's probable profile for success. The summary of observations is followed by additional interpretation of factors, as well as an appendix survey for you to complete to assess your own probability for success in making the move.

While nothing can guarantee success in the transition,

the profile in this chapter is meant to be helpful in understanding some essential ingredients. There are two success factors: perseverance and a positive attitude.

Attesting to these factors, each person participating in the survey had a unique story to tell. Some attained instant satisfaction; some paid their dues over a period of time; two would not repeat their move. 95%, however, felt it was worth the effort.

Highlights of the Survey

The following responses summarize the findings of the survey in relation to the satisfied urban transplant. Specific tallies and comments can be found at the end of the chapter.

As Children . . .

• dreamed about living in a special, less densely-populated spot (mountains, seashore, resort, country, ranch, farm)

• wanted to be financially successful and excel on their own (a performer, business owner, executive)

• were outdoor-activities minded (hiking, fishing, camping, sports)

• resided, or fantasized about residing, in non-urban areas under 50,000 population

• had positive experiences growing up in their communities (regardless of size)

Personality Factors Showed . . .

• ability and willingness to adapt

• positive attitude and belief that they could do anything

• adventurous, risk-taking, in control leadership style

• outgoing, people-oriented nature

• action-oriented and being proactive on their environment

• big-picture orientated outlook

• goals-setting ability while still being sufficiently flexible in the process

• ability to persevere

Pre-move Situations Showed . . .

• had education necessary to offer a variety of work skills and career versatility or were financially independent

• supportive marriage, especially when spouse was familiar with non-urban lifestyle

• no children at home, or, at least, no teenaged children

• age of thirty years or older

• family income of $10,000 to $100,000 per year

• concern regarding quality of life: air/environment, stress level, quality family time in contrast to financial stability or status

In Planning For the Move . . .

• visited their favorite vacation/recreation spot frequently, later purchased property there, which led to their eventual permanent move

• planned for six months or longer to make the move (especially considering their economic situation) researched the liveability (non-economic factors) more than employment or business viability before deciding to relocate

• had living expenses or savings for more than three months (most had over one year's savings)

• dealt with reactions ranging from "mixed" to "skeptical"

from friends and "mixed" to "supportive" from relatives regarding move

Moved to . . .

- locations without immediate family members
- places that let them accomplish dreams they had had since childhood (hobbies, recreational interests, ideal location, ideal business/ownership opportunity)
- places two to four hours from a major metropolitan area
- the northwest, Rocky Mountains, northern California

In Making the Move . . .

- quit their jobs, sold their businesses or retired
- paid for their own move
- started their own business, bought a new business, were self-employed or retired

After the Move . . .

- relatives joined them within five years of relocation
- visited metropolitan areas less than once a month
- settled their new homes as anticipated or more easily
- found employment as anticipated or more easily
- found it easier to make friends and become involved in community than anticipated
- adapted to the new pace as anticipated or more easily
- adapted to cultural differences as anticipated or more easily
- adjusted to the climate as anticipated or more easily
- found the business climate adjustment to be challeng-

ing, not necessarily bad, but different, and needing more understanding and attention than anticipated

• felt a drop in income the first year or two before increasing income substantially or reaching pre-move status within three to five years

• more difficult for those with downward financial adjustment to adjust in all categories, except making friends and community involvement, which remained as anticipated or easier

• said they would do it again

Recommend To Others . . .

• plan the pros and cons carefully

• save up living expenses for extended period of time (one to two years)

• keep an open mind and roll with the punches

• do it

What do these factors mean?—A discussion of the successful profile

The transplants surveyed had a strong desire to be financially successful, own their own businesses, work on the land, or excel in some way. Interestingly, none mentioned being in social service support positions such as nursing, clerical, allied medical support professionals and the like. This may be a phenomenon, as our survey was business and industry oriented.

Transplants liked outdoor sports. Only a handful mentioned reading or other quiet, primarily indoor, activities. About two-thirds responding mentioned they had dreamed about living in beautiful, natural low-density population areas, such as in the mountains, by the ocean, forest, on the ranch, farm or a resort. Additionally, one-third were from small towns under

50,000 in population. One-third were from metropolitan areas over one million in population and one-third were from mid-sized urban areas inhabited by fifty thousand to one million people. From an overall population percentage, small towns were very well represented. Several respondents commented that understanding small town ways was helpful to them in making the transition; likewise, spouses who had *not* been raised in a small town had a more difficult adjustment. This, plus the 75% who expressed childhood dreams of living in non-urban areas, leads us to believe that small town or non-urban experiences or fantasies as children are important to the success of an urban transplant.

Your Childhood Dreams and Ideals

Many psychologists and educators tell us that our childhood experiences are important in forming our attitudes and outlooks on life. Piaget, Bruner, Jung and Montessori are researchers who support this view. There is disagreement as to exactly when attitudes and beliefs are precisely formed. Our minds learn most quickly and absorb patterns and the ways of our world prior to ages six or seven. There is general agreement that by fifteen years of age, we are firmly imprinted in our outlook.

Early conditioning consists of impressions that have been absorbed prior to our brain's full operational, problem-solving development. Hence, as very small children there is frequently no difference between our imagination and reality. Our dreams and desires have not yet met with rational logic which may, at times, unnecessarily limit our possibilities.

When we reach our teens, we use "rational" problem solving, abstract concepts and complex thinking. Of course, by then our imaginations and abilities to absorb new information have slowed considerably.

Our goals and dreams are often formulated because of

pleasurable events, or as antidotes to negative situations. In realizing our goals and dreams, sometimes negative experiences can create memory blocks and, consequently, do not aid us as consistently as pleasurable memories.

Regardless of negative or positive experiences, many of us feel the way we were raised as children was the "right" way. Small wonder that we are drawn to situations that replicate our childhood.

By utilizing the dreams of our childhood, we can get in touch with a strong, yet rarely acknowledged force, that may be a subconscious influence. Connecting dreams and goals with action creates incredible feelings of fulfillment, achievement and purpose.

Releasing your childhood dreams and goals

When you focus on the dreams you have wanted to achieve since childhood, you increase the chances of realizing your dreams. There are a number of books, currently available, that can help you explore and develop insight into this process. Books such as *The Inner Child of Your Past* by Hugh Missildine, *Unlocking the Secrets of Your Childhood Past* by Kevin Leman and Randy Carlson and *Intimate Partners* by Maggie Scarf suggest techniques to gain a positive attitude in order to help you convert past wants into present successes.

Some questions to help you understand your adult desires might include:

- What did you want to be when you grew up?
- Where did you want to live when you grew up?
- What was going to be important to you in your life?

Interpreting your childhood dreams and goals

Besides wanting to live in a special spot, our transplants wanted to be successful. Some were on their way, some had made it and another group of survey respondents were retired or had been working sufficiently long enough to have achieved basic economic and career goals. Once this had been achieved, the questions they expressed was, "What next?" For many, the move to smaller communities helped realize their non-economic dreams. It also provided opportunities to develop relationships, give back to others in the community, and make a difference. Making the move appeared to satisfy self-esteem, and humanitarian/philosophical/spiritual needs.

Interestingly, while apparently not pursuing primarily economic goals, those who served their non-urban community were usually rewarded handsomely after a two to three year "dues-paying" period.

Questions to ask yourself about your initial readiness for such a move include:

- Have you fulfilled your basic economic or career goals?
- Do you feel a strong need to pursue more global humanitarian or philosophical/spiritual goals?
- Do you still have urban-based needs (economic, social or otherwise) for achieving the success you desire?

Personality Factors

Childhood experiences and conditioning shape our value systems of belief and attitudes, which are then expressed and enacted through our personalities. This combination of values and personality is the foundation for who we are as adults, how we behave, and how we perceive ourselves and others. Our personalities form our "filter" systems, by which we interpret and react to the world. Dr. Carl Jung was one of the first modern day psychologists to offer extensive insight into personality theory and research in the inherited key personality traits, especially introversion (internally driven personality) and extroversion (externally driven personality) qualities. Cattell, Adler, and Allport are twentieth century personality researchers who also offered insight into personality traits. According to most of these experts, values and conditioning are environmentally based and at least somewhat modifiable; whereas personality is primarily innate, only in part modifiable by our environment.

Recognizing your alterable personality elements

The most significant personality factors over which we have control are attitudes and the flexibility to change and adapt to situations. Suzanne Kobasai, co-author of *The Hardy Executive,* has done tremendous research in the change or stress hardy personality. Her research was borne out by a study that concluded the hardy personality views change as a challenge, seeks control over the situation and has a strong sense of commitment.

But it is important to remember that for each innate personality trait, there are positive and negative behaviors. We can modify and select whether to function out of the positive or negative side of ourselves. The choice we make is strongly influenced by our conditioning and experiences. The successful transplants surveyed exhibited strong positive behavioral traits rather than the negative behavioral traits.

Vital questions for assessing how ready you are for a major life style change are:

- Do you view change as an opportunity or challenge?

- Do you seek to have a feeling of control over your own destiny?

- Do you really stick by your commitments?

- Do you see yourself comfortably dealing with *all* types of people?

Recognizing your inherent personality traits.

Our successful urban transplants' inherent personality profile makes a good entrepreneur, business owner, marketing person and a challenging, possibly rebellious, employee.

People who have this personality style usually feel more at home in work settings that allow them to be on their own or in a small informal group rather than in a large structured group or organizational setting. This personality often runs into conflict with main stream society, but usually has the people skills to be sufficiently flexible to deal with all kinds of individuals in the process of achieving what he or she desires.

The successful transplant profile thrives on changes. In the public school system, this profile is frequently a student troublemaker for teachers trying to teach structured or standard lesson-plan classes.

Utilizing the Insight Personal Strengths and Stress Profile, the following are inherent personality trait descriptions of the successful urban transplant. In assessing your personality style, after reading the descriptions, ask yourself:

• What traits do I have that are consistent with the profile?

• How would I need to adapt my personality to "make the move?"

• How far am I comfortable and capable of stretching my basic style?

• Where and how do I optimally use my personality traits?

• For which career, industry and type of organization am I best suited?

TRAIT SUMMARY CHART

CONTROLLING < ——— + ——— > SUPPORTIVE

3	2 — 1	SITUATION	1 — 2	3
authoritative blunt commanding rebellious uncompromising need complete control	**assertive** **to-the-point** **confident** **strong-willed** **positive** **need a challenge**	**DECISION-MAKING** **COMMUNICATION** **LEADERSHIP** **FOLLOWER ROLE** **APPROACH TO CHANGE** **BEST ENVIRONMENT**	want support subtle behind the scenes take direction well cautious need peaceful environment	hesitant soft-spoken rely on others cooperative want guidance need strong direction
steam-roller DISLIKE: too many bosses compromise	**commanding** **DISLIKE:** **indecision** **incompetence**	**UNDER PRESSURE** **WORST ENVIRONMENT** **PET PEEVES**	withdraw DISLIKE: no support overbearing personality	seek protection DISLIKE: making final decisions brazen actions

OUTGOING < ——— + ——— > INTROSPECTIVE

3	2 — 1	SITUATION	1 — 2	3
convincing eloquent inspirational eager trusting need opportunity	**enthusiastic** **persuasive** **team-oriented** **cooperative** **optimistic** **need to be with friends**	**DECISION-MAKING** **COMMUNICATION** **LEADERSHIP** **FOLLOWER ROLE** **APPROACH TO CHANGE** **BEST ENVIRONMENT**	analytical reserved quiet non-disruptive questioning need personal time	secretive selective private inconspicuous skeptical need respect
make biting remarks DISLIKE: isolation being left out	**sarcastic** **DISLIKE:** **rejection** **on-communication**	**UNDER PRESSURE** **WORST ENVIRONMENT** **PET PEEVES**	speak selectively DISLIKE: unexpected exposure speaking w/o thinking	silent DISLIKE: constant interaction forced socializing

© 1984, rev. 1989 Insight Profiles, Inc.

RELAXED < ——— + ——— > URGENT

—3—	—2—1—	SITUATION	—1—2—	—3—
procrastinate	unhurried	**DECISION-MAKING**	**quick**	instantaneous
leisurely	casual	**COMMUNICATION**	**fast speaking**	hurried
methodical	planners	**LEADERSHIP**	**action-oriented**	bustling
steady	dependable	**FOLLOWER ROLE**	**active**	demanding
change when justified	deliberate	**APPROACH TO CHANGE**	**swift**	rushed
need harmony	need cooperation	**BEST ENVIRONMENT**	**need variety**	need frequent change
get even later	cover anger with smile	**UNDER PRESSURE**	**abrupt**	short tempered
DISLIKE: pressure	DISLIKE: unexpected demands	**WORST ENVIRONMENT**	**DISLIKE: slow-downs**	DISLIKE: delayed gratification
emotional outbursts	high pressure directives	**PET PEEVES**	**waiting in lines**	complications delays

EXACTING < ——— + ——— > GENERALIZING

—3—	—2—1—	SITUATION	—1—2—	—3—
perfectionistic	analytical	**DECISION-MAKING**	**overview priorities**	big-picture perspective
formal	calculating	**COMMUNICATION**	**unrestrained**	informal
structured	strong organizers	**LEADERSHIP**	**delegators**	free-wheeling
unquestioning	conscientious	**FOLLOWER ROLE**	**self-reliant**	independent
skeptical	careful	**APPROACH TO CHANGE**	**open-minded**	challenge tradition
need standard protocol	need personal security	**BEST ENVIRONMENT**	**need independence**	need to restrictions
fault-finding	refer to book	**UNDER PRESSURE**	**generalize**	disregard details
DISLIKE: unstable surroundings	DISLIKE: no apparent structure	**WORST ENVIRONMENT**	**DISLIKE: bureaucracy**	DISLIKE: detailed accountability
non-factual approaches	mistakes	**PET PEEVES**	**structured settings**	perfectionists

Pre-Move Situations

What was the situation that staged the desire for a different, non-urban, back-to-nature life? By understanding the individuals described in the childhood and personality sections, it is easier to recognize life circumstances that motivated the move. These individuals thrive on change and challenge, constantly push themselves to the limits of their personal potential, enjoy adventure, and measure results by meeting new people and learning new things, rather than in terms of the financial. Most were not running from something, but moving *toward* a goal or dream.

Recognizing your unrealized potential

The successful transplants reached a point where they said, "What next? There is more to life than this." Their dreams were either so strong that they needed to realize more of their personal potential, or, their environmental needs became so critical that a change had to be made.

As pre-requisite for considering the move, the successful transplant already possessed the skills and education necessary for one career. Many have been active in more than one trade or career. All who needed to work expressed that they were willing to do whatever was necessary in order to make a living.

Some questions to ask yourself about where you can best realize your potential are:

- Am I putting up with unacceptable environmental conditions?
- Is the urban lifestyle becoming an intolerable hassle?
- If I need to, do I have a variety of skills to make a living.
- Would it be worth doing something new and unknown to improve my environment situation?

Asking why not?

Change is easier when there are fewer repercussions and people involved. Hence, the pre-move conditions for the typical successful transplant make sense: good marriages to a supportive spouse, no children (or at least not teenaged children—who have and want to follow their own goals and dreams), a savings account, over thirty years old, financially independent or having nothing to lose, and being young enough to start over again.

These individuals apparently weighed what they really wanted, saw they had less, had a pioneering spirit and a close family support system that all said to them, "go for it."

Ask yourself the why not question and others such as:

- Is my spouse supportive of moving to a less urban area?
- Do my children want to make the move?

Planning for the move

A major deciding factor in the planning process phase that influenced or was even a catalyst to the move was discovering the right location. Once this decision had been made, it appeared that the rest of the move was a matter of logistics.

Discovering the right location

The right location for many successful drop-outs appeared to be a blend of their dreams and a chance (or sometimes well researched) vacation or recreation spot.

Many first impressions of "This is the place!" appeared to be primarily based on non-economic factors. Later, the individuals seemed to justify the choices by financial or employment/business research. Important in discovering your right location would be:

• Where is my dream location?

• Where would I rather be than where I live right now?

• If I were to live my life in a place where I'd like to retire, where would it be?

Planning your move

The most significant factor in moving from the decision stage to the actual planning process was the frequency of visits at closer and closer intervals, with more and more time and money spent in the areas that were to become our transplants' future homes. This allowed for reinforcing the pleasures these areas held for the urbanite, a phased economic research of the areas and for an "acclimatization" phase that can never be too long. Many cited the need to understand the local thinking and business ways as having been the only real area for which they were mentally, or emotionally, not quite sufficiently prepared. Most had savings, and all recommended almost twice as much savings—if you are not financially independent—as they had in order to make the move.

In the planning process, ask how ready you could be:

• Have you been to your special spot frequently?

• What would it be like to be hospitalized in this town right after moving here?

• Do you have something put away for a rainy day (at least a year of living expenses)?

• Is there room for a good person, like yourself, doing your trade in the community?

Relocation Sites

The places selected for relocation by the successful transplants in our study were surrounded by naturally beautiful scenery, reflecting a certain tranquility—primarily in the Northeast, Northwest, Rockies and Northern California.

As we lived in Oregon, we had a bias of familiarity with this particular area and contacts; however, we have also included stories of transplants from all geographic locations. Successful transplants have selected sites visited on vacation, childhood dream spots, or places "just like the ideal" all over the face of the United States.

Their motives for moving often seemed the need to accomplish something, not to escape responsibility. Individuals who moved to less urban areas to care for a needy relative often found the transition tougher and not as rewarding as those leaving to fulfill goals or dreams.

The successful transplants did miss the cultural and fast pace activities of the cities. Most, however, felt that the natural beauty, serenity and outdoor activities of their new communities replaced their former urban cultural offerings. Additionally, visits to the city for shopping, cultural events and business became part of their new lives in the more remote areas. With urban areas being an average of two to four hours away, trips to the city happened typically less than one time per month, except for business trips which occurred more frequently.

Additionally, it appeared that the spouse of the person initiating relocation, especially if not working, needed to feel comfortable being out of the mainstream of the national and international information flow. Small town papers are notorious for brief, generalized reporting on national issues, and there is often a one to two day lag time for national paper delivery in rural communities. Difficulties seemed to arise when the spouse could not receive national news or had no social networks for interacting and developing relationships.

Questions for you to ponder regarding the site selection:

• How much of your life revolves around city life on a daily basis?

• Can you get your cultural "city fix" in two or three visits per year?

• Does living closer to nature have a calming influence or does it frighten you?

• How does your spouse feel about losing mainstream contacts?

• Will your spouse have replacement work and/or activity in the new site?

• How much national news do you or your spouse need to feel "informed?"

• Is there current-time national news access through television, cable, newspaper or radio?

The basic questions to ask yourself about your motives for moving are:

• Are you moving to accomplish your own goals or dreams?

• What obligations are associated with this move?

• Is this the time to move to this location?

• Do you have a gut-level feeling that there is another, more appropriate spot that will better fulfill your goal?

Making the Move

The basic moving tasks that face a transplant can be time and energy consuming. Moving to a smaller community can, in many ways, be likened to operating a small business versus managing a mature, large corporation. As in a small business, you pay your own way literally and figuratively. One of your rewards will be the feeling of a sense of control over your own life. Another plus will be the long term relationships you develop with others. In making a transition, there may not be as many people you can ask for help. In fact, your ability to be self reliant will be an important part of making a successful change.

Also, like a small business, you are probably more visible in your community. People in small towns are cautious and have more time to observe you. The importance of your "proper" entrance into the community should not be underestimated.

Several respondents commented on the need to speak and understand the language of the locals from the very outset. Dangers cited were:

- Coming on too strongly
- Being "superior" to locals in whatever respect
- Creating too much change right from the start without knowing the territory
- Investing in the wrong deal or location for a business or your home (until locals trust you, they might not volunteer that essential information)

Questions to ask yourself regarding the move:

- What sort of first impression will I make?
- Do I know the biases this community might have towards me and my family?
- Of which of my "quirks" should I be aware to avoid distrust from a small community?
- What city "baggage" am I bringing that does not fit my new community's standard modus operandi? Do I need it? Instead of giving me pleasure or comfort, will it create mistrust?
- How am I planning to move in? How should I greet my neighbors to best blend in, yet be cordial?

Getting involved in your new community

Your willingness to roll up your shirt sleeves and not be an "arm chair manager" will be recognized positively, and will build a better rapport from the start.

For instance, becoming involved with the workers constructing or remodeling your home, or pitching in and doing a little manual work, will be reassurance to the indigenous population. Not showing class distinctions in dealing with people will be essential in the more rural areas. The more sophisticated your background, the more important it becomes to let your new neighbors see that you are a working person just like them. They will welcome and include you in their community when they see you as genuine. These traits in particular illustrate the common values of the pioneering spirit:

• Willingness to do hard "real" work (no servants)

• Love of developing personal relationships, not just intellectual or sophisticated cultural socializing; by just getting to know your neighbor over a cup of coffee.

• Supporting and attending local community functions (fairs, ice cream socials, politics, buying locally, etc.)

• Helping the neighbor in need, however you can. Showing you care.

To assess your willingness to be involved in your new community, ask yourself:

• Would I enjoy a simpler, more personal lifestyle?

• Would I enjoy dropping a scheduled activity to sit down and talk with a neighbor or acquaintance?

• Am I too accustomed to professional entertainment? Would I automatically judge and compare local talent with professional offerings? Would I consequently not want to frequent these amateur performances or functions?

- Do I feel comfortable in rearranging personal and even business activities to come to the support of a neighbor in need? Would this type of interruption bother me?

After the Move

Somewhere during the first year or two in the new community, a realistic perception of life occurs. New customs either become habits and wear comfortably or become sources of irritation, creating a nagging feeling that "something is wrong with this picture." The keys to feeling in harmony with a new place and life lie first in the quality and depth of the relationships and secondly in the social interactions established. The findings of our survey indicated that if a respondent or spouse made new friends and became involved in the community more easily than anticipated, the *overall* perception of adjustments was also seen as being easier than anticipated. Conversely, where there was more difficulty in connecting with new friends or relationships, the overall perception of adjusting to the new community was also more difficult. Interestingly, whether or not the adjustments were more or less difficult, almost all of our survey respondents felt the move was worthwhile.

With our specialized survey, no major conclusions can be made about overall marriage situations. Prior to moving, only three of the people we surveyed indicated shaky marriage situations, which ended in divorce in two out of the three cases. A single woman stated she married a local. It is safe to say in the case of all our respondents that the move did affect relationships. The outcome had a lot to do with circumstances outside this study.

Within five years of relocating, many of our respondents were joined in their new communities by other members of their family. Parents, in-laws and siblings were the most common family members to arrive on the scene. Only occasionally did adult children join parents who had migrated to smaller communities.

Anticipating the Unexpected

About one half of the working respondents felt a drop in income for the first two years before regaining or surpassing their pre-move income. Eighty-four percent had regained their pre-move income within three to five years. About half of the working respondents increased their income at least by 50% within three to five years. Most of these people were self-employed or started their own businesses. Several of the people we surveyed noted that money goes much further in smaller communities. For the 13% of working respondents whose income did not return to the pre-move level, "more difficult than anticipated" responses in income adjustment as well as other categories were observed, including two expressing they "would not make the move again if they had it to do over again."

Employment for those not working for themselves was a mixed bag. Often the "right" job was not there initially, but did turn up in time. Perseverance appeared to be the key in small town employment, supported by getting to know and be trusted by the "regular" townspeople.

The climate adjustment surprised only a few respondents adversely, while most felt the adjustment was easier than anticipated. Cold was sighted as a problem, as were allergies. Spouses and children of the respondents appeared to have more difficulty in this area than the survey respondents themselves.

The business climate was changeable and uncertain for most of the respondents. Some felt there were negative, narrow-minded attitudes in their new communities. Oddly, this was noted primarily "initially" and then was softened to "I figured out how to deal with them" or "finally found a group of positive thinkers, often other transplants." Traditionally, in the smaller communities, the "new kid in town" goes through a period of being an "outsider" for one or two years, until the local population decides whether he or she can make it. During this time period, information may be qualified or filtered to the new transplant. Keeping a very open mind and getting involved quickly in local activities seem to be good antidotes to this rapport building period. It may be helpful to remember you are probably considered a guest in the community for one to two years and should act accordingly towards the townspeople, yet at the same time keep in mind you *are* at home.

In trying to anticipate the unexpected, the following questions may be helpful:

- What allergies are prevalent in the new area?

- If you need to work to support yourself, how would making half your current salary or less for five years affect your mental and environmental outlook?

- What do you know about "small town thinking?" Do you have an expectation that others must be open-minded in order for you to feel you can operate effectively?

Recommend to Others

For all sorts of reasons, nearly all respondents recommended the move and suggested:

- Know yourself and what you want
- Plan as best you can
- Save your money
- Drop your expectations and go with the flow
- Take some risk and do it.

The amount of good advice was both heartwarming and overwhelming. Perhaps one of the best things you can do for yourself is to contact people in your chosen dream spot who have moved there, and interview them on their experiences and get their recommendations. This may well provide you the first networking opportunity for future community involvement and friends.

Assessing Your Potential to Be an Urban Drop-out

The previous section introduced a successful urban drop-out profile. In the Appendix of this book is a questionnaire based on our survey results and remarks from successful transplants.

Mark your response to the right of the questions. Follow the scoring directions for each section and the overall summary at the end.

If you're really serious, look at the areas where you didn't score highly. Re-read these sections to better assess your situation. You may have special circumstances that this survey has not addressed. Remember, the advice of the urban transplant veterans: Know thyself and what you want, plan, take some risk and then go for it!

§3§

Dropping Out to—Where?

listen: there's a hell
of a good universe next door: let's go.

—e. e. cummings
Times One

The old saying that "one man's ceiling is another man's floor" holds true for urban dropouts. While they all share a common sense of the quest for a better style and quality of life, what that improvement represents is different for everyone. One man may be seeking the solitude and isolation of a forest cabin with a monthly trek to town being his only human contact. For another, a custom home with a few trees on an acre of land outside the bustle of the city may be just perfect.

What is universally agreed upon is the "why" of dropping out. Those simple elements of daily life that many of our grandfathers, and even our fathers, took for granted seem to have disappeared from the hectic everyday existence of most people.

Urban dropouts talk about things like the sense of community they have found in their new town. People know each other and care about one another. Two hundred people will leave their jobs to band together and search for a lost little boy; $10,000 in dimes and quarters can be raised virtually overnight to help someone who is in need of an operation; the whole town turns out for a picnic in the park on the Fourth of July.

With that sense of community comes a new awakening. Dropouts talk about becoming "mini Chambers of Commerce" and are enthusiastic and outspoken advocates of their new home and their new way of life. As the people around them open up and become willing to help, so too does the new dropout crack off the city-bred shell of suspicion and indifference.

These new transplants talk about the self-satisfaction of being accepted for who you are, rather than for your material possessions or the neighborhood in which you live. There is less pressure to compete and compare and more time just to live and let live. Having moved to places where there is a life outside of the workplace, a senior partnership and the two-window corner office seem a little less important to the new arrival. They have gone to a place where big city rules do not always apply.

In small towns, there is a feeling of knowing that one individual can and does make a difference. It is easier to become more personally involved in local government, and have a vote that really counts. A person can stand up at a community meeting to speak out against a potentially-harmful proposal or in support of a worthy candidate. Each person's voice has special meaning.

There is the joy of being in touch with the surroundings, of getting back to the earth. There are animals, both wild and domestic, to watch with respect and enjoy the sheer beauty of their existence. There is an appreciation for how fragile our environment is, and also how wonderful. And there is something pleasurable in learning simple tasks like recycling and conversation, and knowing that, in a small way, these basic things are making a difference.

Although it may sound like a fantasy world, these are not pipe dreams. These are real feelings and real experiences from people who have opened themselves up to a new and better way to live.

THE DRAWBACKS OF THE RURAL SCENE

It would be misleading to offer the impression that all is perfect in rural America, and that there are no disadvantages to moving there. However, we truly feel that leaving the congested, crime-ridden city for the saner environs of the countryside is a wise move that's well worth making. One of our survey questions asked "If you had it to do over again, would you still make the move", and practically every answer was "Yes"—capitalized, underlined, or marked with an exclamation point. To be fair though, since the purpose of this book is to prepare you for the move, here are some additional things to consider:

Availability of goods and services: If you have spent the last ten years in Manhattan, or any major city, you have come to take the availability of virtually any product or service for granted. Whether it's a person to walk your dog or a kosher grocery store, it's all there. This is certainly not always the case in a small town. Although a number of city dropouts have, in recent years, opened a wide variety of interesting shops and service companies in small towns, you may have to travel outside the area or use mail order outlets to find some of the things you want or need.

Many of the dropouts we spoke to make a regular trip

to the "big city" a couple of times a year for shopping. The trip is combined with dining at a top-notch restaurant or a night at the theater or the ballet. Then, having gotten their fill of the city and a good taste of the crowds and all the other reasons they left in the first place, they happily retire back to their peaceful way of life.

Costs of goods: While you will discover that most major items —housing, insurance, vehicles, restaurants, construction services—are less expensive in a small community, some things aren't. Depending on the location of the town, the importation of products from other areas may drive the costs up somewhat, as will the forces of supply and demand. Gasoline may be a little higher if it's being trucked in from a long distance away, as will some fruits and vegetables that are not grown locally. When you make your site visits to places you are considering for relocation, a little comparison pricing in a few different stores is a good indicator of future living conditions.

Taxes and Insurance: Again, these are two items that are almost always considerably lower in small communities, but there are exceptions. Fire insurance, for example, may be higher due to the greater distance between fire stations and the increased use of wood burning for heat. The tax base to support the local school system and community services cannot be spread over as large a number of property owners as in the city (of course, the tax base is also much lower), and property taxes may be a little higher in some areas.

Entertainment: This is an area where your choices will not be as extensive as in the city. There won't be as many restaurants, movie theaters, or other sources of entertainment from which to choose. Television reception may be marginal in some fringe areas, and not every community has cable TV available to its residents.

Transportation: Smaller communities do not typically have international airports. If you travel a lot, for either business or pleasure, you will have to go a little further to get to the airport or an extra connecting flight. However, most communities, no matter how small, are serviced by commercial bus lines, and most have Amtrak available in or nearby.

Health Facilities: Here again, a smaller community may not have the resources for specialized health care. Depending on your particular situation, this is an obvious consideration to explore before deciding on a move to a particular area.

BEGINNING THE QUEST

There are, quite obviously, a vast number of decisions to be made in the course of considering, deciding upon, planning, and executing a rural relocation. Not the least of these decisions is the question of relocating to—exactly where?

The decision-making process essentially breaks down into three broad categories. Number one is the decision to make the move; number two, the choice of where to move; and number three the options of what to do when you get there. All three are interdependent, with each affecting the other to some degree. The most important category, which acts as the pivot on which the other two decision categories will swing, is the choice of where to move.

Where you settle will have a number of ramifications, and should be given a serious amount of thought and consideration. The town you choose, as well as the surrounding community and even the state in which it's located, will affect you economically, emotionally, and physically. Some areas are better for the type of business you would like to start. Other areas have better employment opportunities for your particular field. A desert home may help your health, while a spot high in the mountains may have adverse affects. And while you are certainly not committed to the town once you have moved there, a second uprooting is difficult. This will often aggravate lots of doubts and questions of "did I do the right thing."

Relocating should be—and will be—a move to a better life. So give the choice of where you move the consideration it deserves. Involve the entire family, and let them all have a voice in the final decision. You will find that the whole decision-making process is actually a lot of fun, adventurous and exciting.

This chapter will describe how you can start the research process and narrow down the possibilities of where you might like to move. In the next chapter, you'll learn about visiting the new site, and understanding what to do and what to look for while you're there.

The Town That Finds You

For some people, the decision of where to move was made long ago. Their stories are diverse, but very similar—they discovered a small town in Vermont while on a hunting trip or driving through Oregon on their honeymoon and spending the night in a sleepy little town with which they fell in love.

One couple told of discovering a town while hitchhiking the Southwest on a break from college, then relocating there six years later. A traveling salesman with a route through the Northern states once had his car break down in a quiet rural Michigan community. He became impressed with the friendly assistance he received from the locals and never forgot the town. He moved there when he retired.

Finding the right locale may have been the end result of skiing in Colorado; a seminar at a resort town in Idaho; traveling to a rodeo in Texas or arrowhead hunting in New Mexico. Or it could have been while on an educational sabbatical in Maine; on a fishing trip in Florida; antiquing in Wisconsin; farm hopping in Kansas or touring bed and breakfasts while on vacation along the Washington coast. There were lots of places and lots of diverse reasons to be at those places, but there was one common result—the town was perfection.

Perhaps you've had a similar experience. You are in a town and something affects you about it. It might be a deep breath of crisp mountain air on a fall morning, or the friendly, unsuspicious help of a stranger during a minor emergency. It could be the shops or the hiking, or the silence in the evenings, deep and unbroken. Something gets to you about the place, some little touch of magic meant only for you, and you know that someday, somehow, this is a place to which you'll be coming back.

Steve H. described the experience as "coming home". He was born and raised in the Chicago area, and had gone to college there, but, for some reason, he never really felt comfortable in a big city environment. After graduation, he took a job in Philadelphia and worked there for seventeen years, but again, vaguely and without a lot of conscious thought, he still didn't feel comfortable.

Finally, at the age of thirty-seven, while he and his family were touring the Central farm states, they stopped for the night at a small farming community in Iowa. The next day, they took a leisurely walking and driving tour of the town; Steve and his wife Ellen had a strange feeling of having been there before. Two years later they bought a small farm and moved there. After all those years of living somewhere else, within a remarkable short time, Iowa became truly home.

Like Steve, you may have happened on a "just right" town. But, while the town may have found you without a lot of searching on your part, it doesn't preclude your doing some homework. You will still need to understand the local economy and housing market, the structure of the tax system and the availability of land, the recreational amenities and health care facilities. In short, you will want to arm yourself with as much knowledge as possible of what to expect.

The Town That You Find

Sitting behind a desk that overlooked the haze-enshrouded Los Angeles skyline, Terri R. had never had a divine inspiration while walking quiet streets or buying jam from a roadside stand. All she knew was that she was fed up and had to get out of Los Angeles—and soon. The pressures of her job were overpowering, and the time-consuming commutes and long hours away from home were putting a lot of strain on her marriage.

Days of dissatisfaction stretched into months, and the thought of moving became more and more important. At first, just to relax her mind, she began reading newspaper and magazine articles about rural areas, and about people who had dropped out of the rat race of the city. She methodically began noting the names of cities and towns that sounded interesting, noting additional information as to what these places might have to offer. Finally, as her list grew longer and her resolve grew stronger, she began to gather more information by writing letters to various towns.

Her thoughts of moving began to crystallize, and then her husband got involved and excited about the project. Together, they inventoried their wants and needs and began to narrow down their possibilities. Terri hated rain and cold weather, and thought a desert environment would be appealing. Brad wanted a town that was large enough to have good transportation facilities, so that he could return to Los Angeles as needed to service clients, and a community theatre group where he could devote his free time to his life-long avocation.

Together, they narrowed the field of possibilities to two places in New Mexico and one in Arizona. Not only had they never visited these places, but, in fact, they had never even heard of any of them until just a month earlier. They decided to take a vacation, arranging to visit and study all three towns.

From a purely logical and unemotional standpoint, none of the towns were perfect. Ultimately, however, the town in Arizona was the one that best suited their needs and had the best "feel" to them. Despite taking a very analytical approach to inventorying the pros and cons of each community, Terri still had to admit that emotions influenced them greatly in choosing a new home and one particularly beautiful desert sunset helped make up her mind.

The "Wants and Needs" List

Terri's method of setting out to study all the available data to find a town that is exactly right and Steve's approach of pretty much letting the town pick you, essentially on emotions alone, represent two extremes of selecting a new community. For most people, the quest falls somewhere in the middle. But no matter what approach you use, there are certain common basic elements: you need to know what you're looking for and what you can realistically expect.

Having a solid understanding of why you are making the move and what things you would like your new community to have are essential to your own sense of satisfaction afterward. Whether it is just cleaner air you're seeking or whether it's the chance to own a six hundred acre cattle ranch, poor preparation and over-expectations can quickly lead to disappointment and dissatisfaction. Given the general difficulties of planning and making a major move such as this, the more you know about exactly what to expect, the better off you will be.

Our suggestion as to the best way to set about achieving this is to sit down and develop a *Wants and Needs* List. One person can do this alone initially, but at some point the entire family should become involved. Even younger children need to have a say about what they want, to feel involved from the very beginning in order to help ease their way through the entire complicated process.

Ask yourself the following basic questions, and write down the answers. The information you gather at this point will be essential to the evaluation process, both now and when you visit the towns. It will also give you something to look back on to help gauge your later satisfaction with the move.

Why do you want to move? Be as specific as you possibly can, and list everything that comes to mind. It doesn't matter if you want to move because of high crime, poor schools, congestion, high taxes, or dirty air. No reason is too small or insignificant, and no thought is invalid.

What would you like the move to accomplish? At first glance, the answers to this question seem to be the opposite of the answers to the first question—less crime, better schools, open spaces. But your answer should be more completely thought out than that.

For example, if one of your reasons for moving is congestion, how could your new home solve that problem? Is there less traffic? Are there open vistas where you can see for miles? Do you need fifty acres of your own land around you?

What would you like to do after you move? This is not really a trick question, although it may require more thought than would indicate at first glance. If you are planning to retire, how do you want to spend your time? Passing your days on the front porch of a secluded cabin catching up on neglected reading may sound perfect, but if you are used to an active lifestyle, the seclusion may disillusion you in a short time. Perhaps semi-retirement is more the answer: start or buy a small business, or even find a part-time job.

If you are not going to be enjoying the luxury of retirement and still need to be concerned about earning a living, what do you have in mind? Perhaps you are dissatisfied with your present occupation—in fact, that may be a significant reason behind your relocation plans. If so, what would you prefer to do? Would you like to start a whole new career? Have you dreamed of opening your own business? Perhaps you feel it's time to go back to school to further your education, either for advancement in your present career or to finish getting a degree. Perhaps you may wish to pursue an education in a whole new field. Be honest and introspective, and be sure to write down your answers.

Where would you like to live? The answer to this may be objective, subjective, or a combination of both. You may have specific reasons for needing to be in a certain place, such as a certain climate or a town that's close to a major airport or rail service. Or you may simply have a romantic vision of a white Christmas spent around the crackling hearth of your home in the pine-scented mountains. Again, no reason is too small not to be considered.

How would you like to live? After an hour of head-scratching. The answer to this question may simply be "I don't know." Perhaps you have always wanted to live on a farm, complete with livestock and big red tractor in the barn. Maybe your personal vision is a rustic log cabin, half buried in snow drifts for part of the year. Or, maybe a contemporary home on a rocky cliff overlooking the pounding surf appeals to you? Or a horse ranch? Whichever it may be, it is important to rate the choice.

How are your finances? This subject is covered in detail in Chapter 5, but it bears mentioning here. While you certainly do not need to be rich in order to move, it would be imprudent to think that you can make the move with no financial resources whatsoever. Unfortunately, moving costs money. There is the moving truck, the cost of the trip, deposits or down payments on a new house, and the need for subsistence money until a new source of income is established.

Take a look at your finances—what you have in the bank and what proceeds you might generate out of the sale of your house. Also, consider such things as retirement benefits you might loose by leaving your present job, or important medical benefits you might be without. It may be that your financial situation is fine, and the move would not adversely affect you, or it may be that there are a number of benefits to be gained by simply waiting another year before making a change.

How is your health? For some people, this may not be much of a consideration. For others, it could be the deciding factor between one place and another, or perhaps even the underlying reason for the move itself. If, for example, you suffer from high blood pressure, a move to the high altitudes of a mountain community may be ill-advised. Other communities may be too cold or too damp and humid for your arthritis, or have conditions that aggravate your allergies or your asthma.

As part of your move planning, you will be gaining a variety of demographics on the area, including climatic information. If necessary, you may wish to consult with your physician on the advisability of moving to certain communities, or have him request specific information for you from other doctors in the area under consideration.

Another important health factor is the availability of specialized health care facilities. If you have a specific illness or condition that requires special medical care, make certain that the community you are considering has the capability of providing the treatments you need, either within the town itself or within a conveniently short distance.

How rural is rural? This last question is an important one that often gets overlooked. Different people have various ideas of what "rural" is, and some of those ideas may be somewhat out of touch with what's realistic. Remember the old television show *Green Acres*, with the ex-New Yorker and his wife trying to make it on a dilapidated farm? While exaggerated for comic situations, some aspects of what happened to this hapless couple ring distressingly close to the truth. Farming and ranching are tough occupations, with years of hard-won skill and experience on the land often the only difference between profit and bankruptcy.

Take into consideration the types of things you now enjoy, and try to project them into a more rural environment. Do you enjoy going to the movies? The theater? Are restaurants and shopping an important part of your life? Are the feel of a silk evening gown or the low growl of an accelerating Porsche things that truly makes you happy? And don't be ashamed if they are. The purpose of this move is to find a better life, so don't feel you need to deny your enjoyment of material things out of some sense that getting back to basics involves the suppression of these feelings.

However, many truly rural communities cannot satisfy needs for luxury and excitement. If you can not be happy in a town with a population of two hundred where the closest movie theater is an hour and fifteen minutes away and the diner closes at 7:00 PM, it is important before you move to a country locale that you understand what it is you really want.

Ten Relocation Considerations

While doing the questioning and soul-searching required for the *Wants and Needs* list may be something of a hassle, it's well worth it. You now have some hard data that you can study, plus information about you and your family that can help guide you to the perfect location.

Read back through all your notes, and pick out the signposts of information. Do you see a pattern of answers that show how much your family would like to farm a small plot of land? Does it become obvious that the desert is the perfect place for retirement? Do medical problems preclude your moving high up into the Rocky Mountains?

With a little detective work, you can draw a few conclusions. Try to compile a simple, readable list of major choices, along with the most attractive options to those first choices.

To aid you in compiling this list, and to help focus your thoughts and avoid overlooking anything, we have compiled a list of the ten most important considerations voiced by the urban dropouts we have surveyed. This list of concerns and reasons is echoed by a variety of national surveys and studies that have been done on the subject of relocation and population trends. Simply put, they are the reasons that most people move away from the city.

These ten broad categories are listed below, and are ranked in the order of importance that emerged from our surveys. If you are typical of the majority of dropouts, most or all of these things are important to you, and some of them are crucial considerations—perhaps even the sole reason for moving.

Begin by making a list that contains all ten headings, plus a place for individual rankings. Give a copy to each member of the family, so that they can offer their own rankings of importance. Work through the categories one by one, referring back to your notes and the answers to the previous questions, and determine where your priorities lie.

SURVEY RANKING	CATEGORY	YOUR RANKING
1	Climate/Environmental Quality	_____
2	Size/Population Density	_____
3	Crime	_____
4	Housing	_____
5	Land	_____
6	Employment/Business Opportunities	_____
7	Recreation	_____
8	Retirement/Health	_____
9	Entertainment/Hobbies	_____

10	Geographical Location	______
None	Other Considerations	______

RANKING RESULTS

Climate/Environmental Quality: Among all of the people we've talked with, this category seems to constantly come out at or near the top of virtually everyone's concerns. Most expressed the desire for clean air and clean water, important considerations in this day and age, when it's virtually impossible to pick up the newspaper or turn on a newscast without hearing about another environmental disaster.

We are, as a country and as a planet, slowly poisoning ourselves to death. Environmental issues and concerns are becoming, at long last, more and more important to a growing number of people. People want to live where, as the old joke goes, they can breathe air that they can't see. They also want to feel a little bit more in control of their environment, and feel that their efforts, whether these efforts be recycling, organic gardening or fighting land uses in their area that have a detrimental environmental impact, can and do make a difference.

Climate is equally important. Dan M. was born and raised in the San Francisco bay area. He put a very high priority on moving to a place where it snowed. A white Christmas outside his own door was what he was after, and he wasn't going to move somewhere that he couldn't have it. Joyce L., a native of Washington, D.C., planned to move across the country to escape the high humidity. Others want to get away from the rain, or from the heat, or to live in a place where they never again need to break out a snow shovel.

As discussed earlier, many people whom we surveyed had health considerations. If one of your areas of concern is that cold areas may need to be avoided, or perhaps areas of high rainfall or regions with high levels of certain pollens, place this criterion on your list of restrictions and limit your options to those places which meet your families' health needs.

Size/Population Density: Also at the top of most lists is the desire to get away from the crowds, noise and traffic. Wanting to move to an area without freeways, one couple specifically wanted a town without a single stoplight. Along with clean air, most people are seeking an area where they have room to breathe, where they can go to dinner on Friday night and not expect to have a three-hour wait, where driving to work is a matter of fifteen minutes, not an hour and a half or two hours.

Of equal concern with the size of the area is the population density. Some states, like Connecticut, have very high population densities, with large numbers of people in a relatively small area. While at first glance the population of a town may seem small, if that population is packed into an even smaller number of square miles, you can still have congestion and traffic problems.

Another congestion problem stems from tourism. One man told us that he wanted to live where other people vacation, and that's a common desire. On the other side of the coin, however, you need to remember that people also want to vacation where you live. Quiet mountain towns can burst at the seams during hunting or skiing seasons, and that isolated stretch of beach where you look for shells can have more bodies then grains of sand once school lets out for the summer. This may or may not be a concern of yours, but it bears keeping in mind.

Crime: A low crime rate ranked third in importance with most people, and is certainly an important attribute for any community to which you move. A surprisingly high number of people who have left the urban environment had, at one time or another, been victims of a crime—many more than once. Car theft, burglary, robbery, purse snatching, hit and run, extortion, felony drunk driving, muggings, even gang violence, are just some of the crimes on the list.

For young and old alike, from newlyweds with small children to the elderly on a fixed income, the right to live in a safe and secure environment is extremely important. Many of our interviews reflected the simple joys of being able to jog in the park without worry, or to take an evening stroll around the neighborhood without fear.

Housing: A recent national study shows that the gap between the cost of a house and those who can afford to buy one has widened for the *14th consecutive year.* The greatest of all the American dreams—owning a home of your own—is getting further and further out of reach for more and more people.

Home ownership is a prime motivating factor behind many of the moves that dropouts make. They are either tired of paying high rents while the possibility of home ownership becomes a dimmer dream each year, or else they own a home in an area where property values have risen sharply over the years, and they would like to take their equity out and do something with the money.

There are a variety of publications and statistical sources that show home and land prices in various areas of the United States. If you yearn strongly for your own house, note that here and plan on concentrating your community search in areas where the housing is more affordable. (More on that in Chapter 6.)

Land: Hand-in-hand with housing prices is the price for bare land, for whatever use you wish to put it. If your question and answer sessions with the family have shown a strong propensity for a return to the land, record that fact and make it a priority during your search. Many parts of the country are dotted with small farms and very affordable acreage.

Another land consideration is non-agricultural use.

Many large companies have relocated their offices and manufacturing facilities to rural communities because of the affordability of acreage for expansion—and at the same time they can offer a variety of amenities to entice the best of employees. If commercial or industrial property is important, note that here.

Employment/Business Opportunities: While most urban dropouts have something of the dreamer in them, they also have practical sides. The need to find an area where there is ample opportunity to make a living showed up as an important consideration. While a very small, rural hamlet may sound romantically enticing, if you need to earn a decent wage, it may not be the best place for you.

Doing an assessment of your financial situation has already been discussed, and will be dealt with in more detail later in the book. But as you make and review your lists, you know what your resources are and what they will dictate for your future. With that in mind, you will need to weigh your choice of a new community with care.

In years past, many small, rural farming communities, impoverished and slowly dying as the local economy faltered, saw a continuing downward spiral as more and more people moved away to seek their fortunes in the city. Happily, a tremendous number of communities have experienced a dramatic turnabout in recent years. New people—escapees from the city—have moved there seeking affordable land and a quieter existence.

These new residents have brought with them two important commodities: money and talent. They have opened new businesses, started new services, promoted tourism, and enriched the economy in a myriad of ways. As a result, many small communities all across the country are now havens for entrepreneurs and may represent the ideal place for you to start a unique business of your own.

If you will be seeking more conventional employment and are not moving with a job transfer or a new job opportunity waiting, you will need to do a little more research. Availability in employment is dependent on two basic factors: the type of work you do, and the kinds of companies located in the area.

Certain occupations are fairly universal—accounting or construction work, for example—and, as such, your chances of finding employment are much greater. More specialized occupations may require a town with a larger population, or you may need to specifically seek out an area that has companies which employ people in your field.

Recreation: If you like to fish, you ought to move to a locale where the fish are plentiful. This simple logic was expressed by one potential fisherman with whom we talked, and it holds a lot of weight for a number of dropouts. Many people felt that the availability of recreational opportunities, either in the town or within a short distance of it, was a strong factor when planning their moves.

How important this is or isn't to you personally is strictly up to you, but it is a point well worth considering. If you are an avid skier, for example, what could be better than living twenty minutes from a ski resort? Or for that matter, just living in the mountains where you can break out your cross-country skis for a private jaunt whenever the mood hits? Fishing is often abundant in rural areas, as are the simple pleasures of hiking and bicycling. Water skiing, boating, snowmobiling, diving, equestrian sports, and even hang gliding, whatever your sport, can be found in an area perfect for it.

Team sports abound also. Many communities have long-established softball and baseball leagues, as well as basketball and bowling leagues. Look around, and you are apt to find a football league, volleyball tournaments, or even a group of water polo enthusiasts.

Retirement/Health: These two broad categories were often combined by people with whom we talked and are listed together here. Either or both can be important considerations, depending on your particular situation.

Look back at some of the answers you gave previously, and see how retirement planning fits into your prospective move. You may find that your needs are a combination of some of the categories listed above—a good climate, affordable housing, ample recreational opportunities or the chance for a small business or a part time job.

Perhaps you're considering the possibility of a planned retirement community. There are excellent ones throughout the country, offering beautiful living facilities, individual and planned recreation, travel opportunities, and the chance to meet new people with similar interests. There are several well-written guides to both retirement and retirement communities, and any one of them should provide you with the information you need to get your search started. To find these guides, check with your library or your local bookstore.

You'll also want to research the medical facilities in your new town, something that's an important consideration for people of all ages and at all levels of physical ability and condition. Some rural areas will only be served by one doctor who covers a fairly large area, and hospitals or specialized clinics may be some distance away. However, in a rapidly growing number of small communities you will find excellent health care. Just like you, many doctors have left the urban craziness and set up practices in small towns and cities.

Entertainment/Hobbies: This category emerged as a concern and a consideration that is quite separate from recreation. While the recreation category tended to cover such things as golf and skiing, many people spoke of not wanting to lose the means of entertainment that they now enjoy—movies, theater, restaurants, shopping, and much more.

When taking this ninth category into consideration, take a look at your current lifestyle, and, again, refer back to your earlier notes. Look for what is important to you in the way of entertainment, and plan on adding those things to your list of needs and requirements when deciding on a future home.

Many of the entertainment facilities that you are most used to in the city will exist, albeit on a smaller scale, in a rural community, but much of what you find available will be governed by the size of the town. A very small hamlet may have only one cafe, or perhaps a small restaurant that's part of a tavern. A larger town will probably have several restaurants. If the town has seen any kind of influx of ex-urbanites in recent years, you will probably find a surprisingly diverse, and excellent, collection of menus from which to choose.

The same size considerations will also typically apply to the availability and abundance of movies and live theater, orchestras, nightclubs, choral groups, and rock-n-roll bars, as well as shopping establishments. Don't overlook the availability of some of these amenities in neighboring towns and communities, or even the proximity of a major city. If you only go to the movies once every three months, it may not be a problem that the only theater is a half-hour drive to a neighboring town. If going to an opera or a symphony is a once-a-year occasion, plan a long weekend in the city and combine it with a shopping spree. These are decisions only you can make after weighing all the factors and getting a feel for your priorities.

Hobbies are another consideration for your list and your quest. If you love to garden, the short growing season of a high-mountain community will be a disappointment. If your hobby is model train building and you typically buy everything through mail order catalogs, then where you settle may not matter at all. Again, weigh your options and priorities, and decide accordingly.

Geographical Location: It may be important for you to stay within a certain region of the United States (or elsewhere in the world, for that matter). Most of the dropouts with which we spoke, unless motivated by a job transfer or other outside considerations, chose to relocate to communities within the same basic geographical areas in which they were comfortable. There is the relative proximity of friends and relatives to consider, as well as simply being more at ease with certain regional customs and products.

If you think you would be more comfortable staying within a certain state or region, make a note of your preference in this category. Think about how large or small an area to which you would actually consider moving, and then you can confine your search to towns within those approximate boundaries.

Other: No good list is ever complete without a catch-all "other" category, and this is no different. While you may have reasons for moving that are similar to those of many other people, you may well have reasons for leaving the city or for selecting a particular town that are uniquely your own.

You may be moving so that you can be closer to family members, in which case the town has already been selected for you. One person with whom we spoke had moved because she had inherited from her grandfather a house and a small store in a rural community. Whatever other reasons you may have for making the move, list them here and give them due consideration in your relocation planning.

ARMCHAIR TRAVELING

By now, you probably have a bulging file folder crammed with notes, and you're wondering what to do with it all. Take heart. Knowing what you want from your move is a tremendous first step. It's now time to move into the next phase.

Analyze the Data

For most people, the best next step is to discuss the list with your family. Make an evening of it and go over your conclusions from the questions and list-making you have done. What you want to attain is yet another refinement of your final *Wants and Needs* list. By now, through all the notes and discussions, you should be able to narrow down your quest to some specific areas.

Tim and Cheryl M. had come to the conclusion that they needed a minimum of ten acres in a Western state. They wanted a place where they could raise horses and have enough open areas around them to ride. They also needed a community with convenient transportation, as to allow both the opportunity for occasional commutes to Southern California for business purposes. Their quest led them to Central Oregon and a mini-ranch, which they were able to comfortably afford on the proceeds from the sale of their Los Angeles home.

Deborah C. and her husband, both with business ties in Manhattan that would require their presence two or three times a month, wanted some place that was a convenient train or commuter plane ride away from the city. They had no plans to raise animals, but wanted a good, healthy environment for their two young sons. They settled on a farming community in upstate New York, and bought a rambling old house nestled in an acre of mature trees.

Art M., a single, wanted a community that was peaceful

but not dull. He was looking for a small house that he could afford, didn't want acreage and didn't mind living in town. He also needed to find work. His search led him to a ski resort town in Colorado. He found a small "fixer-upper" home to renovate, a job on the ski patrol team in the winter and on a carpentry crew in the summer. Between the ski lodge and his volunteer work with the community theater, he has had ample opportunity to meet people and make new friends.

All these people were seeking a better life, and they found it. They had diverse goals, however, and specific needs that had to be filled. By taking the time to discover and analyze those needs, each one was able to find the right community for him or her.

Flexibility

One final consideration. As you compile your data and make your choices, don't overlook the need to be flexible in what you are seeking. It is rare to find the right community that possesses exactly the right elements for your situation, so you will almost certainly need to provide yourself with a little room for compromise.

A good job opportunity may lead you to an area that was not your first choice, but is still an attractive possibility. Go for it! Perhaps you find that your financial situation won't let you buy the two hundred acre horse ranch that the realtor led you to believe was affordable. Settle for twenty acres and make the move anyway.

Flexibility and the ability to adjust and adapt were listed repeatedly as important virtues by successful dropouts. These abilities will make your search and your move easier, and help you to avoid unrealistic dreams and disappointment.

FINDING THE POSSIBILITIES

It is time to start the hard work of the search itself. In this phase, you'll narrow down the possibilities and gather some additional information about them. If you have one particular town in mind and have made vacation trips to the area, gathering the necessary information and seeking to make an informed decision will help you to know what to expect after you move.

Even if you think you have definitely settled on one town that you would like to call your own, make a list of alternatives. Keep in mind the rule of staying flexible and adaptable. It could be, upon closer investigation, that the town you selected has absolutely no employment opportunities, or that your kids are allergic to the wood smoke in the air during the winter. Leave some options upon which to fall back. There is more than one pastoral place which will suit you.

If you are like most people, while you've been doing your list making you have also been drawn to magazine and newspaper articles about the rural relocation trend. You may have come across the names of previously unknown towns and communities that sound interesting. Write them down. In talking with friends and neighbors, ask about towns they may have visited on recent vacations or business trips, and make notes of any that sound interesting.

Your next stop should be a visit to your library. With the help of the research librarian, ask to see *The Guide To Periodical Literature.* This guide, and others like it, will direct you by category to articles that have been written about moving, about rural communities, and similar stories. Note the names and issues of magazines that have articles you would like to read, and ask the librarian for help in locating them. Once again, write down the names of any towns in the articles that sound interesting.

Check the card catalog in the library for books that rate towns. There are a number of publications on the subject, probably the most famous of which are *Places Rated Almanac* and *Places Rated Retirement Guide,* both by Richard Boyer and David Savageau. These books list and rate towns and cities for overall livability, and may offer you some interesting choices, as well as providing you with clues to equally livable small towns in other outlying areas. But don't ignore the listings for large cities, either. Seattle, Washington, for example, was rated number one in a recent issue.

Local Chambers of Commerce

Now that you have a list of possibilities, your next step is to contact that venerable source of free information, the Chamber of Commerce. Another stop at the library and a little help from the research librarian will get you the addresses and phone numbers for the Chambers of Commerce in each town you're considering.

Compose a simple letter to each, requesting general information about the town and the surrounding areas. Depending upon your particular needs and interests, ask for details on:

- Demographics—data here will give you population figures, breakdowns of age and income, land area, and a whole diverse and interesting collection of information;
- Climate—figures which will include average monthly temperatures, average yearly rain and snowfall, altitude, length of the growing season, and other information;
- Industrial Base—information on how the community makes its money, and what major companies and industries are in the area;
- Tax Base—information on how the community raises money to support itself. This will spell out income tax, property

tax, sales tax, business taxes, farm taxes, gas taxes, and all the other "devious" little taxes currently in effect in the community;

• Housing—discussions of average new and used home prices, how is construction activity in the area, how available are houses to buy or rent, are there apartments or other rental opportunities in the area;

• Health Care Facilities—included in this listing should be a basic rundown on the number of doctors, dentists, and hospitals in the area. If you have need for specific information, such as the availability of doctors who practice certain specialties, ask for that as well;

• Schools—information on the number of schools in the area by category (elementary schools, high schools, for example), as well as information on colleges. Usually, private school information will also be available;

• Recreation—a listing in this area can include such diverse pieces of information as the number of golf courses in the area, details about nearby ski resorts, how many lakes and streams there are, perhaps even figures on the latest salmon run;

• Business Opportunities—provides you with some specific information about the types and sizes of businesses that have recently been started or bought and sold. You can also find out if there are any local agencies that deal with the promotion of area businesses and the development of new enterprises;

• Transportation—information here will list nearby airports and what airlines serve them, if Amtrak or other rail service is available, what bus lines serve the town, and even such information as taxis and local bus lines;

• Retirement Information—if current or imminent retirement is a concern, you can enquire about specific retirement communities in the area, or the number of retired and senior citizens in the area;

- Vacation Packet—finally, request a Vacation Information packet. This collection of literature is aimed at vacationers and tourists, and will give you a different perspective on many aspects of the area. It will also help prepare you for your upcoming visit to the locale by giving you information on hotels and motels, restaurants, sightseeing, and often will include a variety of discount coupons on rooms, meals, etc.

If you wish, you might also want to ask for a city map, a mileage map (which will give you driving distances to major cities), and a copy of the local newspaper. There may be a small charge for these items, but they can be interesting and enlightening.

State Chambers of Commerce

It's also a good idea to write to the state Chamber of Commerce, which can be found in the state's capital city. This is particularly important if you are considering moving to a new state, and will also provide new and interesting information even if you are a long-time resident of the state.

As with the local Chambers, you'll get demographics, climate information, and details about industry and taxes, but all from a state-wide perspective. You might also want to request a Vacation Packet for the entire state, to help add additional information to your checklist, as well as helping you plan a more extensive future visit to the state.

Videotapes

An interesting idea that is gaining in popularity at a phenomenal rate, due to the electronic explosion of recent years, is the use of promotional video tapes. More and more Chambers of Commerce, as well as tourism and new business promotion offices, have produced videos of their town. From the comfort of your own living room—since it is assumed that most American households own a VCR—you can tour the community in vivid color and stereo sound.

Although a video can give you an overview of the area and highlight what the town can offer, it is important to remember these productions are normally made to enhance public relations. When you write to the state or local Chambers of Commerce, ask if a video tape of the area is available to borrow or rent, either from them or from the office of tourism.

The Letter-Writing Campaign

There are a variety of other letters you can write to help you round out the information you are gathering. You may decide to wait until you get some preliminary information from the Chamber of Commerce, or, if you already have such information, you can go to the library and get names and addresses out of the phone book.

One note about phone books. If you have a specific area in mind, your research will be considerably easier if you take the time to obtain a local phone book for the area. Check the front of your current phone book. You will find a listing for an 800 number to order additional phone books. There is usually a small charge for obtaining a phone book from out of your local service area, but it's well worth the money.

Here are some additional letters to consider:

Potential Employers: As your search for a town becomes more focused and you discover what companies and offices are located there, you can contact a few of the more likely prospects to inquire about employment opportunities. You may wish to send a simple letter of introduction with a brief inquiry about openings at their firm, or you may wish to send a complete resume. Always send a clean, carefully typed, personalized letter—not handwritten and not a form or photocopied letter.

Also inquire about the possibility of visiting the firm in person when you come to town for a visit.

Employment Agencies: In a similar vein, you might consider contacting some employment agencies in the area. Again, your letter should be personalized and typed, and you can either tell them briefly about your qualifications or include a resume. Make it clear the type of work you are seeking. This will result in valuable information about the local job market and salary ranges, as well as possibly opening the door for interviews when you get there.

Community Development Agencies: Many areas have a community development or business promotion office whose responsibility it is to bring new business into the area. If you are thinking of moving a business to the area or starting a new one, a letter to this agency will provide valuable information for you. They can tell you about the availability of land, including zoning and pricing, other competing businesses in the area, the availability of labor and natural resources, the tax and bond base, and much more. You can also get information about the purchasing of existing businesses.

Realtors: A variety of realtors will probably be contacting you soon enough (they'll get your name from the Chamber of Commerce), but you may wish to write to them first. Depending on your needs, you can inquire about the housing market, house and land prices, the amount of surplus inventory on the market (an indicator of how active or static the local economy is, as well as how much bargaining power you will have), property taxes, the availability of rental housing, commercial property, and businesses for sale.

MAILING LISTS

Be forewarned—all the letters you write will almost certainly put your name on a wide variety of mailing lists. Before you know it, you will probably receive letters and brochures from realtors, moving companies, construction companies, insurance agencies, motels, tourist traps, and a wide range of other businesses.

We have found the literature from these businesses to be interesting; occasionally, little gems of really helpful stuff are sent. One person was impressed with a personal letter she received from a realtor, began corresponding, and eventually bought property from him. Another person learned about a company that specialized in work similar to what he was doing in the city, and arranged for a job interview while he was visiting. Although he didn't get that job, he learned about a competitor for whom he now works.

New information increases your base knowledge of an unknown place. But if the thought of being on a firm's mailing list or having your name entered into yet another computer database is more than you can bear, request that the Chamber of Commerce or other persons or businesses that you write not release your name.

RELOCATION SERVICES

Find a trend, and right behind it you'll find an entrepreneur opening a new business to cater to it. Such is the case with relocation services.

It's not that relocation services are new, in fact they've been around for quite some time. For years, employees that were being transferred, or business owners that were moving a business or opening a new branch, could tap into these services to help find housing options and other details about the new city.

Now, with the growing trend to move out of cities and the increasing sophistication of computers and computer software, there are companies which can help you track down just the right rural community to fit your needs. If you wish to decide your future move this way, sit down with the counselor and the computer screen, describe what you're seeking, and the computer will provide you with a list of suitable options. All the details are there, from population to schools to tax bases to climate, and you can ask for specific additional details as you wish.

Thanks in large part to the growing use of interconnected computer networks, many Chambers of Commerce are tied into systems such as these, and are using them to promote their communities. Ask your realtor or your local Chamber of Commerce for more details on relocation services. If there is one available locally, they can help you get in touch with it.

School and Business Services

There are also relocation service systems dedicated exclusively to finding schools and business opportunities, and, being specialized in one specific area of expertise, both of these services can offer you much more in the way of precise, individually-tailored details. Both types of services will allow you to work in either direction. If you have a specific school or business criteria in mind, the service can direct you to an area where that's available; if you have a specific area in mind, they can give you details about the schools and businesses that are available there.

A school locating service, for example, can give you such details as curriculum offered, grade point averages of students, average college entrance test scores of their students, even ethnic and gender breakdowns. From a business opportunity service, you can get information on types of businesses already in an area, new business trends in that region, the labor pool available, and much more.

While the use of a relocation service has some obvious

advantages, it should not be your exclusive source of information for an area, nor should it form your only basis in making your selection of a new community.

For instance, the data you get back is only as good as the data you put in. If you are unsure about what you are looking for—where you would like to be, what you would like to do—the printouts will be equally vague and generalized. The more details you know about yourself and your motives for moving, and here again all your soul-searching and list-making will come into use, the better the computer information will be for your family and your specific needs.

Another problem is that a computer printout is just so many words and demographic details. It ignores the *heart* of a town. One dropout found a town that looked perfect on paper, but found the residents "snooty and rich, with no tolerance for 'outsiders' ". The only way to really know a town is to visit it. Don't ever make a final decision about moving to a town until you have actually walked its streets and talked with the people who live there.

4

An Unconventional Guide to Your New Locale

He that travels much knows much.

—Thomas Fuller,
Gnomologia

If you have followed a few of the suggestions in Chapter 3 and started a letter-writing campaign, by now your mailbox is bulging at the seams. Between the Chambers of Commerce, the vacation packets, the video tapes, and all the brochures and letters from assorted realtors, contractors, insurance agents, and the rest, you have got your share of reading to do.

At first glance, it all looks good. Realtors are telling you about great buys and the three rental homes you can almost have free; contractors are telling you about the castle they can build for less than you could have a garage built in the city; and the Chambers of Commerce have sent you brochures with lots of happy, smiling people doing all kinds of wonderfully happy, smiling things. You must ask yourself how much is true, and how much is just hype?

The truth is, it's a combination of both, probably leaning more toward substance than toward fantasy. For most, a move to the country is a good existence; you can buy more house and more property per dollar than you can in the city, and most of the smiling people really feel happy. However, there are drawbacks.

The trick is to see past the glossy surface—and your own optimistic hopes—and assess your potential new home for what it really is. That's your next assignment, and while you are in for some work, you are also in for some adventure and good plain fun.

The next step in your quest for the perfect new rural home is to make an on-site visit to every town you're considering. For some, this may involve visiting a half dozen towns, perhaps for the very first time. For those with that ideal new community already in mind from previous vacation trips, the quest becomes a little simpler, but there is still a lot of work to do. Analyzing a town as a potential new home is considerably different from just enjoying its amenities while you are there on vacation.

PLANNING FOR A SITE VISIT

As with any important undertaking, thorough planning and preparation are the keys to success. There are many things to see and a lot of stops to make while you are in town, so take the time to get ready for the trip before hopping into your car or motor home.

Before leaving home, consider all the material you have received from all the different sources. By now, you will have read enough material and sorted through enough of your needs and priorities to narrow down the choices for your community to a select few. If you still have ten or twelve places you think you might like to call home, you probably haven't done your preliminary homework thoroughly enough and must further refine your choices. Your final options should be limited to only three or four.

Plotting An Itinerary

Make a list of the towns you'd like to visit, then consult an atlas and plot an itinerary. If you are close enough to the various towns and will be making the entire trip by car, lay out a circle route that gets you from your home to the town closest to you (or the town you'd most like to visit), then around to each of the other areas before starting back home again. This will save you driving time and will maximize the amount of time you have at each stop. An automobile club such as AAA is well worth the cost to join; their travel service can plot out a complete itinerary for you, as well as provide all the maps and motel books you will need. They can even make advance hotel, motel, or even campsite reservations.

If you are visiting areas that are some distance away from the place you now live, you may want to consider flying to the nearest city and then renting a car for the rest of the journey. This is especially important if your time is limited since it allows you to avoid extra days on the road.

How Long To Stay

The longer you can stay in an area while you are on a fact-finding trip the better. A lengthy stay gives you more opportunity to really *see* the town. First impressions can be misleading. After you've been at a place awhile, you will find different areas to see and other people to talk with than you had originally planned, all of which takes time.

If you are planning on visiting several localities during one trip, allocate a *minimum* of three days per town, and more time if at all possible. This is a good argument for narrowing your list of sites down to two or three. Staying less than three days in a town will not give you ample opportunity to form any kind of reliable impression of the area and the people who live there.

Allowing for driving time, the maximum places you could visit in the span of an average two-week vacation would be four towns, and that's pushing it. You will get a bit burned out by the end of the two weeks, and, as a result, the last town probably won't get as much objective attention as the first town received. Probably the only exception to this three-day rule would be if you visit a town and find it is absolutely not what you expected. In that case, spend one night and get back on the road early the next day. You will have more time to spend in other, more favorable areas.

If you are only planning on visiting that one special place on which you've already pretty much decided, how much time you allot is somewhat dependent on how close the move is and how much hard information you need to gather. If you are serious about the move and intend to look at real estate or business opportunities, allow for at least a week's stay. A full two weeks would be ideal if moving time is drawing closer, and you must make decisions.

Our surveys and interviews indicated that most people, as they become more serious, spent increasingly longer periods of time in a new town with which they'd been impressed. They paid more frequent visits to it as the time to make the final commitment and actual move got closer. This is a natural progression, allowing you to form closer ties with the new town to which you will move and start the mental adjustment associated with leaving your old home.

Sam and Joy B. are a typical example of the frequency-of-visit progression. They had made a one-day stop to a town which made a favorable impression on them during a previous vacation. Then they had gone back a year later on another vacation and stayed for three days. The following year, the mental relocation wheels were starting to spin; so they went back—again as part of a longer vacation—but on this visit less time was spent playing and more time spent reading the papers, talking to the locals, and wandering around the town. By the time they got back home, their decision to move was much better formulated.

When their next vacation period rolled around, they took a week off for the sole purpose of visiting the town again to really study things. They also looked at real estate, and made some tentative plans on what type of home they'd like. Six months later they were back for an intensive ten day visit. They put an offer in on a house and spoke seriously with a number of people, including a potential employer for Sam. Their final visit came a month and a half later when they closed the deal on the house, and arranged for utility startups and other services. They went back home and started packing.

Advance Reservations

If any of the communities you intend to visit are located in resort areas or other highly-popular places, you will want to secure advance hotel or motel reservations before heading out, especially if the visit will be during the summer, the peak of the ski season, or over a holiday weekend.

If you received a vacation package from the Chamber of Commerce, there may be brochures for accommodations that look enticing and perhaps may even include some discount coupons. Auto clubs offer another source of names for quality rooms, as do guide books that you can get from the library or your local bookstore. You can also call the Chamber of Commerce for some names, or refer to the Yellow Pages of the community's phone book.

A pleasant alternative to a hotel or motel is staying at a country inn or Bed and Breakfast establishment. This gives you a somewhat less commercial view of the town, and affords you the wonderful opportunity to chat with the owners of the establishment over morning coffee. They can offer a wealth of information to you, and can give you lots of "insider" information as well as tips on local attractions you will want to experience.

If you take your motor home on the journey, you will still want to make advance reservations. Recreational vehicle campgrounds in resort communities can fill up faster than motels during the peak summer months. Also, if you are traveling by motor home, try and have another vehicle with you so that you can explore the area in more comfortable style and still be able to return to an established home base. If you don't want to tow an additional vehicle, you can always rent a car to use during your stay. Many companies offer very favorable full-week rates with unlimited mileage, but, again, be sure and reserve the car in advance.

Some people like to combine their surveying trip with the chance to do a little camping; however, this isn't something we would recommend. While it is good to have the opportunity to relax in beautiful surroundings, this trip is much more than just a vacation. You will be gathering a lot of information and making daily plans for places to go and things that need to be accomplished. That kind of planning is difficult to do by lantern-light inside a tent. Also, you'll want to go out to restaurants and visit stores, so the chance to shower and change clothes will be a necessity. If you do decide to camp, make your campsite reservation early, especially if you intend to stay in a National Park or other major campground.

What To Take

In some ways, your trip is like a vacation, so plan accordingly as far as packing what you really need. You already have a wealth of demographic information at your fingertips, so you know what type of weather conditions to expect. If you are visiting a mountain area, especially during the spring or fall, provide clothing for a variety of weather conditions. Mountain areas are often notoriously unpredictable concerning the weather during these times of the year. There may be a windy morning followed by a 70 degree afternoon, then you might wake up to a dusting of snow the next morning.

Pack some *comfortable* walking shoes. You'll be logging a few miles on foot; so at this point comfort is more important than style. You might want to take along at least one nice outfit. It should be fairly casual, so that you have something comfortable for dinners out. If your trip is to include a job interview, a visit with a potential employer with whom you've corresponded, or even an employment agency, plan on taking along appropriate clothing.

Invest in an inexpensive nylon carry-all bag or shoulder tote for your walking tours. This will allow you a handy place for maps and tour guides, notes, your camera, and maybe a snack. It also gives you someplace to stash business cards, brochures, and other information you will pick up as you travel.

Finally, remember to pack:

- A large folder or other handy container with all of the information you've gotten from the Chambers of Commerce, including brochures, business cards, maps, and coupons;
- Copies of letters you've received from people or busi-

nesses you plan to visit, so they will serve as reminders to them and as introductions for you;

• A list of names and phone numbers of realtors and other people you want to get in touch with;

• A notebook for recording information, as well as for jotting down your impressions of the area;

• If you are using the services of a relocation service, be sure and bring along their printouts for reference;

• A regular camera or video camera so that you can photograph the town, outlying areas, and even the real estate in which you are interested. These pictures and/or video tapes will serve as informative reminders in the future, as well as keeping you presently enthusiastic about the move.

THE PSYCHOLOGICAL PREPARATION

Taking off on a journey of discovery as important as this one requires more than packing clothes and loading film. It also requires a little mental preparation in order to be ready for what lies ahead.

If you are like most potential dropouts, you will have blinders on for the first visit or two. You're thinking seriously about moving, but there are reservations, and, in order to overcome them and prove to yourself that moving is *definitely* the right thing to do, the town needs to be absolutely perfect.

Your eye will see the beautiful old farmhouse, and skip over the dilapidated mobile home right next door. You'll take great delight in reading the real estate ads for the $30,000 and $40,000 houses and mentally start spending all the money you'll have left from the sale of your house, without really considering that these homes are probably not of the type in which you'll eventually want to settle. During this fantasy period, you'll really believe there's not a speck of litter in the park and not an unfriendly person on the streets.

An optimistic outlook is great; in fact it's pretty much essential to all the mental adjustments you'll be making along the way. But there is a lot to be said for realism, too. At first, most people only let themselves see what they want to see. Later, in the tough days and weeks that follow the move (those times when you begin to have doubts) every bad thing about the town, no matter how trivial, comes rushing into your field of vision with alarming clarity.

The simple fact is no town is perfect, and the sooner you accept that the better. The key word in your quest is *better* —better community, better people, a better lifestyle than what you have now.

Another mental adjustment you will need to make, especially if a protective "city-shell" has been formed around yourself, is to open up and talk to people. The most important research you will be doing on any of your site visits will come from just asking questions of anyone who will spare you a few minutes of their time. Store clerks, waitresses, city and county office workers, even people you pass on the streets—each one is a potential source of new impressions and new information that can help you learn what you need to know.

WHAT TO LOOK FOR

During your visits, especially your initial one, you need to open yourself up to what the town really looks like and how it functions. Every town will have specific pros and cons, as well as its own special flavor. The town may be prosperous or plain, sophisticated or a little provincial, but each has something to recommend it or you wouldn't be there in the first place.

While you're in town, there will almost certainly be specific things that you want to see and do, and perhaps specific people to whom you want to talk. But as you walk and drive around the area, there are some more general impressions you will want to note also. Here are a few to which to pay particular attention. They can offer you important insight into the community:

Downtown: The downtown "core" areas are some of the best indicators of how prosperous or poor a town is. In many small and medium sized towns, downtown areas started their decline in the '60s and early '70s when real estate prices escalated. The shopping mall, with its convenient groupings of stores and acres of parking outside the congested downtown, became a regular feature on virtually every horizon, taking customers and businesses away from downtown shopping areas.

Today, many downtown areas are scenes of innovative and exciting renovations. Brick warehouses are becoming eclectic shops, and sidewalk cafes are flourishing. As you wander around downtown, look at the overall face that the town wears. Look at the general condition of the buildings, and the types of stores and offices they house. There may be a vacant building or two, but are most buildings occupied? Are things in generally good condition, or does peeling paint seem to be the primary decorating scheme? Besides the inevitable dry cleaning and haircutting establishments, are there interesting shops featuring bright colors and quality merchandise?

Established Residential Areas: Tour one of the older established residential areas and look at the homes. Are they in generally good repair, with clean yards and a look of attention? In communities where people are doing at least reasonably well, their contentment and financial stability will show in the condition of their homes.

You will want to know if there are areas or neighborhoods considered "good" or "bad". Small towns are much less broken up into specific areas of valuable and less valuable property than large cities are, but it is possible that there are local areas to avoid when considering buying property.

New Construction: Is there any new construction taking place? In towns that have a stagnant economy, you will see very little in the way of construction, while communities that are growing and prospering will have a number of new houses and other new buildings in progress. Also, signs of remodeling on existing houses is another indicator of a healthy economy.

The People: Today's small town often has a much more diverse group of residents than the cowboys and farmers you might expect. It is peopled with an interesting and sophisticated mix of loggers and bankers, ranchers and writers, artists and doctors, housewives and househusbands. As you wander around, look for a general feeling of contentment and at least a moderate mix of people and prosperity.

As you wander around the town and talk with the local people, you will be able to form some opinions about how "open" the town is, and how receptive it will be to newcomers. Some communities, especially very small or isolated ones, may be very tightly-knit, and you may find it difficult to become accepted in such locales. Other towns have experienced an influx of new people for many years and you may find that "everyone there's from someplace else", as one woman we interviewed said.

Businesses and Services: If an area is productive, healthy, and attracting a good mix of people, it will often have a fascinating collection of entrepreneurial endeavors. You are likely to find anything and everything in the way of shops and service businesses—things like hot air balloon rides, pet-sitting services, past-life hypnotists, and caterers that offer everything from dinner parties to champagne picnics for two. Restaurants are also interesting barometers, and may reveal a diverse mix of traditional and ethnic establishments.

As you wander around and as you read, take note of

the shops, services, products, and eating establishments you see. The types of businesses that a town attracts are often great indicators of the types of people that live there.

The Local Paper: Finally, study the local newspaper each day you are there. For that matter, purchasing a mail order subscription before hand is often very helpful. As you read the paper, you can find a number of interesting clues about the town:

Look for the section that gives the meeting times for the various clubs and organizations in town, and note which are active. You may see more religious groups than you're comfortable with, or perhaps a few too many meetings of the NRA for your taste. On the other hand, there may be a number of service organizations in town such as Rotary and the United Way that indicate a healthy business climate.

Read the editorial page for a flavor of the newspaper's political stance. If it's the only paper in town, it may well be reflective of the feelings of the entire community. This will give you a good indication as to whether the town is fairly liberal, fairly conservative, or a middle-of-the-road blend.

Read the "Letters to the Editor" or the "Public Opinion" section to discover what things concern or please the local citizens sufficiently so that they write to the paper. You may even find some clues about major changes in store for the area, if enough people are writing in about them.

Look at the "Community" section and see what types of news articles make the paper. This will also give you some valuable insights into the issues and attitudes in the community.

Read the "Entertainment" and "Recreation" sections to see what's going on around town, from movies and plays to what's on television and what kind of fish are biting.

Look at the advertisements for goods and services.

Also, whenever you're in your room, turn on the local

television station. As with the newspaper, you can get a real sense for what's going on and what interests the local citizenry.

A SAMPLE THREE-DAY ITINERARY

Let's assume you have allocated three days for the initial site visit to a town to which you're thinking of moving. You want to see and do as much as you can, but you also want to get some hard information and form some realistic impressions. What follows is a suggested three-day schedule that will allow you time to gather information and relax and enjoy yourself a little as well.

Day One

Morning: While you are having breakfast, break out the maps and Chamber of Commerce information and familiarize yourself with the town. Go over any notes you made about things to do, and plan a simple itinerary. Stop by the Chamber of Commerce, the library, or the visitor's information office to pick up any additional information that they might have about the area, and introduce yourself to anyone with whom you may have corresponded. Being able to put a face to a name is always helpful, and it helps establish a rapport for future contacts.

Spend the rest of the morning with a driving tour, concentrating on the downtown area and the main residential areas within the town itself. Just go at a leisurely pace. Let your eyes and your mind record the various scenes as they pass by the window. The town may even offer a local sightseeing or visitor's information tour, which is good way to get a comprehensive, narrated overview of the area.

Afternoon: Stop downtown for a casual lunch at a local restaurant or cafe—not a fast-food establishment. Chat with the waitress, and even the person at the next table. After lunch, stroll around the downtown area. Look at various stores and shops, and browse through a few of them. Look at the types of merchandise they carry, at the quality and the prices, and at the general condition of the stores.

Walking is an extremely important part of your research, and the more you can do of it, the better. Walking gives you a much better feel for the town, lets you examine it at closer range, and gives you many more opportunities for talking with local residents.

An alternative to the walking tour, especially if you want to cover a larger area, is a bicycle tour. If you have the equipment, you may want to bring along your own bikes. If not, it is usually a simple matter to find a bicycle store or other local outlet that rents sturdy two-wheelers. Again, as with walking, go slowly and pay attention to your surroundings. Don't miss any opportunity for a chat with people you meet.

Evening: Have an informal dinner in another local restaurant, then sample a little of the local nightlife. Try to get a sense of the pace of the community, both at work and at play, and see if it fits with your concept of where you would like to settle.

Day Two

Morning: Today, start off with a driving tour of the outlying areas. Look at the land and farms surrounding the main part of the town, and do a little sightseeing—particularly those places that either reflect the town's history and philosophy, such as a museum or interpretive show, or that are a large part of the local economy, such as a ski resort. Pack a picnic lunch, and find a quiet spot to eat and enjoy the sound of the birds.

Afternoon: Plan on visiting a realtor in the afternoon. Housing and land prices and availability are important indicators of the local economy, and are of vital interest to you as a potential resident. Have the agent describe some of the homes and property for sale in whatever price, style, and amenity range you're interested. In this way, you can get a feel for what is available, locations, and costs. Get a few addresses, and drive by anything that sounds interesting. Perhaps drive through an outlying subdivision if there is one. Looking at real estate is an important step, both in getting acclimated and in making the choice of a town.

Evening: Take the night off from touring, see a movie or just bring a take out dinner back to the room. Assess what you have seen so far, and jot down any notes about things that are important to see or do on your last day.

Day Three

Morning: After breakfast, visit some of the city and county offices. There you can learn about taxes, services, agriculture, or whatever interests you. Stop by an employment agency, and discuss what kinds of jobs are available and in what salary range. If you haven't already done so, visit the library to find out what local information it has to offer. Talk with anyone you can, both for information and for a sense of friendliness and community pride.

Afternoon: Reserve the afternoon for any specific stops you would like to make that are important to your particular situation. You may want to visit the local elementary or high schools your children might attend, or tour the local college to inquire about what courses are being offered. Ask about the college's Community Education program while you are there. The more informal, non-credit classes that are being offered will often tell you a lot about the type and mix of people who live in the community. Perhaps you would like to visit the local hospital, or look into specific retirement communities or health care facilities. If you are thinking about opening a shop, you might want to wander through the stores in town that are similar to the one you plan to see what they offer.

Evening: Have dinner in one of the town's "pricier" restaurants. Ask for recommendations from the people you have met during the day. Discuss the activities of the last few days, and try to get a handle on your feelings and impressions. Once you start gauging your reactions, you will probably be surprised to discover that you have already decided for or against the area, and can plan your next visit there—or an upcoming visit somewhere else.

MORE LETTERS

After your preliminary round of fact-finding tours is completed, you will no doubt be drawn to that one special place where the people, the homes, and the general ambience of the community has won you over. Whether you are thinking of moving tomorrow or ten years from now, sooner or later you know you'll be back. But, meanwhile, you would probably like to know more.

Armed with the knowledge you've gained from actually being in the town and talking with the local people, you will have a much better idea of the various aspects of the move that need to be pursued further. Between your first visit and your next one, you can continue the research—and the high enthusiasm level—by writing more letters and making more phone calls.

If you were comfortable with the realtor with whom you spoke, you may want to begin corresponding. He can keep you apprised of current market conditions and make you aware of any upcoming changes that might affect your real estate decisions. You might also want to begin writing for more specific tax information, or information relating to specific business decisions or opportunities.

Keep an informal file of who and when you write, so that you'll know what responses you are still waiting for and what further contacts you might need to make. Save every name, address, phone number, and business card that comes your way, and perhaps even make a simplified personal address book just for the new community. It will prove to be an invaluable asset in the months to come.

SUBSEQUENT SITE VISITS

As your plans firm up and you begin to think seriously of a move, you'll want to make at least one additional, more intense visit. At this time, you'll zero in on more specific places to visit, additional people with whom to talk and perhaps even take the giant step of purchasing some real estate.

Plan on going back for at least a week at this time. If you are really serious about buying property and/or job hunting, two weeks would be preferable. If you can, arrange this trip for a different time in the year so that you can see the area in different seasons. Ideally, you should get a feel for what the winters are like before making your final decision.

Planning

On your subsequent visits, think of the trip as being less a vacation and much more of a research trip. Sit down with the family, and discuss the questions that have come up since your last visit. Typically, everyone will have something about which they'd like to know more. Jot down everyone's comments and concerns.

Now is also a good time to look back at your *Wants and Needs* list to remind yourself of those specific things you had listed as being important. You will especially want to make note of those things that you may not have had time to delve into during your first visits—open land, business or educational opportunities, or whatever things are important to know more about.

Arm yourself with a comprehensive list of things to do; then try and get as much done from home as you can before leaving for your visit. If you need information about wells, try to find out who in town you'll need to talk with; if you have specific zoning or land use concerns, who is that person to see? If there are some medical concerns that worry you, find out which doctor or clinic is the one you'll want to visit.

The more names and addresses you can discover while you are still in your old home, the more time you will have available when you get to your new town. Also, as the dates for being in town firm up, you'll have the opportunity to make advance appointments with the people you want to see. Nothing is more frustrating than driving six hundred miles to visit a town, then finding out the doctor with whom you need to talk is away at a conference, or the only guy who knows all the zoning laws is on vacation.

The Tote Bag

For your next visit, a well-organized shoulder tote bag will be a welcome addition to your list of things to take. As before, you can pack your camera as well as some snacks for mid-morning energy. But more importantly, you can stash your ever-growing collection of names and notes in it. Here are some things to include:

• Copies of letters from people with whom you have been corresponding that you'd like to meet and that need clarification or further pursuit from city and county offices;

• Your personal address book of names, phone numbers, addresses, and business cards;

• Employment and tax information if you plan to speak to a lender while you are there (your realtor can tell what specific items you're likely to need);

• Several clean, recently updated copies of your resume if you plan to visit employment agencies or potential employers;

• School records if you are seeking admissions information;

• Tax or financial information if you are pursuing the purchase of a business;

• Notepads, pencils, maps, brochures, and perhaps a small packet of aspirin.

SPECIFIC SUGGESTIONS FOR FUTURE TRIPS

Each person's situation is different, and each potential dropout will have a unique list of things to do and places to visit during subsequent visits to the area. What follows is a list of specific suggestions we think important to add to your own lists, and to help you round out the information you're putting together:

Real Estate: Assessing the local real estate scene in your previous visit has already been discussed, but it is important to mention it again here. Real estate values and inventory are very reflective of the local economy and, to a somewhat lesser degree, the economy of the entire nation. They can fluctuate considerably within relatively short periods of time, and, if it has been a year or two between visits, you should be sure to look into these things again.

Take a look at some houses and property, get a few prices, and compare them to what was happening during your previous trip. If you have the time, stop by a few realty open houses and get a better feel for exactly what's out there and exactly what you can expect for your real estate dollar.

Schools: If you have children, where they'll go to school is of critical importance to both you and them. If you haven't done so before, this time while you're in town, tour the schools.

Call in advance, explain your situation, and ask for an appointment for a brief tour.

While you are at the school, examine the physical facilities and the appearance of the students as well. Both will give you some insight into the educational system. Ask about specific curriculum items, and, if possible, take a look at the school library and even at some of the textbooks being used. Try to determine to which classes your child might be assigned, and talk with the teachers of those classes.

Rural communities often have two problems with their school systems: relatively short budgets and relatively long bus rides. So inquire about what bus facilities are available. If you have a specific area of town in mind where you would like to live, find out how long the bus ride is from there to the school. Also, try to find time to sit in on a PTA or school board meeting. This will give you a quick look at the budget and other political factors affecting the school and the school system.

If you plan to send your children to a private or religious school instead of a public school, then take the time to examine these facilities as well. Apply the same basic criteria as suggested above for public schools.

Local Government: If you have never lived in a small town, you might find the community interaction with local government very interesting. If you have the opportunity, try to attend a city council or county commissioners meeting, and learn how the local government functions, what the political climate and leanings of the town are, and what issues are facing the area in the future.

Local and National Transportation: If you are used to being in Manhattan with its extensive local bus and subway system, most small town transportation will come as a surprise. Local public transportation is typically not extensive—if it exists at all. If you must depend on public facilities to get around, you had better take the time to find out what is available.

In New York you can hail a taxicab on the streets at any time of the day. Most small towns offer some sort of taxi service, although usually one has to call in advance for a cab. Larger communities may offer limited local bus service, typically serving only a handful of well-frequented locations such as shopping centers, the college, hospitals, and the downtown area.

Many towns also have senior citizen transportation services and services for the handicapped, so there's always a way to get out for shopping and other errands. If you are in a resort community, you may also find a shuttle bus that services the ski resorts or other areas frequented by tourists.

If you anticipate doing a lot of traveling, whether for business or pleasure, you will want to check into the local facilities for connections to national transportation. Typically, all but the very smallest of towns will have bus connections going to larger areas. Usually, there are also Amtrak and other rail service connections available locally or near by.

Many mid-size towns or counties have a regional airport that can provide you with short-distance connecting flights to major airports, or even directly to two or three of the largest cities in the area. If there is no airport close by, you will probably be able to find shuttle bus service that commutes to the nearest airport on a fairly regular basis.

Tax and Land Information: If you haven't gotten all of the information that you need in these areas yet, now is the time. Stop by the assessor's office or the farm appraiser's office for specific property tax information, and the Chamber of Commerce for information on sales tax, room tax, gas tax, and whatever taxes might be in effect in the area.

If you have a specific business in mind and need information about land use, you will want to check that out also. The city or county Planning Commission can give you information on residential, commercial, and industrial zoning; housing density restrictions in various areas; predicted future growth patterns and the laws—if any—which regulate them; and specific land-use and environmental impact restrictions.

Shopping: Take a closer look at the area's shopping facilities. In that way, you'll have a better idea of what to expect in the way of product availability and choice after you move.

TALKING IT OVER WITH CHILDREN

Throughout the entire process of self-evaluation, evaluating and selecting a new community, we have stressed the involvement of the entire family. The needs and the feelings of your children should never be ignored or slighted. They need to be involved and informed at each step of the way. Here are some suggestions from psychologists with whom we spoke to help keep your children involved and minimize the trauma of the move.

Discuss the move with the kids as soon as you can, and explain to them what you are planning and why. Be honest with them, but be upbeat and accentuate the positive aspects of the relocation;

Listen to their input on what they expect to gain from the move;

If you have any flexibility as to timing your move, discuss this with them also. Some kids may prefer to wait until school is out to move. Others might prefer to move after school has started so they can make friends and become involved in the community quicker. In this way they won't have to face a long summer without new friends;

Take your children along on your explorations before you move. Seeing their new home and all the wonderful things it can offer is a good way to help overcome their fear of the unknown;

Explain the new situations they will face in a rural environment as opposed to an urban one. Once again honestly accentuate the positive aspects of their new environment.

TAX DEDUCTIONS

One final note on all of your move preparations. If you are moving an established business, buying a new business, being transferred to another job, or are moving to obtain another job, chances are that, if you meet the Internal Revenue Service's criteria, many of the expenses associated with the move will be tax deductible. In addition to the costs of the physical move itself, it may be allowed to deduct some of the preliminary expenses associated with locating a new town and evaluating it.

Only your accountant can give you specific advice relating to your particular situation, but it is never too soon to start documenting things. A simple log book available from any stationary or office supply store will help you keep track of the move-related miles you drive. Save all your receipts from motels, meals, air or train fare, and rental cars. Also, keep track of postage and long distance telephone calls that are related to the move or the preliminary evaluation process.

On any receipt, briefly note the date, place, and the purpose of the expense. Compile the receipts in one place and keep them safely together; then make them available to your accountant at the end of the year for legitimate, itemized deductions on your income tax forms.

5

Analyzing the Rural Economy

Annual income twenty pounds, annual expenditure nineteen pounds six, result happiness. Annual income twenty pounds annual expenditure twenty pounds ought and six, result misery.

—Charles Dickens
David Copperfield

If you are like most people, the realities of making a living in your new town can often dash the hopes of even the most wide-eyed optimists. Financial wealth, of course, is relative—whether your income is in the six-figure range or whether it only reaches six figures including the decimals. In either case, giving it up for a journey into the unknown is tough. The small-town scene may be idyllic, but the call for people of your profession may fall short of your expectations.

There are three basic rules that will help you analyze and adjust to the economic realities of your new home:

Rule 1—Be Prepared
Rule 2—Be Innovative
Rule 3—Be Realistic

BEING PREPARED

To tell someone they need to be prepared for a major move such as this is obvious—to undertake the urban to rural transition on a whim is hazardous. But how do you prepare yourself when you are heading into an unknown area fraught with economic dangers—many real, many only imagined?

For those who will be successful relocators, preparation comes from thorough research and evaluation. This comes from letters and phone calls, from site visits and conversations. It also comes from taking an equally hard and honest look at yourself—at your lifestyle, your goals, and especially how you can fit into the economic reality of your new town.

Translated simply, you need to do your homework.

EVALUATING THE SMALL-TOWN MARKETPLACE

Smaller areas present different economic opportunities, and your ability to recognize and act on them may make all the difference in the world to you and your financial security.

There are actually two ways of looking at the economic potential of the area in which you are considering relocating:

Selecting an area despite the market:

It may be that you have chosen the area to which you want to move based on reasons other than economic ones. You may like the scenery, the climate, or the recreation potential. Whatever the reasons, that town is where you want to live. In this instance, you will have to be more flexible in adapting yourself to what the area has to offer economically. Your initial market research will need to be fairly broad-based, and you will need to keep yourself open and adaptable to business and employment opportunities as they present themselves to you.

Selecting a market despite the area:

Conversely, you may have identified a potential good market for yourself and want to act on it. In this case, the location of the town, while still obviously important, actually becomes secondary. You may have found a new job opportunity in the area, or been offered a transfer; there may be climatic or raw material conditions that are perfect for your business. Or you may have found an area that has the ideal potential for that pastry shop or rare book store you have always wanted to open. Whatever your criteria, you have found a perfect market there and that is the town for you. Your research in this case will have to be more structured, and will focus on the specific things you need to know before taking the new job or opening your new business.

In either case, you need to be prepared and well-informed about what lies ahead. Some parts of your research can be done from home, by letters and phone calls, other parts can only be effectively accomplished through a trip to the area. Every piece of information you accumulate is important. You are to be the one who will be the final judge of what you need to know and what effect it's going to have on your personal relocation plans.

Keep in mind these words of caution as you begin your research: separate the hype from the facts. While much of what you learn will be useful information of real value, always consider the source of the information. The person with whom you are talking may be telling you exactly what you want to hear (or don't want to hear), but are their facts accurate and is their advice realistic? Perhaps they want to sell you a house or rent you a warehouse; perhaps they need your capital for a particular reason; or maybe they see you as a threat to their job or as a potential competitor to their business.

With that in mind, here are three suggestions to help you get started on your quest for the facts:

1—*Gather Basic Research Material:* Find out what the area's newspaper(s) is, and subscribe to it early in your relocation planning. Newspapers are usually pretty unbiased in reporting both the good and the bad news, and they will really help you get a feel for the town and its economic climate. You might also consider subscribing to the newspaper from the state capitol, even if that's not the city to which you're moving. This will keep you abreast of happenings in the legislature, and give you a better state-wide picture of what's happening.

State or regional magazines can provide interesting information and background material, along with advertisements that may yield additional insights. These publications and ads usually contain some overly-optimistic hyperbole, so weigh both sides of the information presented.

Check to see if there are business newspapers or newsletters to which you can subscribe—preferably local or regional but at least state-wide. Industry-specific trade publications might also be available, and they can provide a wealth of information in your particular field or the one to which you are attracted.

Finally, call the phone company and order three telephone books: one for the town to which you want to move, one for the state's capitol, and one for the state's largest city (if different from the capitol). These will be valuable tools for providing local and state-wide numbers and addresses, and for giving you a look at the products and services—and perhaps the competition—you will find in your new area.

2—*Seek Out Other Dropouts:* If you assume that each person who leaves the city and relocates to a rural area would like to keep the area all to themselves, you are in for a pleasant surprise. Most dropouts are very proud of having made the move, and of their accomplishments in their adopted town. You will often find them to be friendly and gregarious—actually "mini Chambers of Commerce" for the area—who are more than willing to share their experiences with you. It will give your morale a boost to talk with others who have successfully made the move. This gives you the added advantage of being able to tap into an invaluable source of impartial, pro and con information about the area.

Don and Kathie G., to whom we talked, placed an ad in the "Personals" section of the local paper and asked for other dropouts to correspond with them. They listed their name, address and phone number with a couple of local realtors with whom they'd been dealing, and asked them to pass that information along to others who were new in the area. They even wrote a small advertisement and sent it to the city's library requesting that it be posted on the library's bulletin board.

The results were amazing. There was, of course, a deluge of ads from realtors, insurance companies, and other businesses—a great deal of which was valuable in its own right. But besides all the commercial mail, they received twenty six letters from other dropouts. Correspondence and phone calls began, and by the time they arrived in the city for their visit, they had a marvelous list of contacts. After that trip, they decided to make the move. In fact, some of those initial letter writers are, to this day, among their closest friends.

Other possibilities for finding people who have relocated to the area would be the Chamber of Commerce, local "Newcomer's Clubs" (the Chamber will know how to find these), schools and churches, singles' groups, or hobby clubs. Just use your imagination and don't be afraid to ask questions.

3—*Use Some Common Sense:* Temper what you hear with some common sense, and compare statements wherever possible. If a realtor tells you that property values have gone up 125% in the last three months, call the Chamber of Commerce or the County Assessor's office to verify these facts. If someone with a store to rent tells you that the town sorely needs whatever business it is you want to open, don't just take his word for it. Find out if there are similar businesses in town, and determine how yours would be different.

Get at least two opinions on everything. This is too important a decision to entrust to optimistic salespeople or plain, dumb luck.

A COLLECTION OF INFORMATION SOURCES

The Chamber of Commerce: As one of the best sources of good general financial information, this is always a good place to start. Plan on contacting both the state Chamber of Commerce for state-wide information and the local Chamber in the city or town where you are moving. This is where you can get listings of businesses in town; population size, including past and projected future growth; general information about the region's industrial and economic base; climatic data which may be important to your particular business; information about schools and the school system, both primary and secondary and; with a little reading between the lines; something of a feel for the moral and philosophical climate of the area.

Probably the most important pieces of information you will get from the Chamber of Commerce are demographics. They can give you regional breakdowns by age, sex, educational level, income, ethnic diversification, and much more. Begin with some general information, then, once you've had a chance to digest that, request specific breakdowns as the need arises.

Visitor's Centers: This is somewhat similar to the Chamber of Commerce, but more oriented toward general tourist information. It is still a good place to visit in the early stages of information gathering. There you can learn about the area's recreational activities, cultural events, special events and celebrations, and more general information about the area. Some visitor's centers have year-long calendars of events that are useful and interesting, as well as general and specialized recreation and sightseeing maps.

Employment Division: This is the best place to find out what job opportunities are available in the area, if they are seasonal, and what current salary scales and benefit packages are being offered.

For some families, making the relocation may also entail a previously non-working spouse returning to the marketplace—either by choice or by necessity. A stop at the employment office will give you a much better idea of what is available within your skill range in the area, and what sort of income you can reasonably expect. Knowing this information in advance of the move can make a big difference if you are depending on two incomes.

Even if you are not looking for a job, this is a good way to find out what you can expect to pay someone else to work for you. It will also help you get a handle on the skill and education levels in the area, the job skills most in demand, and a feel for the general economic condition of the region.

Employment Agencies: Here again, as a potential employee or employer you can gather vital information. Employment agencies may have less information about employment demographics then the State Employment Division (such as unemployment rate and demographic breakdowns, for example), but they have more available job listings and more "inside", real-world information about the region's economy.

Even though you are just visiting (or even just writing or calling), don't be afraid to ask questions. An employment agency's income depends on finding you work, so you will be looked at as a potential future client. In case you have never dealt with an agency, you don't pay a fee until they find you a job. Tell them about your skills and experience, find out what jobs are available and what they pay. If you will be looking for work, this type of hard, practical information is *vital* to your move.

Jill H., a young woman with whom we spoke, was visiting a small town in Vermont with her husband and was looking around with the idea of moving there. She stopped in at an employment agency, and ended up discussing her skills and experience over lunch with the owner of the agency. The next morning, Jill received a call at her motel with a job offer. Her skills were just what one employer had been searching for and he was willing to wait until she relocated to the area. She was even able to negotiate company help with some of the moving expenses. Jill and her husband made the move two weeks later, and haven't ever regretted it.

If you are a potential employer, describe to the agency the types of people you will need, from executives to unskilled laborers. In this way, you will find out if the staff you need is available, and what basic salary range is expected to fill these positions.

Economic Development Office: This is a good place to discover what is being done to promote new business in the area. You can also find out what kinds of funding might be available for businesses moving into the region. This department is often a source of specialized loans for small businesses, agriculture, and all types of industrial undertakings, as well as having information on zoning, bond issues, tax bases, and retail, warehouse, and industrial business sites.

Also, a few friendly questions can usually net you some information on where you as a potential employee can best market your skills, and what type of job competition you'll be facing. You can get information on the type of labor pool on which businesses can draw, what the prevailing wage scales and union conditions are, and what the general skill and educations levels are in the area.

City, County, and State Offices: Here are some other very useful stops for general demographic information and, with a little interpolating, a look at population growth and business trends. Be sure and check out the Assessor's Office for tax and property value information; the Building Department for construction trends; the Census Bureau; and the Department of Motor Vehicles—trends in vehicle registrations can be a good indicator of area growth or decline.

The front of the phone book under the "Government Listings" section will give you leans of other offices to check out. You may want to visit the Planning Commission or the Health Department to get zoning or ordinance information that is relevant to your business, or perhaps to the Board of Realtors to discuss property trends or get real estate planning advice. Be imaginative. You know what you need to learn, so go out there and seek it out.

Community Colleges: Here, you can gather important data, including information on apprenticeship and job-training classes; small business information; and a general look at the curriculum, whether for your own use in completing or expanding your education or simply as an indicator of the type of local job market for which the students are being prepared.

Stop in at the college library, and request a list of the offices and services that are on campus. There might be a wealth of information available about the community and the overall job market.

You may even find yourself in a position like that of Larry B., who wandered into the Community Education office at a small college in upper Washington state. He started talking with the director, and was invited to teach a Community Education class in computers. He had never taught before, but his curiosity was aroused, and working with computers was his specialty. When he made the relocation about six months later, he took the director up on his offer. A night class in basic computer literacy for adults the community was arranged and Larry found that he absolutely loved teaching. He now livens up his retirement and adds to his income by teaching credit classes part time on campus. It is something he never planned on doing, but the relocation and the resulting change in thinking and adoption of a more adventurous spirit helped it all fall into place.

Power Company: This stop is for information on the area's light and heavy industry, including rates and possible incentive programs. Look at what new areas the utility company is planning to serve in the near future. This is a good indicator of what areas in and around the town are growing. You can also check the residential utility rates while there. Compare them to what you are paying now as a guide to help determine your monthly budget after the move.

Title Companies: Here you can seek housing data and trends, plus trends in business property size, growth, and availability.

Real Estate Offices: Realtors will supply similar information as above, but will also have specifics on prices for retail and service space and businesses for sale. If you are in the mood and find a salesperson you enjoy, spend an afternoon touring the town and looking at houses and property for sale.

The Post Office: Post offices are often gathering places in small towns. Information on mail delivery and box availability can give you insight into the services and/or ruralness of the town.

Department of Environmental Quality, or similar offices: This is a good place for specific environmental ordinances and other information that may affect your future business. A stop here will also give you a feel for how serious the community is about maintaining the clean air and water that brought you there in the first place.

Airports, Train Stations, and Bus Stations: Here you can find out what passenger and freight services are available, and also look at passenger loading and unloading information with an eye toward the region's growth. You might also want to visit a trucking company for additional freight service information if that is important to your business.

Book Stores and Community Library: Always a good source of specific books about the region. If you are lucky enough to meet some local authors, you will find they are usually staunch advocates of the area, full of information, eager to talk, and generally very enthusiastic about relocating.

Local Museums: This is a great place to learn about the region's economic base and its history.

MAKING AN INVESTMENT IN YOUR FUTURE PIECE OF MIND

Not everyone is an economic overnight success in their adopted community. Some dues usually have to be paid first before you become firmly established and functioning. It may help if you can think of it as an investment in your future, keeping an eye toward improvement and a brighter economic future.

Some people make the relocation only when a solid job offer has been received; others move on a whim, putting their economic fate in the hands of whoever or whatever watches over disgruntled urbanites. Some struggle, some don't. Some are more successful and settled-in than others. Virtually all have said two things: thinking about the move and trying to make the decision was much harder than the move and the adjustment itself; dropping out of the urban rat race has been the greatest and most satisfying change ever made in their adult lives.

BEING INNOVATIVE

As your research is probably beginning to show, rural areas and small cities present some unique opportunities as well as some challenging economic realities. The business and industrial base is usually not as diverse as in larger cities, and there are not as many high-paid positions available as would be found in New York or Los Angeles.

As a result, your rural relocation may well involve a little innovative job searching. Of course, innovative doesn't mean holding down three jobs or compromising your ideals or integrity. It simply means that you need to adapt yourself to the new economic realities that surround you, and use them to your advantage.

What follows is a list of suggestions and possibilities, designed to start you thinking about ways to make relocation work from an economic standpoint. These suggestions will give you some idea of what others before you have done—and what you can do.

TRANSFERRING YOUR PRESENT JOB

Let's start with one workable possibility—a job transfer. If the company you currently work for has a branch office in an area where you would like to live, give some serious thought to applying for a transfer there. Making a major move such as this one is considerably simplified if a good job is waiting for you at the other end.

The biggest drawback to applying for a job transfer is that you may not like your present job, or the company for which you work, in which case transferring may not be all that enticing. It will, however, at least get you out of your present city and into a new town where you truly want to live. Once you are living there, with an income you can rely on, it is much easier to find new and exciting opportunities in the job market.

Harry W., another of the people we surveyed, transferred from Boston to a little town in New Hampshire. He liked the town, particularly the slower pace of life, but, since he had retained his old job and merely changed locales, his unhappiness with his firm remained. In less than two months, one of his company's local competitors, who was desperately in need of experienced, qualified people that couldn't be found locally, offered him a job. He is much happier now at work, and has had an increase in salary. Harry has become so involved in his new community that he's volunteered his free time as a softball umpire for the parks' department.

However, you may also find that your job and your company are much more tolerable in new surroundings, with new offices, new co-workers, and, hopefully, a new and brighter outlook on life. A perfect example of this is the story of Bob C., a quiet and friendly person who had worked for years under a dominating manager. He transferred from Washington, D.C. to a smaller city in upstate New York where, under the guiding hand of a new and innovative boss, his talents are finally being recognized.

Still, one potential problem transferring locations is that if you like your firm, but don't like your job, it may take some time until a new position opens up for you.

On the other hand, if you like your present job, but not the working environment, you might create a similar position for yourself. Perhaps there's an existing branch office somewhere you would like to live, but your particular job title doesn't exist there. Do a little homework, assemble facts and figures, and prepare a case to prove to your boss why that position should exist in a new locale, and why you are the best person to fill the new vacancy.

Probably the most innovative of all transfer possibilities comes into play if your company doesn't have a branch office in the area to which you want to move. Explore the possibility of convincing your boss to open one there. It may sound a little farfetched, but it does happen. If the economic climate is right for the company and the move makes sense, you might just make it a reality.

A NEW JOB IN THE SAME FIELD

If you're good at what you do, and you like what you do, but there is no possibility of a transfer, the next easiest solution is to find a new job in the same field. If you are an accountant or a nurse, and there is an accounting firm or a hospital in the area that has an opening, this is an obvious possibility for you to explore.

Many urban dropouts with whom we talked adopted this solution and it has tremendous potential for a lot of aspiring dropouts. There is excitement and challenge in a new job, but in a field you know and in a position where your skills are equal to the task. You also have the advantage of an immediate income, which makes the move a lot easier and more enjoyable with which to deal.

Try and stay abreast of openings in your field that occur in other areas. Trade magazines and industry newsletters often have job information. There are a number of specialized agencies, reports, and services that can help you match your skills with a job in a new area.

We found that a commonly-asked question is what to do about area-specific jobs such as publishing, aerospace, or even auto making? Again, you can find any number of open, innovative avenues. In publishing, for example, Manhattan may seem to be the only real center for the industry. But what about smaller publishing houses in smaller areas? What about regional magazines or publishers? Perhaps freelance writing or editing is a possibility, especially if you take some of your old contacts along with you when you move? What about starting your own magazine or newsletter?

Another possible solution to the area-specific dilemma is to commute, even if to another state. That may seem completely far-fetched to many, but a surprisingly large number of people are doing it.

Dale and Carolyn R., a middle-aged couple from Hollywood, California, were two people with highly-paid, specialized, very industry- and location-specific jobs. He is a well-recognized and sought-after makeup artist for the movies, while she is an independent producer of television commercials. At first glance, these jobs seem to have virtually no potential in any other area. A number of stress-reducing vacations to Oregon convinced them to move, and they bought a ranch house on nine secluded acres in the middle of the state. Now, Dale commutes to Hollywood, at studio expense, three to four times a year to work on selected movies. Carolyn has linked up with the Oregon Arts Council, and produces local fine arts events. Both also work with visiting television and film crews who periodically shoot films in the rustic beauty of their newly-adopted home.

These successes were achieved by people using a creative approach. They illustrate how a positive attitude and flexibility can create innovative solutions that make a move to country living possible.

STARTING OVER WITH A NEW CAREER

It could well be that the time has come for you to move to a new town *and* a new career—a change that may be just what your life needs at this point. Perhaps you have always thought of making a career change, whether related to your field or whether it is something totally different. In analyzing your job skills, interests, and education, you, better than anyone, know what you have to offer and in what direction you would like to go.

If you discover you lack a specific skill or education, why not take this opportunity to gain them? Either prior to changing locations or once freed of the seemingly unbreakable and unmanageable restraints of your old job, go back to school, or perhaps enroll in a technical training course.

A good example of this approach is shown by the experiences of Sue and Roger B., a young married couple from Chicago. He was a successful certified public accountant and she was an equally successful computer technician. They were tired of urban problems and apartment life, and felt some changes were definitely due. On a camping trip to Montana one summer, they became enchanted with a particular city, and vowed to return.

They began communicating with a local realtor who specialized in selling businesses. Knowing of their joint love of cooking, he found a small, moderately successful general store and bakery for sale. They made the relocation, and reorganized the store into a bakery and specialty spice shop. Roger put his accounting training into restructuring the business. Sue set up a computerized inventory of where specialized herbs and spices can be found. She now has a growing reputation and is writing a cookbook in her spare time.

A point should be made here about money. This couple, while successful, were like a number of Americans. They had a few material trappings, but very little money in the bank. They took the modest proceeds of $11,000 from the sale of their condominium and combined it with $4,000 in savings and a $5,000 loan from her parents, and made the move based on $20,000.

They bought into the store, which was already producing a small monthly income, for under $10,000 on a contract with the previous owners. Roger initially did some freelance accounting work for a couple of local businesses to help pay the bills. They tightened their belts, and dipped gingerly into the remaining savings only when absolutely necessary. Much of their initial profits went back into the store until the business was restructured and profits increased.

The point is that these success stories didn't happen overnight, and usually not without some risk and a lot of very hard work. But successes do happen, and they can happen *without* a six-figure bankroll.

THE HOME OFFICE REVOLUTION

Two electronic marvels of the twentieth century, in tandem with the old reliable telephone, are rapidly changing the way America goes to work. Armed with a computer and a facsimile machine, virtually anything is possible from the privacy of your own home. You can write, edit, research, draw, analyze, revise, calculate and compute, then have your work anywhere in the world in just minutes.

Your day, which once started with a bumper-to-bumper commute to an office in the overcrowded city, could become like that of this New York dropout: as the sun is rising over the misty fields outside her lovingly restored Vermont farmhouse, Judy R. pours a second cup of coffee and retires to her cozy loft office. The computer is warmed up, and she makes a few revisions on the report she prepared the previous night. In another hour, she is one phone call from her computer to a data bank computer 2600 miles away. She has her supporting graphs, charts, and statistical information ready. She activates her modem, and within seconds the report is in the computer at her office in Manhattan. Judy FAXs over the graphs and charts and, just to drive the people at the office completely crazy, includes a photo of herself hard at work in jeans and a sweatshirt.

Consider these rather startling statistics. In 1982, there were 2.4 million computers in American homes. That number had grown to 22.8 million by 1988. In 1983, there were a paltry 70,000 FAX machines sold in the United States. That number has grown to 1.5 million in 1988.

The home office, once berated as a second-rate alternative for those who could not afford a real one, is now the desire and the envy of many executives and entrepreneurs. People are moving out of the conventional office setting and into their homes without ever having to give up their present jobs. They're finding that instead of wasting three or four hours of productive time each day commuting, they can spend that time getting something accomplished.

In fact, it is possible to have your job and your office hundreds or even thousands of miles away from where you live, as is the case of Richard G., an advertising executive from Chicago. He dropped out of the urban rat race two years ago in favor of a medium-sized town in northern Wisconsin. He now freelances for the company he used to work for, mainly by phone and FAX, plus a two-day trip back to Chicago once a month.

Richard worked out these figures one afternoon, just to satisfy his own curiosity:

Old job: Driving, parking, cab fare, lost productive hours getting to and from the office—$935 a month.

New job: Round-trip air fare to Chicago, plus expenses —$365 a month.

By his own estimate, he's putting an additional $570 a month into his pocket, plus having a rather incredible *sixty hours a month* of additional, productive, income-producing time that is freed up by not having to commute to the office. That's not an unusual number, if you consider wasting three hours a day, five days a week, four weeks a month just getting to and from work.

Working at home is not a fairy tale only for "other people." It is a very real and very rapidly expanding part of today's working environment. As of 1988, an estimated *24.9 million* Americans were working at home, either full- or part-time.

That number is steadily increasing at the rate of 7% per year, adding about *two million* new home offices to the American scene each year.

BECOMING A CONSULTANT

Another rapidly growing trend in today's society is the use of outside consultants. If you have a skill or specialized training, give some thought to selling it to someone else, perhaps even the company for which you used to work.

Many companies have learned that it is much less expensive to seek out and pay for specialized advice only when it is needed, rather than incur the costs of training and maintaining a person on staff for only occasional use.

The mechanics of establishing yourself as a consultant will vary with your skills and the particular field you have chosen as a career. Once again, trade publications are a good place to start. You can comb them for leads concerning companies that might need your services, and you can also place advertisements there. A comprehensive, professionally-prepared brochure, used in conjunction with a purchased, specialized mailing list of potential clients, might be the answer.

Keep in mind that a consulting business is not established overnight. You may need to find a job in your new town while you work at getting your new enterprise off the ground, or you may even get started before you make the relocation, while you are still employed in your present job.

STARTING YOUR OWN SMALL BUSINESS

For most people, starting your own company is the most exciting and intimidating possibility of them all. For many, independence and financial security, without the eyes of the boss peering over their shoulders, are truly glimpses of heaven.

Here are a few things to consider in the early planning and fantasizing stages:

1) Analyze your skills and interests, and plan a business accordingly. It is much easier to succeed in something you know than something you don't.

2) Attend some small business classes, and learn the ins and outs of proper management.

3) Have a sufficient amount of capital available, and don't depend on the business to earn your living immediately. It takes time to become successful.

4) Think seriously about purchasing an existing business, or even a franchise. It is often easier to get an existing business running smoothly and making a profit than it is to start from scratch.

To offer any further advice on the creation and running of a small business is outside the scope of this book. There are hundreds of excellent books, tapes and training courses available for that purpose. The decision to start a business, with all its potential problems and rewards, is solely yours. However, do not overlook the very real possibility that you, like many others before you, can have your own business and can make money —maybe lots of money—operating it.

What follows is a partial listing of some of the more innovative and successful businesses that have been started by urban dropouts in various parts of the country. It is offered as an example of what others have done, and to add a little bit of inspiration:

- Bed and breakfast
- River guide and outdoor chef
- Organic vegetable gardening
- Mail order marketing of regional crafts
- Christmas tree farm
- Llama ranching
- Handyman services for motels and rental property
- Freelance technical writing for computer firms
- Wooden jewelry manufacturing
- Commercial heating system design consultant
- Continuous guttering manufacture and installation
- Freelance time management consultation
- Mail order marketing of alcohol-free perfumes and cosmetics
- Residential and commercial energy conservation consulting
- Freelance editing and review of new manuscripts
- Real estate, insurance, or securities sales
- In-house pet and plant sitting service
- Party and entertainment planning and organizing

BEING REALISTIC

Without a doubt, in some ways you are already being realistic. You have certain expectations already in mind—a cleaner environment, lower crime rates, less stress, a more wholesome environment for children. These are the things you have been dreaming of during your daily commutes or while waiting for a cab, and they're all valid goals.

Money, however, seems the one area where people who

plan to relocate have trouble facing reality. For most, the first line of thinking when facing the economics of relocation is the "What The Hell" Syndrome. You're frustrated and fed up with your present life, the mountains are beckoning, and you want to move—NOW. You're infused with a reckless, new-pioneer spirit, and you're convinced you can make it. You'll take whatever life throws your way.

This optimistic attitude has its good points, to be sure. A little foolhardiness, mixed with a light sprinkling of overconfidence and reckless abandon, can be a real asset in two regards—it gets you up and moving, and it can sustain you during those discouraging times when things in your new home are not all you had imagined.

A surprising number of people, initially at least, feel that they will make the move no matter what has to be done to earn a living. For example, Jack A. was a man who had been a $75,000-a-year, desk-bound executive for twenty-three years. He was being treated for stress-related ailments and was absolutely certain that he would welcome the chance to move to a country setting and work with his hands. He was planning on cutting firewood to sell, and sitting at the farmer's market on weekends peddling the chemical-free apples he planned to grow. He even thought of taking a booth at the local crafts fair to sell his hand-made cribbage boards and a few of his wife's quilts.

It was a nice thought while gazing out the window of his Detroit office, but when Jack finally moved, he soon learned that money is still a necessity no matter where you live. He found it was realistic to have maintained that he'd be willing to live on less money in order to improve his quality of life; he found it was realistic to assume that it would take less money to sustain a comfortable lifestyle in a rural setting than it would in an urban setting. But he also found that once he was used to $75,000 yearly income, and his lifestyle was based on that amount of money, the overnight transition to a considerably lower sum was not something to be taken lightly.

Jack was one of the lucky ones. He saw his mistake not long after moving, and took a new job with a smaller, less stressful company. He now earns about 60% of his previous salary, but his expenses are down by almost 40%. He truly feels that his new way of life and his improved health are enough "income" to make up the difference. And he does sell his apples and his cribbage boards—he just doesn't rely on them for his entire income.

EXAMINING YOUR ECONOMIC EXPECTATIONS

Now is the time to begin examining exactly what your monetary needs and expectations are. This is something only you can do. This book can offer guidance and suggestions, but you are the final authority on how much money you have and how money you need. Only you can decide your true motives for the move, and only you can decide how much, if anything, you would be willing to give up in order to relocate.

Each person entertains the possibility of a move having different wants, needs, and goals. For some, their personal expectations are carved in stone and, if making the move can't achieve these expectations, they'd just as soon not move. Others have goals that are much more subjective, more intangible, more a whimsical product of imagination than a realistic assessment of what's possible or perhaps what is even truly, honestly desirable.

The recent college graduate will have an entirely different set of goals than the executive on the verge of retirement. A couple with children face the move with a different outlook and a different set of priorities than a childless couple, and the needs of the confirmed bachelor aren't the same as those of a newlyweds.

Each individual also brings a unique set of assets with themselves when they move. Education, job skills, specialized training, hobbies and avocations are all packed along with the furniture. They, more than anything, will determine any future economic course.

Being realistic most certainly DOES NOT mean being a pessimist. It simply means that, to ensure yourself of the very best chances of success in your new home, you need to temper those slightly rash, "back-to-the-woods", "I'll-do-anything-to-survive" fantasies with some wisdom and realism.

By this point in life, you are probably used to a certain type of lifestyle and have grown accustomed to some of the trappings of success. While you may despise the lifestyle that got them for you, a realistic assessment will probably show that there are certain things you'd rather not be without. Whether it's a new Mercedes every other year or just electricity and hot running water, be honest with yourself about just how much you want to give up to move.

A rural relocation certainly does not mean a strict austerity program either. It's certainly very possible to move AND enjoy the finer things in life. Thousands before you have done it, but it helps immensely if you know what those finer things are. Sooner or later for virtually everyone, no matter how pure the motive for the move, concerns about money will set in. You might as well be prepared; then it won't be such a shock to find out you're only human after all.

ANALYZING YOUR RESOURCES

It may surprise you to sit down and discover what a wealth of resources are open and available to you. You've gained more knowledge over the years than you probably realize, and now is the perfect time to take stock of what you know.

You must realize that not every asset has a dollar sign in

front of it, although many translate to dollar signs in the future. What you are looking for is an honest evaluation of your personal situation at this point in your life, monetary and otherwise. Inventory and analyze your assets and, while you're at it, your liabilities as well. You'll have a much better picture of what you can bring with you when you move.

What follows is a guide for self-evaluation—a do-it-yourself manual of introspection and assessment. Allocate a quiet, uninterrupted block of time for yourself and your family to really evaluate this move.

FINANCES: While not every resource is financial, many are. Begin with a realistic look at your financial position.

Ask the obvious questions first—how much money do you have available? How liquid is it? What portion of it is available to you to help with the move, as opposed to that portion that must remain untouched (tuition money for the kids, investments for retirement)?

It would be foolhardy to assume that you could move yourself and your family to a new area, find work and a home, and establish yourself in the community, all without a financial reserve. Unfortunately, things don't happen overnight, and you will need funds until you are settled.

The size of the reserve is, as with so many aspects of this move, up to you. It is dependent on your particular situation, and what's awaiting you when you have moved. If you are being transferred or if you have a new job waiting for you, the equivalent of a month's salary in the bank might be all you need to get set up—*not* including the cost of the move itself. If you plan to look for work after you arrive, you might need three to five months' salary. If you plan to start a new business, or perhaps go back to school or write a novel, six to twelve months salary might be more realistic.

List your current bills and ask yourself how many of them could realistically be eliminated before moving. Again, be honest. For example, you may decide to sell your present car, figuring to eliminate a $300-a-month payment. But is the car something which you can do without? What will you replace it with after you move—both for transportation and self-satisfaction?

Prior to moving, Sal R. reluctantly parted with the Porsche he'd been driving for two years. It was an awesome sacrifice, as that car represented the realization of a dream he had since college. It was the visual proof of an important financial goal he'd set for himself. But the car payment and insurance represented $530 a month; money that, in the initial flush of self-denial and sacrifice, he felt was better off in his pocket.

No more than a month after the move, his longing for his Porsche was overwhelming; so he began shopping for a new one. To his delight, that particular car was less in demand in Colorado than in California. He was able to buy a newer version for less than the amount for which he'd sold his older one. In Colorado, his insurance cost less, his registration cost was lower, and he saved the necessity of investing $850 in a car security system. He's now driving a newer model Porsche, and his monthly payment has dropped to $465.

Sal's initial sacrifice helped him have the financial peace of mind to make the move; he found after moving that rural didn't mean poor, and he's now got an extra sixty five dollars bucks in his pocket.

THE AFFORDABILITY FACTOR: Perhaps the most commonly asked pre-move financial question is "How can I go from $60,000 a year to $30,000 and still be happy and comfortable?" An honest answer to that question may not be easy. It involves a lot of truthful self-evaluation, and in the end, only you can arrive at and interpret your conclusions. First, you need to ask yourself how much income it takes to sustain you and your lifestyle at the present time. Next, and this is tough, but important to answer, how much will it take to sustain you *after* you move? Try to look at the big picture here, and take as many things into consideration as you can. More phone calls and letters may be necessary, even another site visit or two to track down the hard numbers you need, but this information is vital to your future happiness.

One of the most pleasing aspects of relocating is that you will almost always find it substantially cheaper to live in a rural area than in an urban one. This difference in the amount of money that it takes to maintain a comfortable lifestyle can often be the deciding factor in determining that you *are* financially capable of making this move. We call this the Affordability Factor. In fact, monthly expenditures for people who have relocated dropped an average of 25% to 35% with very little reduction in the quality of their lifestyle.

For example, if your mortgage payment now is $1,300 a month, could you realistically drop that payment to $800 after the move for a comparable, or at least a desirable, new home? You will be very pleasantly shocked to discover that real estate prices in many rural and semi-rural areas are running 30% to 50% below their urban counterparts. Consider these figures of *average* home prices from a 1988 housing survey conducted by the Federal government:

- Anaheim, CA—$231,200
- San Francisco, CA—$228,100
- Boston, MA—$182,800
- New York, NY—$178,500
- Hartford, CT—$165,000

The other side of the coin:

- Jacksonville, FL—$90,300
- Richmond, VA—$90,000
- Colorado Springs, CO—$88,278

- Lansing, MI—$87,833
- Louisville, KY—$85,817
- Boise, ID—$81,000
- Billings, MT—$79,267
- Bend, OR—$75,000
- Charleston, WV—$66,967

Think for a moment about what that house you own in New York or Los Angeles would sell for at current market conditions, then consider what you could buy elsewhere and how much you'd have left over. The profits from the sale of your existing house could easily tide you over while you get settled, emotionally and financially, or it even might be enough to set you up in your own small business.

Auto expenses are another prime example of cost savings. Remember Sal, the man with the Porsche that he loved so much? As was noted, both his car payment (based on the lower initial selling price of the car) and his insurance (based on less drivers on the road, less chance of an accident, less chance of having the car stolen, and less chance of having the car vandalized) were lower in the country. Now factor in two other items: lower mileage costs (his monthly commute dropped from 1320 miles to 360 miles) and lower parking fees. Here are his figures:

	Was	Is
Car payment	$400	$370
Insurance	$130	$ 95
Mileage $0.24	$317	$ 86
Parking	$285	$ 40
Total	$1,132	$591

Monthly Savings: $541

In this one example alone, Sal reduced his monthly car allowance over 52%, with no drop in lifestyle. In fact, he feels even better about his signpost of success because there's not a Porsche on every corner, making the realization of that earlier financial goal all the sweeter. And this is not an isolated case.

Here are some other financial points to consider, keeping in mind their impact on the Affordability Factor:

Insurance: The actuarial tables don't lie. It is cheaper to get insurance in a rural area than in an urban one. There are less people, less crime, less traffic and inevitable traffic accidents. There is less of virtually everything, including premiums. Here are three examples of average insurance rates (based on 1989 car, owner married with no accidents):

Los Angles, California—$1,900
New York, New York—$1,750
Miami, Florida—$1,300

Now compare that to:

Bend, Oregon—$550
Flagstaff, Arizona—$650
Richmond, Virginia—$850

Reduced theft, vandalism, and other potential personal and business hazards are reflected in lower rates for virtually all types of insurance: home, auto, medical, liability, business, or inventory;

Transportation: Besides insurance, there are other transportation costs that will decrease. Your new geographical base will be smaller, so your commuting time will be substantially reduced. If your daily commute drops from fifty miles to ten, you'll save $9.60 a day at the Internal Revenue Service's allowance of $.24 per mile. Also, licensing and registration fees will probably be lower. And this is not even taking into consideration the additional hours each day that are now freed up for productive work;

Taxes: Many areas of smaller population have a comparably smaller tax base (less schools to support, small police forces, no massive public transportation programs), with a resulting

drop in property taxes. Business taxes are much less in many areas, and, depending on the state, you can conceivably find yourself paying no sales tax, property tax, or income tax;
Entertainment: Not to be overlooked is the general reduction in entertainment cost, which can be a real savings if you're a businessperson who makes dining out part of the overall business plan. The amenities won't be lacking either. Chefs and restauranteurs are among urban dropouts, and many small cities and towns, particularly those in tourist-oriented areas, offer dining rivalling any big city's. And without big city prices and a three-hour wait;
Education: Many states have excellent colleges and universities which offer first-class quality education at lower tuition than the "name" colleges. Your new community may also be the home of a good, low-cost community college. You will probably find reduced tuition rates at private schools of all types and grade levels. Again, our survey assessment looks only at the financial side. Remember, too, that classrooms are less crowded and entrance waiting periods do not stretch into what seems to be an eternity.

JOB SKILLS:

Next on the self assessment list are your job skills. List the obvious first, such as your current employment. Then start delving a little deeper, and give yourself credit for all the things you've learned and the skills you've acquired, both on your present job and from previous ones. Do you have computer skills? Management skills? Writing skills? Can you swing a hammer or fix a car?

Be imaginative, resourceful, and thorough. Look at the grants you've written and the reports you've analyzed, at the homes you've built and the real estate you've sold, at the seminars you've conducted and the books you've kept. Such accomplishments and skills may not be related to what you do now, but they are assets to be listed, remembered, and, perhaps, drawn upon in the future.

EDUCATION:

As with your job skills, take a close look at your education. Remember, noting "college graduate" on your list is not enough. What classes did you take, and what grades did you earn? Which ones did you particularly enjoy, and which ones did you excel in? Are you lacking only a few classes to finish your degree, or perhaps acquire a new one? Is this the time to get that high school diploma about which you've been thinking?

Don't overlook business or trade schools either. Attending college does not always equal success in life. Have you taken any business classes? What about apprenticeship classes or specialized training in a given field?

Finally, look at seminars you've attended, even if it was only a half-day workshop. Everything counts in your inventory at this point, no matter how small it may seem.

HOBBIES:

Here's a part of the personal inventory to which you may not have given thought, but it could be crucial. You never know when another garage project will turn into a multi-million dollar industry. Over the years, your interests have probably varied. Perhaps there are some for which you haven't had time lately and wish you had.

It's very possible that what may seem like relatively unimportant interests, such as creating science fiction characters, tying fishing flies, building cabinets, or making that salsa about which everyone raves could actually have the potential for a new business or career. Many urban dropouts have taken their hobbies and turned them into successful vocations—with that enviable extra of being able to work at something they enjoy.

By all means, write these interests down. What do you like to do with your spare time? Is there any income potential in it, as it currently exists or with a little revising and innovation? Give in to your imagination here, and be creative. It may not lead anywhere, but you never know.

ADAPTABILITY:

Look back on your life to this point, and take a hard look at how adaptable you've been when faced with other important changes in your life. This could be an asset that's every bit as important as money in the bank. Were you ever fired or laid off from a job, only to bounce back and forge ahead better than ever? Have you ever started a business of your own, even if it never made the Fortune 500? Have you ever spotted an opportunity and been able to take advantage of it?

Many successful dropouts have had the ability to roll with the circumstances as they present themselves. A very surprisingly high number of them are in new careers or businesses today that they would never have imagined themselves a few years ago.

UTILIZING THE INFORMATION

The information that you have compiled provides you with the tools and the raw materials, but what you build with them is up to you.

Look back over what's been written down, and search for patterns. All the indicators may point to your need to find a job in the same field, or to ask for a transfer. However, you may see a pattern of responses that brings the realization that you will never be happy unless you can own your own store or finish your college education.

On the other hand, you may even find that your resources are such that a move is possible without immediate economic concerns. This may be the perfect time to make the relocation decision, and then spend your time working on the novel you've always dreamed of writing.

INTANGIBLE

There is a real, intangible factor of your move on which you will not be able to put a price. but one that must be weighed heavily. After all, it's realistic that even after accounting for the Affordability Factor, the chances are that you still won't be at the income level that you were in the city. Most rural and semi-rural areas simply can't match it.

You know you want to move, to get away, to make a change—your brain, your body, your spirit are crying out for it. So the question becomes, how much is a better, slower, safer, saner way of life worth to you? $100 a year, $10,000 a year? Only you can supply the answer. But give it serious thought; there truly *are* things that money can't buy.

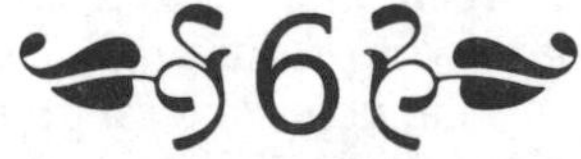

Choosing Your New Homestead

My idea of a home is a house in which each member of the family can on the instant kindle a fire in his or her private room.

—Ralph Waldo Emerson
Journals

Pick up any newspaper and look at the rural property section and you will find some of the most seductive ads ever written.

Try this one for example:

CENTRAL OREGON
Are you contemplating a change of lifestyle? Looking for just a nice place to live, raise a family, work and retire? Well it's time to take a good hard look at Prineville, in Crook County, Oregon. We're the geographic center of the state and in the heart of vast

Central Oregon recreation playground. We offer more of less than a lot of communities: less people at your favorite fishing hole. The list goes on, but you catch our drift. For information on real estate here in God's country call or write today. Central Oregon Real Estate, P.O. Box 573, Prineville, Oregon 97754.

Sound appealing? How about this one?

MOUNTAIN RETREAT

Log home on five pristine acres located in the heart of the gold rush country. Handcrafted from scratch by the owner, this home features large country kitchen, huge master suite with views of the Sierras and two additional bedrooms for your weekend guests from the big city. Huge beams and plank floors add to the rustic feeling of this magnificent home. Enjoy the clear mountain air and spring-fed water as you gaze through acres of ponderosa pines. Truly a one-of-a-kind opportunity, $34,000 call today. Ripp Off and Run Realty, P.O. Box 13, Nevada City, CA.

People have been known to spend hours fantasizing while reading ads like these. They all sound too good to be true, and the prices are unbelievable. The truth is that any property can be made to sound better than it is in print, and real estate companies have become masters at making even the worst properties sound appealing.

It's not that realtors want to deceive people—some properties are so bad there is no way to get exposure without a well-written ad. Also, real estate companies spend a lot of money on specific advertising meant for their clients, who think their house is the best one on the market. The point is, don't believe too much of what you read in the classifieds.

GATHERING INFORMATION

One of the best ways to get information on real estate, especially if you can't visit the area yourself, is to subscribe to the local newspaper. Look for the real estate companies doing the most advertising and write to them requesting information on real estate which is in your price range. Be sure to ask for pictures, or a copy of one of the many photo books, such as *Homes and Land Magazine,* that can be found in many communities around the country. As you read and study, you will begin to develop a feel for the prices and relative quality of available housing in the area. This information will give you a base of knowledge when you actually visit the community. This will also help you calculate what financial resources you will need if you are thinking about buying a house in your new location.

If you should visit the community to which you are moving prior to selling your old house, do not, repeat, *do not* buy a new house until you have sold your old one. Many people get caught up in the excitement of finding just the right property and let their emotions take hold. This can lead to a situation where you own two houses at the same time—a situation you definitely want to avoid.

FINDING YOUR NEW HOUSE

Just as your wants and needs in moving and in selecting a new community will vary from another person's, so will your needs in housing and your particular situation for purchasing a new house. But there are a number of similarities between most people's experiences with moving and looking for real estate, so let's begin by working through the typical step by step process of finding a new house.

Evaluate your Resources

Assuming that you have found the area of your dreams and have decided to move, what should you do first? Obviously, you need to decide whether you are going to rent or buy.

If you intend to buy a house, then your next step is to do a thorough assessment of your financial resources. Begin by determining exactly how much equity you have in your present house. Most real estate companies in your area will provide you with a free competitive market analysis showing the approximate value of your house. The analysis is free of any cost to you, but the agent will try to solicit your business when it comes time to list your house on the market.

Realtors use a variety of means for establishing value, probably the most accurate of which is a computer search of "comps," other homes in your area that have recently sold and are comparable to yours in size, condition, location, and features. The realtor can then compare selling prices, and adjust the value to take your house's drawbacks and special features into consideration.

You will probably have done a little research on your own by this time, including reading advertisements in the paper and perhaps even snooping through an open house or two, so you should have some idea of what your house is worth. If the realtor's value seems abnormally high or low, get a second opinion. As long as you don't sign a listing agreement with the agent, you are under no obligation to use their services, and you are free to contact as many companies as you wish.

Another more accurate method of determining your house's value is to employ the services of an independent real estate appraiser. Having a professional appraisal done will cost between $100 and $300, depending on the size of the house, how much acreage surrounds it, and the difficulty of finding comps. The advantage of this kind of service is that the appraiser has no conflicting interest in the matter of what your house is worth. He won't inflate the value to entice you into listing the house for sale, and he won't lower the value in the hopes of making a quick sale and an equally quick commission.

You also need to determine approximately how long houses take to sell in your market area. Add thirty days to this figure as a buffer. For a sale to occur in a normally healthy market, it is advisable to list your house at the market price plus five percent. Any more than this will lessen your chances of selling and thus prolong your move. Remember, what you may give up in price at your old residence can, and often is, made up for in what you pay for your new house.

If the market is sluggish or heading down in your area, you may want to consider renting your house until things improve. Many urban dropouts will also rent their homes instead of selling them just in case they should decide to return. This is a good way to hedge your bet if you are a bit unsure about making the relocation. Either way, you want to be absolutely certain that you take the trouble to find good tenants and don't ignore the need to check references. Also, pay a trusted neighbor to look after the house in your absence, or hire a property management company to do the overseeing. There is nothing worse than returning to a house you once loved and cared for to find that it has been reduced to shambles while you were away.

When calculating the return on your house, be aware that you are going to have certain selling expenses, and that there are also some tax considerations with which to deal. Ask your real estate agent for a "seller's net income statement." This will show you the bottom line dollar amount you'll be seeing after sales commissions, title and escrow fees, and loan payoff. As far as taxes are concerned, your accountant should be able to help you determine any capital gains you might have based on the expected sales price of your old house when compared to the purchase price of the new one.

After all this research, you should now have a good idea of the market value of your house. Since it is likely you will pay less for your new house than you recovered from the sale of the old one, there should be some money remaining. Getting settled in your new location may take a little time, and moving, unfortunately, isn't free. Try to invest the money wisely for future use. If possible, open a money market account and don't touch the principal amount unless it is absolutely necessary.

One small note of sobering reality: While it will feel good to buy a less expensive house in your new location, remember that if you have to go back to your old city, or to any other major urban center, it will probably cost you more than the price you received when you sold your previous home in the city. This is something to remember until you've made the final decision to stay in your new location.

ASSESSING THE REAL ESTATE MARKET IN YOUR NEW LOCATION

During the 1980s, the real estate market has experienced a number of ups and downs. Some areas of the country have been afflicted with declining values while others, like Los Angeles, have seen sky-rocketing increases of twenty to forty percent a year.

It is important to look beyond current market conditions and to develop a historical prospective concerning real estate values. For example, what current factors are influencing the property values in the area you're considering? Things like employment, investor activity and population trends are all areas that should be studied. Have values been going up or down? How do these rises and declines relate to the activity of prior years, and what factors are currently impacting the market?

For most new arrivals from major urban centers, real estate seems like an absolute bargain in the rural areas. Many people are so overwhelmed with this perception of "cheap land" that they pay full price for a property when it might have been possible to pay less. Others have purchased everything in sight, and have ended up "real estate poor". Every market has its own unique set of characteristics. It is important to look at the facts. Don't trust anyone but yourself to gather the necessary information. This also offers you a good opportunity to get a feel for the pulse in the community, and a chance to meet some nice people in the process.

REAL ESTATE AGENTS

Assuming you don't already have one, your first contact when searching for your new home will be a real estate agent. Don't be enticed into an office by a big sign, and settle on whichever agent happens to be there and offers the first hello. Do some research first. Find out the best companies in town with which to deal, and which people in those firms are considered the best agents. Cheaper land values or not, you are about to spend a great deal of money on a real estate purchase. Why leave it up to some part-timer who does this as a hobby instead of a full-time professional who comes with a sound recommendation? Most Chambers of Commerce will have a list of all the real estate companies in town, along with their dollar volume per year. Checking a few newspaper ads will usually get you the names of the "Top Listers" and the "Top Sellers" in those companies. If you know anyone in town who has bought or sold real estate, ask them for specific recommendations of companies and agents. This way you will have a place to begin your search for the real estate agent who can meet your needs.

Once you form a relationship with an agent, assuming you trust the person and get along well with him or feel the person is doing a good job for you, try to remain loyal. It is frustrating for an agent to spend hours or days trying to help you with your real estate needs only to discover you are making the rounds of every real estate company in town. It is also counter-productive, since it takes time for an agent to get to know you and your specific needs, and to direct his search in the best direction.

Most companies share their listings through the Multiple Listing Service (MLS), so they have access to one another's inventory. If they don't belong to the MLS or don't have some way of sharing inventory, then it probably isn't a good idea to consider that particular company. Many agents also have "pocket listings", special listings known only to them or to their office. These listings are new on the market and have not yet made the MLS books. You typically need to work with an agent for awhile before you will be made aware of these special listings. This is another good reason for staying with the same agent.

Trust is a crucial commodity in working with an agent. You need to be comfortable with what you're being told, and you need to feel that you're getting the agent's honest attention and effort, not just a pat sales pitch. If you work with an agent for awhile and are not fully satisfied with the relationship that's developing, move to another agent or another office.

Be totally honest with your agent and let him know that you expect the same in return. It is extremely hard for an agent to meet all the requirements of a client if the client withholds some important information. Be frank about how much you have to spend and what you can afford in monthly payments. You should have already decided on a price range, and this will influence the inventory available for you to see. Look at as many houses as possible until you get a good feel for the market and what's available.

If you don't yet have a job, or if you've only been on the job a short time, you are probably going to have trouble qualifying for a mortgage. However, there are other available means to remedy these situations, such as seller-assisted financing or lease-options, so again, look to an agent you trust to give you the right advice.

OTHER SOURCES OF INFORMATION

Real estate agents are only one source of information. You will want to contact a variety of other sources before making the final decision to purchase a home or land. Again, gather as much information as possible so that you can verify what others are telling you is the truth, and also be certain you are comfortable by having all the facts.

To help you in your quest for the facts, here is a list of agencies that can answer specific questions related to your real estate purchase:

Lending Institutions: Take the time to speak with a variety of banks, savings and loans, and mortgage companies in the early stages of your real estate search. They can provide you with information about the types of loans available and also give you some idea of what it will take to qualify for a loan with them. Some won't lend on parcels over five acres, or on farm property, while others won't lend on mobile homes or make construction loans. If possible, try to get preapproved for a specific loan amount so that you know exactly what price range of houses you can afford;

The County Assessor's office: This is the place to go for information on property tax, both general information and exact taxes on specific parcels;

Farm Appraisers Office: Some communities are heavily agricultural and have a separate office for the appraisal of farm and ranch property. If you are looking at acreage, be sure and stop by this office to get specific tax and assessment information on the property, and also to find out if there are any regulations pertaining to that specific piece of land or that region with which you will need to comply;

City or County Planning Department: This office will provide you with information on an area's zoning laws, as well as those affecting zone changes and housing density. They can also provide you with plat maps of the property in which you are interested, so you can see its exact dimensions and ascertain if there are any variances or restrictions on the property;

Building Department: This agency can tell you about building permits, and whether the necessary permits and inspections were taken out on any home you are interested in buying;

Department of Environmental Health: This agency (it may go by another name in your community) can give you information regarding septic systems. If you are looking at a piece of property that is not served by a city sewer system, it is imperative that you know if you can get approval to install a septic system on the land. Without that approval, the land is virtually worthless;

Chamber of Commerce: You probably already feel like you are a permanent fixture here, but this is the place to check for information on your town's population growth.

Employment Department: This agency can give you information on job growth, another crucial consideration both for your own employment and for the future growth of the area;

Economic Development Department: Here is another agency that can provide you with information on area growth;

Title Companies: Any of the area's title companies can provide you with data on local real estate conditions, as well as covenants and restrictions that might apply to any particular subdivision you might be considering;

An Independent Appraiser: For information of locations that have shown marked appreciation value;

An Insurance Agent: Talk with an insurance agent for rates on homeowner's and fire insurance, renter's insurance, and other rate information;

State and County Highway Department, or the County Department of Public Works: These agencies can tell you if any road changes are planned for your area, or if the dirt road leading to that property you like is going to be paved soon. They can also give you information about winter snow removal. You should have some idea of how snow affects local traffic and where your particular area is on the list of snow removal priorities—some parts of town wait longer than others for the snow plow to arrive;

Watermaster: Many towns have a Watermaster, whose responsibility is to oversee water wells and irrigation in the area. If you are purchasing land that has a well, or if you anticipate the need to drill one, the Watermaster can tell you about the depth of the water table, rock and soil conditions, and the going rates for drilling in the area;

Irrigation Company: If you are looking at acreage, you will need to know if any irrigation water rights are adjudicated to that parcel, or if you can purchase water rights. For further information, check with the irrigation company that supplies water to that area. Your real estate agent, title company, or the Watermaster will know which company to contact;

Private Water Companies: Many rural communities with land outside the city limits have private water companies that supply domestic water to outlying areas. If you are looking at a house or piece of land that is served by a private water company, check with them for information regarding rates and services;

Forest Service and Bureau of Land Management: If your property abuts theirs, they can provide you with any pertinent rules and restrictions about land usage;

Department of Fish and Wildlife: If you want to put fish in your pond, raise certain types of exotic animals, or use the land in a way that may be at odds with the protection and safety of the area's wildlife, this is the place to check the regulations;

Utility Companies: For information on the availability of services, as well as current rates, most utility companies have customer service departments to answer all pertinent questions;

Department of Agriculture: This is the place to go for information on growing seasons, and for the possibility of raising certain crops in the area;

County Extension Office: A similar source of crop and gardening information;

Fire Department: For information on the availability of fire crews in your area, water pressure, and response times;

Police Department: For information on crime rates in specific areas of town;

County or City Library, or Historical Societies: There are always interesting places to visit for historical information about land you'd like to purchase, as well as about the area in general.

There may, of course, be other agencies with which you may like to talk as the time and need dictates. The important thing is to speak with enough people so that you feel comfortable about your purchase and are reasonably knowledgeable about the area.

Location

It has been said that there are three things to consider when buying real estate—location . . . location . . . and location. When you find that special property in which you are seriously interested, its location is one of the most important things to consider. You do not want the best house in the worst neighborhood, but would not mind the worst house in the best neighborhood.

Here are some important questions to consider when evaluating the location of a piece of property:

How will the value of other properties directly influence yours? Rural areas are often known for a lack of distinctive "good" and "bad" neighborhoods, and it is not uncommon to find an aged, single-wide mobile home nestled in the trees next door to a $200,000 custom home. Look closely at the neighborhood or surrounding area to see what's there, and if you can tell what the trend for that area might be;

What is the distance to town? Some perfectly beautiful pieces of rural acreage are quite a distance from town. This drawback might not become apparent until the winter snows set in. Take into consideration such things as to how far away you will be working, where the nearest shopping center is, and any other factors that may influence how far you want to be from town;

Is there a view? Views cost money, so think about what you want to see and how much you want to pay for it;

In what condition are the other homes in the neighborhood? Even in an area where all the homes are relatively the same in size and quality of construction, there can still be tremendous differences in condition and upkeep. A neighborhood of poorly kept homes reflects the owners' lack of interest in the values of their property—and in the value of yours;

Is there a homeowners' association? There are pros and cons to homeowner's associations, and you need to weigh these carefully. Some people like them because they impose restrictions on the types of homes to be built in the area, the kinds of animals that can be kept on the property and the models and number of vehicles that can be parked at the home. They also oversee maintenance and upkeep and have the power of approval or denial over remodeling projects that affect the home's outward appearance, which results in maintaining property values. Opponents dislike homeowners' associations for exactly the same reasons.

Purchase Agreements

When you have finally made your choice and are ready to start the purchase process, the writing of a purchase agreement is the first step. Here you will really need to rely on your agent to help build in the necessary protective clauses. Remember that being unfamiliar with the area, you will want to pay special attention to every detail. All of the intricacies concerning the various component parts of a real estate agreement are too numerous to go into here, and will vary from deal to deal. If you have a good agent working with you who's familiar with the local customs (and since you have been so good about doing your research before hand), there is no reason why things should not go smoothly.

Depending on the area of the country in which you settle, you may, or may not, have an attorney present at the closing. Either way, if there is seller-assisted financing being provided, either on a land contract of sale or a note and deed of trust, there will be a number of legal documents to review and sign. Be represented by your own attorney. Your real estate agent or the state bar association can recommend a lawyer well versed in real estate law for the area.

RENTING VERSUS BUYING

Many urban dropouts choose, at least initially, to rent rather than buy a home. Your choice depends upon your personal plans and situation, but renting may well be the best alternative, especially if you are unsure about your long term plans. If you decide to rent, the next question is whether to rent a furnished unit and put your belongings in storage, or rent an unfurnished place and have to move twice should you eventually decide to buy a home and stay in the community.

There are also some tax considerations if you sold a home prior to moving. Currently, you have two years to reinvest the proceeds from the previous sale in order to avoid capital gains taxes on the full amount. If you purchase a new home that is less expensive than the price for which you sold your previous home, the difference between the sale price of your old home and the purchase price of the new one will still be subject to tax. The rules, just to complicate things a little more, are slightly different if you intend to build a new home. Since these laws are continually changing and are affected by a number of different factors, it's best to consult with your accountant or the Internal Revenue Service prior to making any final decisions.

Should you choose to rent, there is the added consideration of the dollars spent for rent versus dollars spent on a mortgage. The interest expense you pay on a mortgage is deductible on your income taxes, while rent is not. Also, if you buy a house, you can deduct the amount of property taxes you pay. If you are renting, you are, in essence, paying the property tax payment as part of your rent, but the landlord gets to take the deduction.

Bear in mind that if property values go up while you are renting, the home you eventually buy will ultimately cost you more. You will have lost the appreciation you would have gained if, instead of renting, you had purchased a home right away.

The decision to rent versus buying a home is a personal one. No one can tell you what the value of having peace of mind is worth. After all, you have already taken a big step just in relocating to a totally new area. Perhaps you would just as soon not have to worry about what might happen if things don't work out as well as hoped. There is also the risk that property values might decline after you buy, or that interest rates could rise, either one of which would make it more difficult to sell your new home and recoup your investment should you decide to leave.

If renting is your choice, the classified section of the local newspaper is usually your best resource, or you might want to register with a property management company or a real estate company. Some realtors maintain a property management division, and others may have unsold inventory that the owners would rather rent out than leave vacant—but most realtors do not deal in rentals.

In some areas, particularly those desirable rural communities that have recently been "discovered", the rental market may be very tight. In most rural communities, there has been very little construction of apartments and other rental units in recent years. As a town becomes popular, you will find that the demand for rental housing has quickly outstripped the supply. This is especially true of seasonal communities that offer recreational amenities such as skiing, and in areas where an abundance of seasonal service jobs exist. As with purchasing a house, you will find that the more rent you can afford to pay each month, the greater your choices of available rental units will be.

Plan on beginning your search for area rentals prior to moving, either through site visits or by working with a local property management company. If the market is tight, be prepared to act quickly, perhaps even sight unseen, if the management agent comes up with something promising. In an area where rentals are more plentiful, arrange to see pictures of the house or apartment complex and negotiate the best rental terms prior to signing an agreement.

Should you ultimately decide to stay in the community

and buy a home, be sure to begin negotiations prior to the expiration of your rental lease. Discuss your situation with your landlord to gain some flexibility on move-out dates, and try to arrange them to coincide with the closing dates for your escrow. Most landlords are cooperative if you are honest with them.

Storage

If you are moving into a rental unit or purchasing a home that is smaller than your old one, you may be forced to store some or even all of your belongings. Many small towns have not yet built up a large inventory of "mini-store" units, and finding storage facilities may be difficult. Your mover will store items for you, but this is an expensive and inconvenient alternative, since your items will be stored in crates that make access to individual items virtually impossible.

When storing items, try and arrange early for dry, secure, easily accessible storage. You may even be able to arrange to rent a garage or small storage shed from a private individual. If you need to have the mover store your belongings, try to anticipate which of your goods you will need and either move them separately or separate them from the main shipment. It's far better to have access to something than to have to replace it.

CHOOSING THE RIGHT PROPERTY

You have been reading all the advertisements and looking at all the magazines in order to locate the perfect property only to find out over and over again that things aren't always as good in reality as they sounded in the paper. Carl and Diane P. told about the "mini-farm" that was advertised as "the perfect place for the gentleman farmer". The ad said that the property had "a large main ranch house with accompanying out-buildings". Special features included "a large pond stocked with fish", and "complete wood fencing", and the property is located next to "750 acres of open land". All for just $124,500. They immediately called their real estate agent for a showing. To Carl and Diane, the place sounded like such a great deal that they didn't want to lose out to another buyer who acted faster than they did.

Upon inspection, the "large ranch house" was indeed just that—a large house that looked like a ranch inside. They chased out the goats, dogs, cats and other assorted animals from the living room to discover that the house had, to put it mildly, a well-lived-in look. It had been built in 1906, and still had a hand water pump and screw-in fuses. One of the upstairs bedrooms had about a 12% list to port, apparently the result of one of the rocks in the foundation having given way. The house did have plumbing, complete with one of those bathtubs with claw feet and a shower curtain that hung on an oblong metal ring.

The barn had a number of ragged holes that are part of most old buildings built around 1906—holes that look great in rural photographs but leak like a sieve during the slightest hint of rain. Carl and Diane weren't sure about the condition of the rest of the barn. The sag in the roof discouraged further inside investigation.

The pond was so mud-encrusted that the little swirls they saw in the water could have been fish or they could have been something else. The wood fencing hadn't been painted for years and each post leaned in a different direction. There was no well, but "ditch water" was available—irrigation water that ran straight from the canal into a wooden cistern. All this "rustic charm" was set on one-and-a-half, rock-strewn acres that couldn't be cleared with dynamite. And the 750 adjoining acres? Just before they left the site the agent informed them that the county had the property under study for a zoning change to allow its use as a rock quarry.

Carl and Diane T.'s case is an extreme one, but does serve to illustrate some of the dangers that are inherent in buying rural property. Things like the availability of domestic water, irrigation water rights, easements, and land use laws are some of the many things you will want to evaluate prior to making a purchase.

This is especially true when buying raw land with no history of use. Consider Pat and Emil C., who bought forty acres of raw land twelve miles west of town for $1,000 per acre. It seemed like quite a bargain, even by most country standards. But when they applied for a building permit, they discovered there were no irrigation water rights attached to the property. Water could only be found at the 1,500 foot level. At a cost of $15 a foot for drilling, plus pump and pipe, sinking a well would add almost $30,000 to the initial cost of their land.

Not only was there no water, but there was no fire protection in the area—not even a lone volunteer. Unless they invested another $5,000 in a private fire protection system, their homeowner's insurance rates would be so high as to be almost unaffordable. This is another case of a "too good to be true" rural dream turning into a nightmare.

RURAL PROPERTY—SOME DIFFERENT CLASSIFICATIONS

When you are dreaming of those wide-open spaces and the lure of owning your own land becomes too strong to resist, there are a few things you should know before heading to your realtor's office. There are actually several classifications of acreage, depending on size and intended use. The following breakdown may help you better understand what type and size of land parcel to look for, and what its possible use might be.

UNDEVELOPED ACREAGE

This type of land is usually in the five to twenty acre range, and is typically what most dropouts have in mind when looking for rural land. Zoning for these parcels varies, but are typically classified agricultural, farm, or forest zones, and, as such, may have certain restrictions. You will want to be sure to check the applicable zoning regulations for the area before making a final decision.

Some Initial Considerations

Relocation and open land seem to go hand in hand for most people, and owning some acreage of your very own is a worthwhile dream shared by many of the people we interviewed.

As you read on, it may seem that the number of drawbacks and expenses and conditions to consider associated with rural acreage make the endeavor totally unworkable for all but either the most wealthy or the most foolish. But this is not actually the case.

What we have tried to do is give you a realistic look at what buying and owning land entails. This is not meant to discourage you or push you in another direction, but to offer suggestions for protecting your interests and to guide you into the undertaking with both your eyes open.

Perhaps the biggest question with small acreage is what you intend to do with it. If you envision living in a park, remember that five acres is a lot of lawn to mow. "Mini farms", "mini ranches", and "gentleman ranches" are all cute phrases that realtors apply to parcels such as these, and indeed they are large enough to farm, but only as a hobby. Twenty acres is large enough to actually plant a cash crop, but not return an income that will resemble anything close to a living wage. As a ranch, fifteen or twenty acres will allow you to raise a number of animals such as sheep, goats, or pigs and will also even allow some profit from their sale to supplement your regular income. But, again, it's not enough for you to actually live on.

What To Look For

As with the actual farm acreage, there are several things that should be closely checked when buying rural undeveloped acreage. Here is a checklist for reference, with some explanations following:

UNDEVELOPED ACREAGE CHECKLIST

1 _____ Domestic (house-use) water is included or available
2 _____ Irrigation water rights are included or are available
3 _____ Ingress and egress to the property is clearly defined
4 _____ Easements across the property are clearly defined
5 _____ No restrictions exist to prevent building permits
6 _____ The property has septic system approval
7 _____ Utilities are available at or near the property line
8 _____ The land has been surveyed and the boundaries are clear
9 _____ You understand the tax status of the land
10 _____ Zoning is compatible with your intended use
11 _____ Land use laws are compatible with your intended use
12 _____ Soil and climate is adequate for your intended use

(1) As mentioned previously, water is a major selling feature for any land. You will want to know if drinking water is available on the property, either from the city or a private water

company, or determine if a well is there or can be drilled. A note about wells: Well drilling is expensive, averaging $10 to $20 per foot for the hole alone, plus the pump and related equipment. Existing wells may be subject to state or local regulations governing pressure and water quality, and will need to be checked and certified, usually at the seller's expense, prior to closing escrow. Another common situation is the shared or co-owned well, in which several adjacent families share the expense of drilling and maintaining the well. If your land has a co-owned well, *be certain* that a legally-recorded document exists that defines the rights and responsibilities of each well partner. There are horror stories in abundance concerning problems arising from well agreements that are too loosely drawn.

(2) Irrigation water is usually available from private irrigation companies or from the state, and you will pay so much per "acre of water." An acre of water is the equivalent of one acre of land covered with water to a depth of one inch, or about 7.5 gallons of water per minute. You will also pay a minimal charge on a yearly basis for shared maintenance of the canal and its various components. Many states have irrigation water usage laws that relate to the "beneficial use" of the water; if you don't use the water for irrigation purposes, you may loose your rights to it. Be sure and verify all these details with your irrigation company.

(3) Some parcels are "land locked." You will need to get special permission to cross someone else's property in order to get to your land. Be certain your access to the property is clearly defined and legally protected. Also, if your access road is shared by other property owners, find out who is responsible for maintenance, and how the responsibilities are divided. Ideally, you would like to have a formal "road maintenance agreement" (some lenders even require this before granting construction or mortgage loans) that clearly defines the rights and responsibilities of the road owners.

(4) It is not uncommon for other people to have easement rights across your property. These may include utility easements, for water or power lines to cross the property; irrigation easements, for a pipe or ditch to cross the property so that a neighbor can get water from an adjacent irrigation canal; or ingress and egress easements. Easements should be legally recorded, and you can get copies of them from the title company.

(5) Some areas, particularly agricultural and forest areas, may have restrictions against the construction of single family homes. Check with the building department for full information.

(6) Not all types of soil are capable of sustaining a septic system. Before buying the property, check that septic approval has or will be issued for that parcel.

(7) If your land is fairly remote, utility lines may still be some distance away, and to get them to your property may require some very expensive "line extension" charges from the utility company. It may be necessary to bear the expense of having a transformer installed to get electricity to your land parcel. Check with the electric company and the phone company to see how close to the property their lines are and what the cost will be of serving your land. Even if the lines are at your property line, you may still be looking at considerable expense to get them across twenty acres of land to the spot where your house will be built.

(8) Many pieces of rural acreage have vague boundaries defined by years of usage. To prevent future problems, your parcel should be surveyed and the boundaries clearly laid out and marked.

(9) Some parcels of land may fall into special tax categories, granting various forms of tax relief if the land is used exclusively for farming or certain other purposes. Check with

the county assessor's office or the farm appraiser's office for specific details.

(10) Depending on what you want to do with your land, local zoning and land use restrictions may prevent certain usages, as may the local soil and climate conditions. Some areas restrict livestock, or raising certain "exotic" animals if they pose any kind of threat to the surrounding areas. Extremely rocky soil may need to be cleared, which is a tiring and often expensive undertaking. Soil that is high in clay content may have a special drainage problem during the rainy season. Be sure to verify that the land is, in all ways, compatible with your intended usage before buying it.

Costs

All too often overlooked or ignored are certain aspects of owning rural undeveloped property such as the cost of ownership and improvement and the work involved for their improvement.

If you are starting from virgin land, you may have to pick up twenty acres of rocks by hand before you can plow. There can be what seems to be miles of irrigation pipe to be moved during a growing season, or trenched and placed underground at a fairly high initial expense. That beautiful white fence will need painting every two years, and animals have a tendency to scratch and bump some interesting contours into the fence line. There are also taxes to pay on all that land. If you don't qualify for farm tax credits, the tax total may be a considerable sum.

There is also equipment expense to consider. Irrigation pumps, pipe, and other equipment—perhaps a tractor and related implements—even things like a chain saw and a variety of picks, shovels and other hand tools will be necessary to maintain your property. You needn't buy everything at once, and some items can easily be rented or borrowed, but these are definitely some expenses overlooked by many people.

Rural acreage is beautiful and peaceful, but it didn't happen overnight. Don't lose sight of the fact that your own personal Eden will take a few years of hard work and more than a few of your extra, hard-earned dollars—but it will be worth it in the end.

FARMS AND RANCHES

Farms and ranches are a very specialized category of rural property intended for the actual business of producing crops or animals to sell. Buying a piece of property such as this is actually like buying an established store. It needs to be analyzed for its inventory and its ability to produce a profit.

Very close attention needs to be given to adequate water rights, especially in a dry climate. Without the water, the land is essentially useless. These types of properties also may have buried tanks for heating or fuel oil, and these will need to be inspected to ensure compliance with local and state environmental laws. Once you purchase the property, you will become responsible for the future condition and upkeep of any buried tanks. You may also have some liability should the tanks be discovered to have been leaking even *prior* to when you bought the land. The same caution needs to be applied to the storage and use of pesticides and fertilizers. Most universities in or near rural areas have an agricultural department that will analyze soil samples for you. The added expense of having this done is well spent if you have any questions about the condition of the soil, the types of chemicals that have been used on it in the past, or if you are considering planting a crop that is not indigenous to the area.

RURAL SUBDIVISIONS

Another type of land possibility is the rural subdivision, which typically consists of semi-developed land in one to twenty acre parcels. Depending on the development, improvements might include water and other utilities at the site, paved roads, common recreation areas, and common maintenance agreements, as well as some covenants that limit or restrict certain types of usage.

There has been a great deal of abuse surrounding the sale of this type of land, and sales may or may not be state regulated to any great extent. The first rule when buying property of this kind is to never make a commitment sight unseen. These so called "map sales" have been going on for years, with many buyers finding out too late that the promised improvements to the property never materialized. All too often, after finally inspecting their little piece of paradise, they find it to be nothing more than acres of sagebrush baking under a treeless landscape.

There are, of course, many reputable rural subdivisions and most competent real estate agents are aware of them. Make arrangements to tour the subdivision. If it is still in the early development stages, be certain there are legal stipulations in your purchase agreement that clearly define what amenities to which you are entitled, and when these amenities will be in place.

Most communities offer many different types of subdivisions. Some cater to specific segments of the market, including retirees, families, and young, first time home buyers. It is sometimes possible to buy a lot in a subdivision where there are many different builders at work, which gives you the advantage of seeing their work first hand. Once again, you will need to place your trust in your realtor to find just the right opportunity.

BUILDING SITES

Building sites are typically classified as quarter to half acre parcels on which you will build your dream home. Many of the same cautions mentioned earlier apply here, with the exception of the environmental issues. As in buying any kind of real estate, location is always one of the most important considerations. If you can find a vacant lot in a good neighborhood offering sewers, water and other city services—and buy it for the right price—this might be the ideal approach for your particular situation. Keep in mind that you very seldom get a "steal" on quality land unless the market has gone down or you find a distress situation.

When buying this kind of lot, keep in mind the nature of the homes in the surrounding area. You will want to build in a way that is consistent with the character of the neighborhood, both to avoid resistance from the neighbors and to maintain the home's value at the time of resale. Check if there is a homeowners' association and an architectural review board, since these organizations were set up by the original developer to control certain aspects governing the community. If either of these two exist, ask for copies of the covenants, conditions and restrictions along with the by-laws, as there may be certain restrictions concerning the type of dwelling unit you build, or even the color you can paint it.

DESTINATION RESORTS

Another type of real estate that is growing in popularity, especially in areas offering recreation amenities, is the so-called "destination resort." This is usually a planned subdivision consisting of one or more golf courses, swimming pools, tennis courts, a lodge with restaurants and meeting facilities, and perhaps even a small community airport. The product mix consists of single family homes in various price ranges, condominiums, townhouses and time share units. Some of the larger resorts are valued in the hundreds of millions of dollars, often taking fifteen to twenty years to fully plan and complete.

Destination resorts appeal to many dropouts for a variety of reasons. Recreation and shopping are close at hand, and there is the opportunity to meet new friends with similar interests. There is usually a wide selection of real estate available, maintenance is fairly low, and there is a sense of security when living in a controlled environment.

Property in this type of subdivision usually costs more than in other areas because the developer has a larger investment in the recreational amenities being offered. You will generally be asked to pay some form of homeowners' dues to help support these amenities, in addition to your other normal housing costs of property taxes and insurance. If looking at property in a destination resort, be sure and balance the value and cost of having these amenities available to you, versus the cost of buying or gaining access to them separately when and if you want them.

When buying property in a destination resort you will typically have two options. The first will be to purchase a lot or developer-built property directly from the resort. If you buy early in the life of the development, you can count on regular price increases as they release future lots and homes for sale to the public. This is generally done as an inducement to get you to buy today before prices go up tomorrow.

A word to the wary: Real estate salespeople in some developments can be exceedingly aggressive. They are trained to make the sale *today,* since many potential customers are only visiting the area for a short period of time and may not be back soon, if at all. They can be extremely persuasive and usually have all kinds of inducements to get you to buy. Take your time, don't be pressured into anything, and look carefully at anything you are asked to sign. Be aware that most states allow a short "cooling off" period to allow you to reconsider and back out of a contract that was signed under pressure without any recourse against you.

The second option you have is to visit a local realtor, either at the resort or in a nearby town. They may not be able to sell you developer-owned property, but they should have access to many resales that exist in these communities. Since many properties were bought as second homes, there are always motivated sellers, especially during recession periods.

If you are buying a home or condominium, be sure to check comparable sales of similar properties to make certain you are not overpaying. Also, since these properties are generally used on a seasonal basis and rented during the owner's absence, it's a good idea to have the property inspected to be sure it is in prime condition. Be sure to get a copy of the original developer's Covenants, Conditions and Restrictions governing the development before you sign anything. Also, check with the Homeowners' Association to find out if there are any pending changes in fees or assessments, then find out what the current rental rates are from a local property management company.

Here's one other consideration. A major problem for most full-time residents of destination resorts is the influx of renters during the winter and summer months. There are a high number of second homeowners in this type of community, and since they are there only occasionally, their homes or condominiums are usually offered for rent. While bound by the same rules and regulations as homeowners, renters do not have the same concerns for an area that a full-time resident does, leading to animosity between renters and year-round residents.

CONDOMINIUMS AND TOWNHOUSES

Condominiums and Townhouses have become a popular alternative to traditional single family housing over the past twenty years. Offering ease of maintenance and security, they are generally more affordable than the traditional home. Most resort communities have a good selection of condominiums for sale, and they can be purchased through a realtor or directly from the developers.

There are a few things to consider when looking at this alternative. Condominiums have been called "glorified apartments", and in many ways that's exactly what they are. The primary difference is that you own your own unit, along with an undivided interest in whatever recreational amenities and common areas that may exist. Condominiums are governed by Homeowners' Associations, allowing you a vote and the opportunity to become an office holder.

Successful condominium projects sell out quickly, and usually work well as investments. Units in less successful developments are often rented in order to generate cash flow for the developer until they sell. Remember that it is illegal not to rent to families with children in some states, and this may adversely affect the peace and quiet you were looking for when you first moved there.

If you are retired or an "empty nester" (a person or couple without children), then a condominium might be just the right choice for you. There are always people around, and in larger projects there is usually some kind of security patrol. If you travel a lot and would like to just close the door behind you and take off for a month or longer, condominium living is one of the most convenient ways to own property.

Many of the same precautions that apply to buying a house also apply to buying a condominium. Check the builder's reputation, talk to a few people in the development about the quality of the units and how well they're maintained, and be sure to read and understand all the documents governing the complex.

RETIREMENT COMMUNITIES

If you are getting older and prefer a totally hassle-free method of home ownership, consider a retirement community. Some of the more successful retirement villages cater exclusively to senior citizens and will not allow occupancy by young people with families. The minimum age is usually forty-five to fifty, and there are very attractive amenities packages designed around less strenuous activities.

Homes are built on a single level and are designed for maximum efficiency. There is usually a security patrol and a wide variety of planned activities for active seniors. Some retirement centers offer a form of ownership, which usually includes an apartment with cooking facilities and 24-hour medical care for those who need it.

MULTI-FAMILY DWELLINGS

Another hybrid form of home ownership is to buy a duplex, triplex or fourplex with an owner's unit. The beauty of this plan is that your tenants help to make your mortgage payments and other ownership expenses. At the same time, you have a place to live. You shouldn't expect to recoup 100% of your expenses, but it is a nice way to help offset your cost of living. Another advantage, as with condominium living, is that you can usually leave for extended periods without a lot of worry—just leave one of your more trustworthy tenants in charge for a small concession in their rent.

Income property transactions are different from buying a single family home. You will want to pay close attention to such things as tax benefits, vacancy rates and rent levels. A good real estate agent with experience in this area should be able to help, and you will want to consult with your accountant.

BUILDING YOUR OWN HOME

Having looked at all the major forms of home and land ownership, no list of possibilities would be complete without a look at a secret dream that most relocaters share—a custom house. Large or small, rustic or contemporary, contractor-built or built with your own two hands, what can compare with designing and constructing a space that is uniquely your own, perfectly suited to your tastes and desires.

Many people have spent countless enjoyable hours in the evenings poring over plan books and moving scale furniture around on little floor plan grids. Building your own home is like an artist's painting. It's your statement to the world.

Lot Layout

Whether you use an architect, designer, or purchase stock plans from a plan book, the first thing you should do is spend a lot of time on your building site. You can't move the house once it's built, so be sure to consider as many things as possible: like where the sun comes up in both summer and winter; what the possibilities are for solar heat; are there particular orientations that will capture a view; and how to deal with the natural terrain and vegetation. Ask about the prevailing winds in both summer and winter, and determine from which direction the major winter storms come.

If your new house is to be built by a lake or river, check the data on the last one hundred year flood plane to determine how far back the house will have to be from the water's edge. Riverfront setback is an important building code consideration, so check for local restrictions and regulations. The proximity of a lake or river will also affect both the well location and the location of the septic system, so verify those setbacks.

Selecting A Contractor

Selecting a contractor is one of the most important parts of any construction project. He can make the building process one of the most enjoyable experiences of your life—or one of the most miserable.

Some states, such as California, require that contractors verify four years of experience in the building trades and pass a very tough, day-long examination before becoming a licensed contractor. Other states, Oregon for example, will allow virtually anyone to "register" as a contractor, regardless of their background or experience.

Before searching for a contractor, check with the state to see what licensing, bonding, and insurance requirements there are for contractors, if any. If there are licensing or registration requirements, be certain that the contractor you choose meets all the legal requirements, and call the state board to verify it.

The best way to find a contractor is through a personal, "word-of-mouth" recommendation. Ask friends and neighbors for recommendations, or stop by and talk to someone who is having a house built to see an example of the builder's work, and talk with some clients, if possible.

Soliciting Bids

Most problems between builders and clients arise from a simple lack of communication over what is expected. If you are unfamiliar with the building process, and especially if this is the first home you have ever had built, take the time to do a little research. Study books and magazines, tour other new homes to fully understand exactly what you are looking for in your new home. The more clearly you understand what you want and the more clearly you can convey your thoughts to your contractor, the better your chances are of getting the house you want with a minimum of headaches.

When you know what you want and have a set of plans ready, contact at least two contractors to bid the project. Provide each with an *identical* detailed set of plans and specifications. This is the only way to be certain that both contractors are bidding the same fixtures, materials and other details.

When the bids come in, compare them side by side. If you have been good about providing both contractors with the same plans and specifications, you will have a much easier time of comparing the details of the bids. Make sure that the materials are consistent with one another, and that neither has left anything out. If the bids are considerably different, you may wish to have a third contractor bid the job to give you an additional comparison.

If the prices are close and they have both bid the same items, then the final choice usually comes down to how you feel about the contractors themselves. Remember that you will be working very closely with this person for a number of months, so even if his bid is a little higher, go with the one you feel most comfortable working with.

Pricing and Payment Schedules

Most subcontractors will give you a set price for a set amount of work. Assuming no changes are made during the course of the job, that is the price you will pay.

Another method is time and materials, or cost-plus. In this case, you will pay for the exact hours or days worked, plus the cost of any materials used, including an agreed-upon markup. If you enter into a time and materials contract, agree on the price per hour or day, the percentage of material markup, and a "ceiling" price that the contractor cannot exceed without your knowledge and approval.

Your contractor will set up a payment schedule, detailing the amount of each payment and when that payment is due. Payments, also called draws, are usually made as specific phases of the project—the foundation, the drywall, etc.—are completed and approved.

The Contract

Most contractors use simple, easily-understood contracts that can be read and comprehended without spending a fortune to have an attorney read them. There are, of course, certain points to look for and verify:

—Details of the job are *completely and clearly specified,* whether in the contract or on an attached sheet. This may seem like a tedious extra step, especially if you are working well with the contractor and have a "verbal understanding", but having the details in writing is the best way to avoid future hassles;

—The price for the job is correct, and the payment schedule is clearly described;

—Dates for beginning and completing the job are specified;

—Names, addresses, license number, and other details are correct, and there are no spaces left blank.

Construction Liens

Most states have construction or mechanic's lien laws that deal with non-payment of bills for materials and labor. If you hire a general contractor, pay him as required by your contract, but then he, in turn, does not pay his subcontractors or material suppliers, these parties can still take legal action against you to collect what's owed to them, providing they have filed the necessary lien notices within the required time periods.

Each state varies in the details of its lien laws, and most require that your contractor provide you with written information about the laws in that state. Talk with your contractor, the state contractor's board, or your attorney for additional details.

Being Your Own Contractor

With growing frequency people are succumbing to the whir of a saw and the smell of fresh cut lumber, and are choosing to act as their own contractor. There are definite pros and cons to doing this, and you should weigh your decision carefully before undertaking it.

On the plus side, there is the satisfaction of doing the job yourself, plus the possibility of saving some money over the course of the project. Exactly how much you'll save is, in large, dependent on how active a role you take in the construction.

On the other side of the coin, there are some definite drawbacks. The biggest problem is that running a construction project is *very* time-consuming, and involves phone calls, meetings, material runs, and constant scheduling problems.

Scheduling is the single most difficult task to face, especially if you are not overly familiar with construction and the normal sequence of events. Scheduling mistakes can actually cost you money in delays, ruined materials, and subcontractor back-charges for wasted time. You will have to make literally hundreds of decisions, large and small, over the course of the project.

Finally, any problems are yours alone, from dealing with county officials and building inspectors to your ultimate responsibility for zoning and building code violations. You'll need to see that everyone is paid on time, and arrange for subcontractors to come back and fix any problems that arise.

BUYING BEFORE YOU MOVE

Many people relocating to a rural area will make their purchase years before the actual move, especially in the retirement segment of the market. There are some benefits in doing this, and some pitfalls you should consider.

There are a variety of motivations for buying before you

move. You may want to buy now, pay on a piece of property and retire debt free. Or you may want to buy property before the prices escalate. Perhaps you want to use the property for a second home or as a rental property for the time being; or maybe you'd like an "anchor" in your new community which will give you the extra push to make the relocation at some future time.

There are specific tax laws that currently allow you to use your property for not more than 14 days each year and still retain the tax benefits associated with investment property. If you decide on this as an alternative, be sure to check with your tax advisor, since the laws are always changing.

On the negative side of this approach is the fact that nothing in life is more constant than change. We never know what's going to happen in five or ten years that can lead to an abrupt change of plans. Unfortunate things such as a death in a family or a divorce can leave many dreams unfulfilled. Owning property hundreds or even thousands of miles away as an absentee landlord can also have its risks.

When making any land purchase, try to control your emotions and be realistic about your future plans. Many people have bought into a community this way and were very glad that they did—just be aware of the possible down side if things don't work out.

LOOK BEFORE YOU LEAP

Many people, caught up in the excitement of buying real estate in their own little rural corner of the world, find out later that they overpaid or didn't have all the information necessary to make an informed decision. The economic ebb and flow of communities around the country is determined by many local, regional and national factors. Real estate markets that are up today could be down tomorrow depending on any number of factors—some predictable, many not so predictable.

It wasn't long ago that Texas, Arizona and almost the entire eastern seaboard were flying high. But, as of this writing, their real estate markets have experienced a serious downturn. When choosing a community, look for steady growth rather than boom and bust cycles. Be skeptical of a one-industry town where the majority of jobs are concentrated in one segment of the economy. There should be a good mix of manufacturing, service and either trades or tourism to give the community a balance. If all the young people are leaving to find jobs elsewhere, you can be sure that's a sure sign of limited opportunity.

Due to the changing demographics discussed earlier, there will be areas of tremendous growth and opportunity over the next twenty years. There will also be areas that might well go bust. In selecting the right community, you need to look at all the aspects—the emotional and lifestyle factors as well as the economic ones.

Whether you end up on that gentleman's ranch on the back forty or in a spiffy little condominium in town doesn't really matter. What does matter is you and your happiness. You are the new American pioneer who has gained control of his own destiny once again. Enjoy it, you only live once.

7

Moving Day—Relocation Realities

Unless one says good-bye to what one loves, and unless one travels to completely new territories, one can expect merely a long wearing away of oneself and an eventual extinction.

—Jean Dubuffet,
quoted in the *New York Times*

A good argument can and will be made by dropouts everywhere that deciding to move, selecting a new town, and the other decisions that go into relocating are child's play compared to moving day. Not even previous moves ever seem to completely prepare one for that awesome moment when the day arrives.

Perhaps it will help to think of moving day as the last really stressful thing you will do in the city, and that a new and more serene life awaits.

Throughout, much has been made of good planning and the making and keeping of lists. At no time during your entire rural relocation will planning and lists be more important than in the preparation and execution of the physical move itself. Organization is the key word. No move is ever easy, but the better organized and prepared you are, the less stressful it will be.

To help with your planning, the move has been broken down into four basic segments: *Moving Companies,* including how to select and deal with one, insurance, delivery dates, and damage claims; *Moving Yourself,* for the hearty and adventurous souls who will be trucking themselves to their new destination; *Organizing The Move,* including preparing a master checklist, starting and stopping services, forwarding mail, cleanup, and even such commonly overlooked necessities as readying the car and packing suitcases; and *Special Considerations,* with tips on preparing your pets and plants for the journey, and transporting vehicles.

As you read through this chapter, the whole moving process may seem more complicated than it really is. But don't despair—we've been through it, all the other dropouts have been through it, and we're all just fine. Start early, stick with the tips and outlines given below, and you'll be moved before you know it.

MOVING COMPANIES

Employing the services of a moving company offers you an easier, albeit more costly, method of getting your belongings from Point A to Point B. They handle the loading and unloading, do the driving, are responsible for damage, and, if you wish, will even do your packing.

If your employer is paying your moving costs because of a job transfer, they will probably have a moving company that they deal with regularly, and will handle many of the arrangements for you. If you are footing the bill for your own move and are moving for health reasons as directed by a physician, or relocating an existing business, remember that many of the costs associated with the move are tax deductible. Consult with your accountant for specific details as they relate to your specific situation.

The Interstate Commerce Commission

All moving companies are regulated by the Interstate Commerce Commission (I.C.C.), and are subject to their rules and restrictions. As the governing body, the I.C.C. has established rate guides, mileage guides, and other regulations designed to protect the consumer and make comparing moving companies a little easier. As a result, much of what is said by various moving companies will be the same, as will be their paperwork.

However, in 1980 Congress passed a little-publicized piece of deregulation known as the Motor Carrier Act. As a result, while movers will still quote rates from the I.C.C. rate books, consumers have a little more latitude in negotiating rates for transportation and services between various movers. You will also find a number of differences in reliability, safety, and even the mover's general attitude. A little homework on your part can save you both money and headaches.

The I.C.C. maintains local offices in at least one major city in each state, as well as regional offices in Boston, Massachusetts; Philadelphia, Pennsylvania; Atlanta, Georgia; Chicago, Illinois; Ft. Worth, Texas and San Francisco, California. For local offices and phone numbers, check the phone book under "United States Government", or contact them directly at the main office:

Interstate Commerce Commission
Office of Compliance and Consumer Assistance

Washington, DC 20423
(Phone 202-275-0860)

Selecting a Moving Company

As with selecting most goods and services, word-of-mouth recommendations are the best forms of advertising. Talk with family, friends, and neighbors who have used moving companies to find out if they were satisfied. If you notice someone moving in down the street, introduce yourself and ask them about the moving company they used. Personal experiences—good or bad—are your best source of information.

Your next source would be the Yellow Pages. Local movers may be best if the load is small and the distance short. If you have a lot to move a long distance, or you are crossing state lines (many small, local movers are only licensed for one state), then one of the bigger, interstate companies will be better suited to your needs. Call several companies to be certain they service the area to which you are moving. Don't expect rate quotes over the phone. A company representative will need to visit your home and do a walk-through in order to fully explain the options and give you an accurate price estimate. It's something of a bother, especially if you are dealing with more than one company and time is short, but it's a necessity of the moving industry, and is actually for your protection.

While searching for the best company, you may want to contact your local Better Business Bureau or Chamber of Commerce. It may help if they have any information about a particular mover. Also, you can contact the I.C.C. in Washington, D.C. to request a copy of its *Performance Report,* which contains statistical information on movers that have completed more than 100 interstate moves during the previous year.

If possible, have at least three movers come out for an estimate. Try to begin this search about two months in advance of your move, in order to ensure ample time to schedule the estimates and evaluate and compare the results.

The Company Estimate

When the moving company representative visits your home, be prepared to have them do a thorough tour of the house—disorganized closets and cluttered garage included. Their purpose is, obviously, to see what and how much you have to move. Your final bill will eventually be based on the weight of what is actually moved. So don't hide your grandfather's antique anvil collection—it will just give you an unrealistically low initial estimate.

The estimator will begin by explaining his company's services and some of the options open to you. He or she will give you a copy of the required I.C.C. publication "Your Rights and Responsibilities When You Move", and a variety of company literature. You will be asked some preliminary questions, such as where you're moving to and when you expect to move. Then the estimator will request a room-by-room tour of the house.

Try to present the house as reasonably clean and organized as possible. This will make the estimator's job easier and more accurate and be less embarrassing for you. Walk along through the house and be sure to point out any items that you will be selling or transporting yourself. Don't overlook the garage, the contents of storage buildings, and basement and attic if there are a lot of things to be moved stored there.

The estimator will use a fairly detailed estimate sheet that gives approximate weights for most common household items, as well as an approximation of how many cubic feet of space will be required on the truck. In each room he or she will check off the appropriate items on the list and the number of items there are such as one bed—queen, two nightstands—small, one dresser—large. The estimator will look at the contents of closets and perhaps in some of the drawers, all with an eye toward making an educated guess about how many boxes will be required for clothes, linens, dishes, and everything else that will need to be packed.

Pay close attention to the inventory list that is being made by the estimator. It is the basis for your estimate. If you choose that particular mover, a copy of this initial inventory will go to the truck driver. The driver will also make an inventory list on the actual moving day, which should closely match that of the estimator's.

After the tour, you will be asked about other services you may require. For example, you may wish to have the mover provide all the boxes and do all the packing, or you may intend doing all the packing yourself. You may want to request packing services only for those items you would rather leave to professionals—a large crystal chandelier or a collection of antique china, for example—in order to ensure that the item is correctly packed and that someone else will be financially responsibility in the event of damage. You can also buy boxes and packing material directly from the moving company, particularly specialty boxes for clothes, mirrors, and pictures.

Some of the other services that might be offered would be unpacking, temporary storage, and Saturday pickup or delivery. The estimator will provide you with a complete list of what the company offers and at what cost.

When the estimate form is completed and you have agreed on which services will be provided, an estimate will be prepared, usually right then and there. Basically, the mover will first total the estimated weight of the load based on the tour of the house. Then the applicable rate will be determined, which is based on the distance of the move and the weight category of your load. Weight categories typically change with each 1,000 pounds of total weight. Finally, the estimator will multiply the weight in hundreds of pounds by the rate in dollars per hundred pounds to arrive at a price, adding the cost of packing, boxes, insurance, and any other items you have requested to the total cost.

The estimator will use a thick volume called the I.C.C. Tariff Book, which lists the I.C.C. maximum rates. Since the deregulation of the industry, however, you may be able to negotiate a lower rate than those listed in the book. Depending on the competition in your area and when you intend to move, you may also be able to get discounts on packing. Some movers will provide previously-used packing boxes at little or no charge in order to get your business. It doesn't hurt to ask.

Also, be aware that rates are highest in the summer—especially the first four weeks after school finishes. This is the most popular moving period and, therefore, the busiest time for movers. Planning your move for non-peak times can save you money. You can also save money by planning far enough in advance, so that the mover has some freedom to schedule your load onto a truck going to or near the same destination. Remember that you will usually have to pay extra for rush service, and for loading or unloading on a Saturday.

Your estimate will be provided in one of two ways:

Binding Estimates: The estimator may give you a Binding Estimate, which is preferable. This estimate tells you exactly what services you are contracting for and what they will cost. Unless you substantially change what is being moved, you will know exactly how much the move will cost. If you agree to a binding estimate, you will be required to have that amount of money ready—in cash or a certified check (no personal checks are accepted)—when the movers arrive at your new home. In most instances, the truck will not be unloaded until payment is made.

Be certain to ask the estimator for the length of time the price is guaranteed, and have it put in writing. In most instances, you should be able to persuade the mover to guarantee this price for sixty days, an obvious benefit to you. The I.C.C. allows movers the right to charge for a binding estimate, because of the amount of time involved in the preparation. Most movers will not charge, however, because they would rather have your moving business than to make a few dollars providing an estimate. If the mover does charge you for the binding estimate, you may want to consider taking your business elsewhere.

Non-Binding Estimates: A non-binding estimate is just that—an estimate of the costs of a move to which the mover is not yet firmly committed. Under I.C.C. regulations, a mover is not allowed to charge for a non-binding estimate.

Once again, the estimate will be itemized as to what is being moved and what services are being provided, and will contain a dollar figure at the end. But, the mover is not allowed to charge more than ten percent above the original estimate at the time the move is completed. For example, if the non-binding estimate was $2,000, you cannot be charged more than $2,200 for the move. You will also only be required to pay the amount of the original estimate—in this case $2,000—at the time of unloading. You will have an additional thirty days in which to pay the remaining amount.

INSURANCE

You will, of course, want to take out insurance on your belongings while they are in transit. Minor damage can occur in loading and unloading, and it is certainly not unheard of to have an entire van-load of furniture destroyed in a fire or highway accident, or even to be stolen.

You can obtain liability coverage for loss or damage directly from your mover, through your own insurance company, or through a third-party insurance company. Coverage takes a variety of forms and has a variety of rate structures, so choose carefully the plan you need.

Minimum Coverage: Your mover is required to assume a minimal amount of liability for your contents at no additional charge to you. Called "released value", the mover is required to pay you sixty cents per pound of shipping weight of the items transported. For example, if you shipped 4,000 pounds of household goods and the entire shipment was destroyed, the mover would only be liable for $2,400. This option should only be chosen if you have arranged for outside coverage. While there is no charge for this option, *you must specifically request this coverage and sign for it on the Bill of Lading.*

Depreciated Value Coverage: If desired, your mover can provide you with an option policy that is based on value and not on weight. The cost is, approximately, $5.00 for each $1,000 of declared value of your shipment. Therefore, should you insure the items being moved for a total of $30,000, the coverage cost would be $150.

Under this plan, lost or damaged items would be replaced at their *current, depreciated value,* rather than what it would cost you to replace them. For example, if you bought a stereo system 10 years ago for $1,500 that today has a used value of $600, you would be paid the $600.

One warning. If you do not specifically declare a value for the shipment, its value will be established on the basis of the ICC's antiquated rate of $1.25 per pound. Using the example of a 4,000 pound shipment worth $30,000, if the total value of the shipment was not declared as $30,000, its value would be established for you at only $5,000 ($1.25 × 4,000).

Replacement Value Coverage: Under this third option available to you from your mover, your contents would be covered at their *full replacement value.* If that 10-year-old, $1,500 stereo system was damaged and it would cost $2,100 to replace it, you would be paid the full $2,100.

This type of coverage, while clearly preferable, is more expensive. Rates vary from mover to mover, and currently average around $9.00 for each $1,000 of declared value. With your $30,000 shipment, cost for coverage would be approximately $270.

If you are shipping expensive items, particularly antiques, their value should be specifically noted for the mover, in addition to declaring a value for the entire shipment. An antique desk valued at $5,000 shows up on the driver's inventory list as "Item 327—desk, old-fashioned—multiple nicks and scratches, broken top drawer". Claiming $5,000 for the desk later on will no doubt cause some additional, unneeded hassles if you did not previously established its value. For a rare or extremely valuable piece, the mover may insist on a written appraisal of its value before it is shipped.

Private Coverage: Perhaps the best way to insure your belongings—and also often the least expensive—is to work through your own insurance agent. Your existing homeowner's or renter's policy may automatically cover you during the move, in which case you don't need any additional coverage. If you are not already covered, your agent can usually write a rider policy for a reasonable fee.

Be sure to ask if any items are *excluded* from the policy coverage. Things like jewelry, large amounts of camera equipment, and even phonograph albums are a few of the items people have found that are not covered. Also, clarify if the coverage is at depreciated or full replacement value.

Whatever coverage option you choose, whether through your mover or your own agent, be sure you *fully understand* the details of the coverage, and that you get verification of it *in writing.* Jodi B. related the story of an aggravating experience with an insurance company that luckily wasn't a lot worse. After talking with her agent prior to the move and being assured over the phone that her belongings were covered, she told her mover she didn't need any additional coverage above what was automatically included in the price of the move.

The moving van arrived safely at her new home, but, upon unpacking, Jodi discovered a number of small items were damaged. The total cost to repair or replace the items totaled $260.00, so she filed a claim with the moving company. Since the mover's valuation was based on 60 cents per pound of *actual shipping weight* and the damaged items totaled 22 pounds, Jodi received a check for $13.20.

Her next claim was to her old insurance company. The agent told her that he'd apparently made a mistake, and her personal belongings actually *weren't* covered under her old policy. Threatened with legal action through small claims court, the agent settled with her for $150.00, and Jodi had to absorb the rest, plus all her time and aggravation. Six years after the move, she still has nightmares about what would have happened if the entire shipment had been lost.

The Order for Service

The moving company representative will prepare a form called an *Order For Service,* which you are not required to sign unless you are certain you will be selecting that mover. It is not a contract, and, should you sign it, you are not obligated to use the services of that mover. However, to avoid any future problems, it is simply best to avoid signing an Order For Service until you have interviewed and received estimates from at least three companies.

After selecting your mover and signing the *Order For Service,* for your own protection and that of the mover, be certain that any changes you make are *in writing.* The mover has Addendum forms for just this purpose. If you choose to add or subtract items that substantially change the weight of the load, or should you request or cancel additional services, have the mover fill out an Addendum, and attach a copy to your copy of the Order For Service.

When making your final selection, do not be swayed by price alone. If you did not get a good feeling from the company representative, or if, for whatever reason, you just don't think a particular company will do a good job for you, then by all means look elsewhere.

Pickup and Delivery Dates

At the time you choose a mover and make final arrangements, immediately establish the dates on which you would like to move. This is another reason for starting the selection process early—the sooner you start, the more assurance you will have of securing the dates you want. Most movers need a minimum of two weeks advance notice, and it could be twice that in busy areas or during busy times of the year.

Pinpointing the exact loading date should be no problem; however most movers will specify a time spread of three days for delivery. This allows for problems while in transit, and for time needed to load or unload other shipments that may be on the same truck with yours. If you need a specific unloading day, such as on a weekend or a holiday—for whatever reason you might have—specify that no other shipment be loaded on the truck with yours and plan on paying extra for this service.

Be sure that the agreed-upon dates are listed on the Order for Service. Should you or your mover need to change these dates prior to the move, execute an Addendum showing the new dates in writing. Finally, try to provide phone service at your new home, arrange for a message phone somewhere, or leave a location where a telegram could be delivered. Should your shipment be delayed in transit past the expected arrival date, the mover will need some way to contact you.

The Bill of Lading

The Bill Of Lading is your actual contract with the mover, and, as such, is the most important piece of paper you will receive from them. It is required to match the details on the *Order for Service,* and will contain all the pertinent information regarding your move, such as cost, destination, loading and unloading dates, and services requested.

The Bill Of Lading will be presented to you by the driver on moving day. Read it *carefully* and *do not sign it* if it contains any wrong information or if you do not understand any part of it. If you have a dispute, contact your moving company representative and resolve it before preceding any further. Once you have signed it, obtain a copy and keep it safely with the other papers you have relating to the move. Many movers will provide you with a folder to keep all these documents together.

The Inventory

Having dispensed with the details of the Bill Of Lading, the driver will now make a thorough tour of the house and inventory those items being shipped. As he goes, he will note each item, or box of items, on his inventory form, make notes as to its condition, assign it a number, then place a self-stick tag on the item with a corresponding number. When you reach your new home, if you have children, they can be occupied for three or four weeks removing all the stickers.

Accompany the driver on his inventory tour, and make notes of your own. He will be writing down things such as "103, Dresser—Master Bedroom, large scratch on top, 2 nicks on left front drawer". This is not a critique of the condition of your furniture, it is simply his notes to himself in the event of future claims for damage.

When the tour is over, he will then have you sign the inventory sheet. Once again, *read it carefully,* compare his notes to yours, and discuss any discrepancies before signing it.

He will give you a copy to add to your files. The inventory will also include the number of your shipment which you will need in the event of making future claims.

Weight Determination

Before arriving at your house, the driver will have weighed his truck to give him the weight of the vehicle and contents prior to loading your shipment. Whether the truck is empty at the time of weighing or whether it already has another load of furniture (large moving vans will often transport two or more entire households of goods at the same time) doesn't matter. The driver is interested only in its weight before your shipment.

After loading, the truck will be weighed again. The difference between the pre-loading weight and the after-loading weight is the figure that the movers will use as the weight of your shipment.

The driver receives a written weight slip from the weigher, and a copy should be attached to the Bill of Lading for your inspection. Under I.C.C. regulations, the mover is required to notify you of the location of the scale he uses so that you can be present at the weighings if you wish.

Claims and Disputes

Should there be a problem with your move resulting in loss or damage to any of your property, I.C.C. regulations allow you nine months from the date of delivery, or the date delivery should have been made, in which to file a claim. However, file the claim as soon as possible. In some states, filing a suit after 120 days has elapsed may make you ineligible to recover attorney fees even if you win the case.

Make your initial claim to the mover, and to your insurance company if you obtained outside coverage. Both your mover and your insurance agent will have an established claim procedure and a number of forms to be completed. Be patient and follow their specific instructions as carefully as possible.

Remember that the I.C.C. will not arbitrate or otherwise resolve any disputes you may have with your mover. If you are unable to reach an agreement, you can file a civil lawsuit for damages. You can also submit your claim for arbitration, which is a less stressful and certainly less expensive alternative. Your mover may have an established arbitration program available, using independent, impartial arbitrators, or you can arrange for an arbitrator on your own. Look in the Yellow Pages under "Arbitration Services", or contact:

American Arbitration Association
Household Goods Dispute Settlement Program
140 West 51st Street
New York, NY 10020

MOVING YOURSELF

For many people, the dollar savings associated with moving themselves is too attractive to pass up and adds to the excitement of leaving the city. In fact, surveys of Urban Dropouts indicated about a 50-50 split between those who used a moving company and those who moved themselves.

Self-moving offers, in addition to economy, more freedom of time and worry. You control the moving and delivery dates; your belongings are never out of your sight; and you avoid the bother of moving company estimates and all the paperwork that is necessary for these estimates. It is also a lot of hard work. Besides doing all the packing, you will have to physically load and unload the truck, plus undertake the driving chores.

Equipment

Self-moving has grown in popularity over the past few decades, and the new generation of rental trucks and equipment have made things considerably easier. Many of the newer trucks have air conditioning, AM-FM radios, air-ride suspensions, and comfortable cloth-covered seats to make the long trip less of a strain. Lower body heights and built-in loading ramps simplify loading and unloading.

The primary piece of rental is the truck itself. There are a wide variety of sizes and types available, ranging from as small as ten feet up to as large as twenty six feet. There is some guess work involved in selecting the right size truck, but the rental company can help guide you based upon the number of rooms of furniture to be moved. Look for a truck with a built-in loading ramp. Virtually all trucks are now equipped with this feature. The ramp-equipped truck is usually best for most household moves, but if you have many heavy items to move, consider a truck with a hydraulically-operated tailgate.

Trucks are often available with diesel engines when you rent one of the larger sizes. Driving a diesel truck is essentially the same as driving a gas-powered truck, and your dealer will provide you with complete instructions on the few minor differences. The main advantage to the diesel trucks is that they are more fuel-efficient. Unless you are traveling in very rural areas, locating diesel fuel should not present any problem.

For smaller or shorter moves, or to supplement the capacity of the truck, you might also want to rent a trailer. These are available in several lengths, and in both open and closed models. Most rental trucks are already set up for trailer towing, with all the proper lights and safety equipment. If you intend to tow a trailer with your car, have the rental dealer examine your vehicle to ensure that it is the proper size with which to safely tow, and have him equip your car with the necessary tow bar, safety chains, and lights.

Other rental equipment available from your dealer includes tow bars for towing automobiles; horse trailers; dollies and hand trucks for safely moving furniture and other heavy items; and quilted pads to protect furniture. He can provide you with locks, rope, and other small items. Many dealers also sell boxes and other packaging materials.

Rental Options

In addition to a number of equipment options, there are also some options open to you concerning rental rates. The first basic choice is local or one-way rentals. For most moves, you will be renting one-way, which means you pick up the truck at the local dealer and drop it off at a dealer in the town to which you are moving. If you are not moving too great a distance, and can pick up and drop off the truck at the same dealer, it may be somewhat cheaper, but this is usually impractical.

For one-way moves, there are a variety of rates and rate structures, depending on the dealer and your destination. Some dealers have a straight per day and per mile charge. If the rental rate is $30 a day and 40 cents a mile, and you keep the truck for four days and travel 500 miles, the charge would be $320 ($30 + 40 cents × 500). Other dealers may offer discounted or combined rates, such as $150 for up to seven days use, or $40 a day with up to 100 free miles per day. There are all kinds of rate combinations. You may even find an all inclu sive package rate—five days and 500 miles for $250, for example. All prices do not include fuel, for which you will pay extra while on the road.

Drop-off Charges

If you are moving to an area which is not overly inhabited—which is basically the whole point of this undertaking in the first place—your dealer may assess a drop-off charge on one-way rentals. For example, if you are moving to a small town in northern Wisconsin that does very little business in rental trucks, it may be necessary for the dealer there to move the truck from where it was dropped to a large city where it can be available for rent. You will probably have to pay these moving charges, which in some cases can be substantial. Be sure that you inquire about drop-off charges before making the final rental agreement.

Repairs and Insurance

When renting any equipment, ask about the company's policy regarding breakdowns and repairs. Some companies allow you to pay for repairs out of your own pocket, then reimburse you when you drop off the truck. You may also be given a toll-free phone number to use in the event of a breakdown, or be instructed to take the truck to the nearest dealer, which can be problematic. For short moves, you may save a little money by renting from a small dealer, but for long distance moves, especially crossing from one state to another, it is best to choose a larger, well-established rental agency. It will have more dealers, a more comprehensive network for you to use in the event of problems, and its equipment is usually newer and better maintained.

Some dealers can also provide you with insurance for your contents while in transit. Check first with your own insurance agent for the most comprehensive coverage at the best rate. But if your existing policy doesn't cover moving, this will give you an option. Ask your rental dealer for specific information on any insurance programs they might offer, and be sure to *read and understand* everything before you sign an agreement.

No special license is required to drive a rental truck. Check with your insurance agent, however, to be certain that you are covered under your existing auto insurance policy in the event of an accident while driving a rented truck.

Loading and Unloading

Here are a few basic tips for loading a truck or trailer. Plan on loading the heaviest items first, and place them on the floor at the front of the truck. Load from side to side, working your way to the back as you go. Use smaller items to fill in, and place light items toward the ceiling and at the back of the truck. This keeps the weight properly distributed and balanced, making the truck smoother-riding and easier to handle.

Most trucks have tie-down rings recessed in the side walls. As you go, wrap ropes around the load and secure it to the rings to prevent the cargo from shifting while the truck is in motion. Use plenty of pads—they're available from the rental dealer and are cheap protection for your furniture. You can also use your own blankets, pillows, and rugs as additional padding.

Don't underestimate the amount of work involved in loading a truck full of furniture, and don't overestimate how much you can lift. Arrange for plenty of help on moving day and have help lined up at your destination. If you don't know anyone in your new town to help you unload, contact the local employment office when you arrive. They can usually provide you with one or two laborers at a reasonable daily or hourly rate.

ORGANIZING THE MOVE

Even as apprehensions start to run high as the transition from your old life to your new one approaches, you need to mentally begin planning well in advance for your move. Two months is actually the ideal length of time. It may seem like an extra long period of time, but this allows you a somewhat more thorough and leisurely approach to such time-consuming things as selecting a moving company and arranging for estimates. Six weeks will still allow you time to properly plan and execute the move, especially if you are moving yourself, with four weeks being the minimum time for a reasonably organized move. Arrange your schedule accordingly. To allow yourself less than four weeks is tantamount to unnecessary headaches.

The Master List

Just like a military operation, you will have your Master List, forming an overall strategy.

Invest in a large, sturdy sheet of poster board, which is available from most office supply stores. If you're feeling reasonably serene about the move, choose white poster board, or any vibrant color to catch the family's undivided attention. Also purchase some felt pens for use on the Master List—at least two colors—and some red and black marking pens. You will use these later for packing.

Divide the poster board into fourteen sections. Split it any way you like, but allow more space for seven of the sections than for the other seven. Label the seven smaller sections Week 8, Week 7, down to Week 2. Label the seven larger sections, which comprise week 1, Day 6, Day 5, down to Day 2 and finally Moving Day.

You have now created a central processing point where you and your family can plan and write down well in advance what chores that need to be done in the weeks before the move. Then, as the "Things To Do" lists become larger and more hectic, they can be broken down into day-by-day lists for the final week. Depending on your personal preference and how organized you are, you can also break Week 2 down into day-by-day categories.

Following is a list of things to remember in the weeks and days preceding your move. Not all will apply to your particular situation, of course, and there may be other items you need to include. You may wish to rearrange the suggested days or weeks in which these things get done. But however you choose to alter, amend, or rearrange it, the Master List should help to get your move-planning correctly started by helping to jog your memory for all the things that need to be done.

The schedules shown here do not include any pertinent details about selling your house. How far in advance you will need to begin that process is determined by the real estate climate in your area and the selling price of your home (see Chapter 6). You may, however, want to include such items as escrow closing dates and bank meetings on your schedule.

One final note concerning the Master List. At first, it may seem an unnecessary extra thing to do. But people who have moved several times will tell you that it is easy to overlook some of the smaller details of the move while driving yourself crazy worrying about the bigger ones. The Master List allows for a central spot in which to compile and organize your thoughts. You will discover a tremendous feeling of relief to know that each detail of the move is written where it won't be lost or forgotten. The Master List also keeps you on schedule as moving day approaches.

Week 8

Contact Moving Companies: Now is the time to begin the process of locating and contacting moving companies. Ideally, you will want to have at least three moving company estimators visit your home, inventory your furnishings, and prepare an estimate of moving costs for you. This is a time-consuming procedure, and by beginning early, you will assure yourself of enough time to assess and compare the companies to make an unhurried, informed choice.

Advertise Vehicles For Sale: If you have a car, truck, camper, boat, snowmobile, or vehicle to sell, the time to start the process is now. Some of these can take weeks or even months to find a buyer, especially out of season sporting equipment, so the earlier you advertise, the better. This also allows ample time to transfer registrations, handle bank paperwork, and take care of the other details related to the sale of major items.

Vehicle and recreational vehicle advertising two months in advance has two other benefits worth considering. First, it allows you more time get a fair price for what you are selling, rather than being forced to accept a low offer—or perhaps even take a loss—simply because you have to get rid of it. Second, if the item doesn't sell right away, there is still time for you to pursue other means of disposing of the article.

Tom and Suzanne R., for example, decided that their Porsche 944 would not be an ideal car to take to Vermont, because of the heavy winter snows where they were relocating. Pricing the sports car at $19,000, they were having no luck attracting buyers through the newspaper advertisements and were starting to despair. A friend then suggested they contact a leasing company, who, in turn, had a client who wanted a Porsche. The company negotiated the outright purchase of the car from Suzanne so that they could make it available to lease to their client. Another couple assigned their customized camper van to a Recreational Vehicles dealer, who ran a consignment lot in order to sell it. As you can see, there are options open to you, but they may take time, so plan accordingly.

Week 7

Sort Out What's Not Going: Here is another time-consuming process that should be started early. Virtually everyone who moves takes the opportunity to sell, donate, or simply discard unwanted or unneeded furniture, clothes, and other items. It lightens the load that has to be moved, lessens the packing and unpacking chores, alleviates clutter and frees up storage space, and has an added benefit of perhaps generating a little extra cash to help defray moving costs.

Start the sorting process in the attic, basement, or wherever you have stored items that seldom see the light of day. Start a pile in one corner of the things you want to take, and don't get caught up in cleaning, fixing or pricing anything. That will come later.

When you are finished with the storage areas, tour the house and ask yourself some questions. If the home you're moving to is smaller, will you have room for all of your furniture? It doesn't make sense to pay to move something that you will have to store when you get to your new location. Will you have a guest bedroom, or is it the time to get rid of that extra spring and mattress? Is there room for the freezer or extra refrigerator you have in the garage or basement?

Pay particular attention to heavy, bulky items that are well past their prime. A perfect example would be a washer that needs repairs. If it is expensive to move and expensive to fix, now is the time to sell it and buy a new one when you get to your new location.

As the sorting process continues, include all the family. Children in particular will already be off balance thinking of moving to a new town. If they come home and find their bike on the "to sell" pile—even if it hasn't been ridden in years—this will add to their feelings of disruption and abandonment. Discuss the sorting process with them, but let them make their own choices about what goes and what doesn't. Let them participate in the sale of their things and keep the proceeds—that usually gets their closet cleaned out in a hurry.

Advertise Expensive Items: If you have larger or more expensive items to sell, such as furniture, appliances, or antiques, you'll command a better price for them if you advertise in the classified section of the local paper rather than relegate them to a garage sale. The garage sale comes later, and you can invite the people who respond to your classified advertisement to come back then to see what else will be sold.

Week 6

Final Moving Company Selection: By now you have had ample time for at least three moving company representatives to visit your home. Make your final selection, and firm up the dates for loading the furniture at your old house and delivering it to your new one. If you don't have an exact moving date yet, try to determine one as soon as possible. Some moving companies are booked well in advance, especially during the summer months.

Week 5

Contact Truck Rental Companies: If you have decided to move yourself, it's not too early to begin contacting truck rental agencies. Various companies will offer different equipment and different rates, depending on when you are moving and how far you are going. Some offer discounts for advance bookings, others require early reservations for certain types of trucks and trailers that are in heavy demand.

Book Airline Reservations: If you or any members of your family will be flying to your new town in advance of the movers, it is the time to book the flight. Reserving your seats early will assure their availability, and allow you to take advantage of the advance reservation discounts available with most airlines.

Begin Address Change Notifications: Most magazines need five to six weeks notice to change your subscription address. Notifying them now will allow your magazines to arrive at your new address without interruption, and you will avoid paying any forwarding charges. Change of address forms are available at the Post Office. Also, as you remit monthly bills, you can complete the "Moving" section that is included on most account statements to get your address change into their computer systems.

Week 4

Garage Sale: This is the week to hold your garage sale, preferably over the weekend. During the week, finish collecting and organizing the things you want to sell, clean them and price each article. Place an advertisement in the classified column to announce the date and location of the sale, and title your advertisement "Moving Sale" instead of just a garage sale. You'll get a better turnout on sale day.

Anything that doesn't sell in the garage sale donate to a charity, otherwise it will just be hauled back into the house to be packed and moved. Keep an itemized list of anything you donate and get a written receipt when you deliver the items. This allows you to deduct the donations at tax time.

Transfer School, Medical, and Veterinary Records: Contact the office at your child's school, and request that his or her records be transferred to the new school. You will, of course, need to have all the pertinent information for the new school.

Medical records are handled a little differently, depending on the doctor and the nature of any medical conditions you may have. If you have an ongoing medical condition and have already been in contact with a doctor in your new town, he can help you arrange to have the records transferred directly to his office. In some instances, you'll be allowed to take your records with you, but you'll need to discuss this well in advance with your current doctor. If you have hospital records that are important, have your doctor contact the hospital, as well.

If you have no particular ongoing medical need for your records, you need not worry about them just now. Just make a list of the name, address, and phone number of any doctor, dentist, clinic or hospital you have visited during the time you lived in your present city, and keep the list filed for future reference. Your new doctor can always request your records should they be needed at a future date. You should, however, get a copy of your eyeglass prescription, and a record of any prescription medications you take, in case they are needed in an emergency after you have moved.

If you have pets, you will want to get a copy of their veterinary records. Again, this is primarily important if they have an ongoing medical condition, otherwise your new veterinarian can request them as needed. As with your own medical records, keep a list of the names and addresses of any vets or clinics your pet has visited so you have them for future reference.

Week 3

Make Pet Travel Arrangements: If you have pets, preparing them for a safe and healthy move is of prime importance (see the "Moving Pets" section below). If the pets are being transported by air, make the necessary airline arrangements now. You will need special, airline-approved pet crates. Talk with the airline representative for instructions and details. Also, take your pets to the veterinarian for a checkup and any special instructions or medications. A mild tranquilizer or sedative may help make the airline trip easier.

If it will be a few days between the time you arrive in your new location and the time you settle into your new home, you may want to arrange temporary boarding for your pets. You can leave them with friends or family at your old location, then have them flown out when you are settled. Another alternative is to fly them out in advance with the family, or take them with you in the car if you are driving, and board them in a kennel in your new location.

Complete Address Change Notifications: Notify the post office of your new address, and arrange the effective date to begin having your mail forwarded. Send address change notifications to people or companies not previously notified. Notifying casual friends and acquaintances can wait until after the move and you are settled. You have enough to worry about now.

Begin Using Perishable Foods: Begin planning meals around what's in the freezer and refrigerator, and don't grocery shop for anything other than necessities.

Begin Using Flammable Items: Flammable items such as barbecue lighter fluid, gasoline, solvents, and ammunition cannot be transported, so start using them or giving them away. If you have questions about whether or not a particular item is safe to transport, contact your moving company or the truck rental agency.

Arrange Appliance Repairs: If your refrigerator, freezer, washer, or other major appliance needs repair or servicing, get it done now. That way you won't be without its services when you arrive in your new home, and you won't be searching for a serviceman or a laundromat in a strange new town. Tell the serviceman that the appliance is about to be transported to find out if he has any specific suggestions or instructions regarding its care.

Make Hotel Reservations: If you need a hotel at the new location until your furniture arrives, make those reservations now. If you are moving in the summer months or moving to an area that is frequented by tourists, you may want to make these reservations even earlier.

Arrange to Transport Vehicles: If you have a car that is going with you to your new home but that you won't actually be driving there, you will need to make arrangements for its transfer. (See the "Transporting Vehicles" section below).

Week 2

Make Packing Decisions: Tour the house, and make a list of the items you will want to pack yourself, if someone else is doing your packing, or the items you want the movers to pack, if you're doing your own packing. Also, list the items that won't be loaded onto the truck, such as a vacuum cleaner, suitcases, and the like.

Finalize All Moving Arrangements: If not already completed, finalize any and all moving company or truck and equipment rental arrangements. If you are self-moving, arrange now for assistance in loading and unloading.

Close or Transfer Charge Accounts: In addition to change of address notifications, there are charge accounts that require transferring to your new location, and some local accounts that you'll need to terminate.

Arrange Utility Stops and Starts: Contact the utility companies in your current location, and arrange the effective cutoff date for services. In most instances, if a new occupant is moving into the home shortly after you leave, these arrangements will simply be a transfer of the account at that address from your name to the new tenant's name, without any actual disruption of service. If the house will be vacant after you leave and services are actually being shut off, make the effective date the day after you move. It is worth paying for an extra day to assure an uninterrupted supply of electricity and heat while you pack and load. Don't forget to arrange for the refund of any deposits due you to be sent to your new address.

It is also time to arrange for utility service at your new location. This may involve some long distance phone calls, or perhaps even a site visit if you're close enough to make that practical. Your realtor or rental agent at your new location can usually help with this arrangements.

Here is a checklist of utilities to contact, depending on what services you have or will need:

- Electric Company
- Gas Company

- Water and Sewer Services
- Garbage Company
- Cable Television Service
- Newspaper

Arrange Telephone Service: Contact the telephone company for service in your new home, and for a cutoff date of your old service. Once again, don't shut off the telephones on moving day, and have a telephone ready at your new home (or a place where you can get messages) in case the movers need to get in touch with you while in transit or upon arrival.

Ask the telephone company about their forwarding services, so that a person calling your old number will automatically be referred to the new number, if you wish.

Transfer Insurance: Meet with your agent, and arrange for any insurance needs you require. This includes confirming coverage of your personal belongings while in transit; continuing coverage of automobile insurance until a new policy is in effect in your new location; finalizing details on current homeowner's or renter's policy; transferring or changing addressees on life insurance policies; and checking details on health insurance coverage. If your health insurance is through your place of employment, check with your current employer about temporarily continuing the coverage. This is usually available for an extended 60-day period to allow you to arrange coverage in your new location without a lapse in health protection.

Service the Car: If you are driving your car to your new home, have it repaired, serviced, and inspected before the trip. Car trouble is one extra headache you won't need during this transition period.

Final Week—Day 6

Clean the House: That's right, clean the house—dust the furniture, do the laundry, organize the paperwork on the dining room table. You will find that packing is a lot easier when the house is organized.

Measure Large Furniture: This is a simple task that will greatly simplify your moving. Measure the bed, sofa, dresser, and other large pieces of furniture, and make a list of their sizes. Keep this list handy with your other papers, and don't let it get packed away.

Final Week—Day 5

Visit the Bank: Arrange with your banker to have your accounts transferred to a branch office or a new bank in your new location. If you haven't yet arranged for a new bank, have your old bank close your accounts and hold your funds there, then wire them to your new bank after you have moved. There may be a fee for this service. Your banker may have other suggestions, but however you arrange it, the goal is to be able to transfer your funds without the necessity of your physically transporting them from one location to another.

While at the bank, get a certified check for the amount you need to pay the mover. Remember, they won't accept your personal check and they won't unload until they're paid, so make sure to cover this detail. Also, buy travelers checks in an amount sufficient to tide you over while in transit, and keep $100 or so in cash.

Set Aside Items for the Car: If you plan on driving one or more of your vehicles to your new home—whether you are self-moving or using the services of a moving company—you will want to set aside a few items that you'll need while in transit or upon arrival. Find an unused corner and begin compiling these items now, but keep them accessible. Here are some suggestions:

- Vacuum cleaner, broom, mop, and dust pan;
- A box of cleaning supplies, including all-purpose spray

cleaner, cleanser, window cleaner, oven cleaner, furniture polish, dish soap, rubber gloves, cotton gloves, trash bags, and a few light bulbs (for your new house);

• Tools. A small tool box with a supply of the basics such as hammer, screwdrivers, pliers, and an adjustable wrench will come in handy. Be sure and include a flashlight—and don't forget batteries;

• Personal hygiene and entertainment supplies (other than those packed in your suitcase), including towel, washcloth, soap, pre-moistened towelettes, books or magazines, playing cards;

• Supplies for the children, including books and games for the trip, snacks, pillow and blanket, and *quiet* toys;

• Pet supplies, including leash and collar, food, bowls, toys, and perhaps their own towel and blanket;

• Camping supplies, if you intend to camp out while making the trip, or if you anticipate having to rough it before your furniture arrives, you might want to set aside sleeping bags, camp stove and lantern, tent, and other supplies as necessary;

• Automobile supplies, including tire chains, jumper cables, flares, a water-proof tarpaulin, and other emergency roadside supplies.

Final Week—Day 4

Verify Insurance: Take the time to meet with your insurance agent so that you can finalize and verify the transference of your insurance coverage. Be certain your auto insurance will remain in force during the move, including insurance on cars in transit that you are not driving yourself, or that you have a policy rider that extends the coverage for a set period of time. Also, be sure to *verify* that you have insurance on your personal belongings while they are in transit, and get this verification *in writing.*

Finalize odds and ends: Last minute details, including banking, real estate and other business transactions, should be finalized now. Empty your safe deposit box and store the contents at home or with a neighbor. Pick up boxes and packing materials, or arrange for the mover to have them delivered. Arrange for the carpets to be cleaned, if needed, after the furniture is loaded on the truck. Stop at the grocery and buy some snacks, paper plates, and the ingredients for simple meals. Discard or give away whatever remains in the refrigerator.

Final Week—Day 3

Clean Refrigerator: Unplug your refrigerator and thoroughly clean the inside. Wipe the inside dry with a towel, and place a box of baking soda in both the freezer and refrigerator compartments. Leaving the doors open will help to completely dry the unit. If you have small children in the house, remove the refrigerator doors completely or securely tie them open.

Begin Packing: Start with those items you can most easily do without, such as pictures and the contents of storage closets. Move on to the attic, basement, spare rooms and the garage. As you finish packing each box, seal it and *stack it out of the way.* Be sure each box is clearly and informatively labeled— "Master Bedroom", "Tom's Room", "Kitchen", for example. This will make unloading much easier.

Final Week—Day 2

Continue Packing: This is your primary packing day, and you should be 90% finished by the end of the day. Work room by room in an orderly fashion, and move the boxes to a central, out-of-the-way area as each is filled. Stay calm, have music playing in the background, take short breaks whenever you feel the need, and don't forget to eat.

Prepare a "Load-Last, Unload First" Box: This is a box that will go on the truck, but one that contains items that you will need right away. Some suggestions about what it should contain include the coffee pot and tea kettle, coffee and tea, and some cups; paper plates, glasses and plastic utensils; easy-to-fix, non-perishable food; items to occupy the kids and the pets; aspirin; a portable radio; more trash bags and cleaning supplies; and any other items you think necessary to have handy on moving-in day without having to sort through all the boxes.

Final Week—Day 1

Pack Suitcases: Prepare your suitcases and those for the kids. They should contain just the basics—comfortable clothes, socks and underwear, an extra sweater or light jacket. Plan ahead for the length of time it will be until your belongings arrive. Remember that you are not packing for vacation. It is unlikely you will be going to the theater or to an expensive restaurant for the present time, so formal suits and evening dresses can be stowed on the moving van.

Pack Your Valuables: Small, very expensive items such as jewelry should not travel by moving van. Carry them with you, or mail them to yourself—registered and insured—and keep an inventory list and photographs of the items. Important papers and computer disks should also be hand carried. Don't pack large quantities of cash; carry a small amount with you, and convert the rest into traveler's checks. Be sure to check with your moving company or truck rental agency for any restrictions regarding transporting firearms and ammunition.

Take Pets to a Neighbor: Your final packing and loading chores will be made much simpler if a friendly neighbor can babysit your pets—at their house—until just before you are ready to leave.

Finish Packing: Complete any last-minute packing. By

day's end, everything should be packed and sealed except your "load last" box.

Pick Up Moving Truck: If you are moving yourself, pick up the truck and other equipment this afternoon. Be sure it has a full gas tank and that all the paperwork is in order. If you're using a moving company, verify that everything is still on schedule, and find out what time they will be arriving.

MOVING DAY

Thanks to your Master List, when moving day finally arrives you'll be ready for it. It will still be a hectic day—nothing can completely simplify it—but you won't be wondering if you forgot anything or frantically packing odds and ends. Now here is your list for the big day:

Be Ready: Get up early, make coffee, and have some pastries ready for breakfast, including enough for the movers or your helpers. If possible, have a neighbor watch your kids for a few hours while the loading is being done.

Meet With The Movers: If you are using a moving company, be on hand to meet them when they arrive. Show them through the house, answer any questions they might have, and sign the required documents. As they inventory your belongings, they will be making notes about each item's condition. Follow along, pay attention, and make notes of your own for future reference during unloading.

If you are having the moving company do some or all of your packing, take the packers through the house and answer their questions also. Keep those things that are going in your car separate, and point them out to the movers, Once the movers are ready to load, stay out of their way.

Load The Truck: If you are moving yourself, it is time to start loading the truck. Have plenty of help, work carefully and methodically, and, as with the packing, take breaks as needed, and don't skip lunch.

Pack The Car: Finish your "load last, unload first" box, and load the car.

Final Check And Cleaning: As each room is emptied, check it over. Look in all the closets and cabinets, and be sure everything has been removed. Don't forget to check the attic, basement, garage, and storage sheds. Do a final quick dusting and vacuuming, room by room, then close that room off so you know that it is finished.

Secure The House: Make sure all the windows and doors are locked, lights are off, and the heat is turned down (but not off if the house is to remain unoccupied for a while). Leave the keys with the realtor, a neighbor, or whomever you have arranged to take them.

UNLOADING DAY

Be Ready: Be at the house well in advance of the movers, and have the rooms vacuumed and ready for the furniture. Tour the house, making as many advance decisions as possible about where furniture is to be placed. Refer to your list of dimensions to make sure that large pieces will fit where you want them. The movers—or you and your helpers—will find it a big help if they know exactly where the big heavy stuff goes.

Direct the Unloading: If you used a moving company, try to have two people available to direct the unloading. As the movers take things off the truck, one person can check things off the inventory list and look for damage, while the other is inside to direct the placement of furniture and boxes. If obvious damage is noted (that doesn't mean you have to unpack boxes while the movers are still there), point it out to the driver and make the appropriate notations on the inventory list.

SPECIAL CONSIDERATIONS

Moving Your Pets

Pets are a very special part of any household, and moving them to their new home requires care and planning to ensure their health, safety, and comfort. For the family pet, the disruption of familiar surroundings, the rigors of the move, and the acclimating to a new home are every bit as stressful and traumatic as they are for any other family member. What follows is a compilation of the guidelines suggested by the Humane Society and leading moving companies and airlines regarding your pets.

Some things require quite a bit of advance planning and notification, so familiarize yourself with the guidelines early on in your moving plans, and make entries on your Master List accordingly.

Know The Laws

Many states, and even many counties within the states, have specific laws and guidelines governing the importing of animals from other areas of the country, especially more exotic animals. While it's highly unlikely that there will be any difficulty moving your Golden Retriever from New York to Vermont, your monkey or your son's boa constrictor might be another story. Some animals may require special vaccinations or even a quarantine period; others may need special safety equipment or restraining hardware while being moved. Animals classified as livestock—family pet or not—may fall under different classifications.

During a pre-move visit to your new area, check on the local and state laws governing interstate transportation of pets. You can get this information at the Chamber of Commerce, the City or County Clerk's office, or at a local veterinarian's office. For more unusual animals or for information on moving pets to locations outside the United States, contact the Animal and Plant Health Inspection Service (APHIS) of the United States Department of Agriculture. Check the phone book under U.S. Government for listings in your area.

Contact Your Veterinarian

Your next step is to take your pet to your veterinarian. Have him or her give your pet a complete checkup, and issue a health certificate or letter. The certificate should provide information about the pet, including its physical appearance, and certify that the pet is in good health and free of contagious diseases. Make certain that all vaccinations are up to date, including those for rabies, distemper, parveau, and feline leukemia. Get the necessary certifications. Obtain a current rabies tag, and be sure to attach it to your pet's collar.

If an entry certificate is required in order to bring the pet into another state or country, have your vet arrange it. Make a copy of all these health and immunization records, attach one securely to your pet's cage for the trip, and carry a copy with you. Also, be sure to obtain and carry with you a copy of any prescriptions your pet requires.

Now is also the time to arrange for sedatives, safety equipment, or any special in-flight cage that your pet may need during transit. Consult with your vet for specific suggestions.

Finally, ask your vet to recommend a new veterinarian or animal clinic in the town to which you are moving. A personal recommendation from a trusted doctor will ease your mind about finding quality services in your new home. If your vet is unable to recommend anyone, you might want to check with the American Veterinary Association, the American Animal Hospital Association, or the American Association of Equine Practitioners for a recommendation. Your vet should be able to supply you with addresses and phone numbers of these associations, or ask for them at the reference desk of your local library.

Get A Name Tag

In addition to the rabies tag on your pet's collar, be certain there is a name tag there, too. Most airlines require this, and it's a good precaution for protecting your pet whether it's required or not.

The tag should contain your pet's name, your name, and at the very least a telephone number where you can be reached. You may need to change the tag when you get to your new home, but remember to keep your pet tagged and the phone number current.

Your Transportation Options

There are basically three ways that you can transport your pets: by private automobile, unaccompanied on an airline, or accompanied on an airline. The regulations of the Interstate Commerce Commission forbid the transporting of animals aboard moving vans, and the Animal Welfare Act stipulates that airlines cannot transport puppies or kittens which are less than eight weeks old, or that have not been weaned. The airlines may also place their own limitations on transporting animals that they feel to be vicious, dangerous, ill, or otherwise hazardous to passengers and airline personnel.

Transporting By Private Automobile

Here are several tips that can make transporting your pet by automobile safe and comfortable. Remember that anytime you transport your pets, you can endanger their lives by careless or improper handling, so take necessary precautions.

Don't feed your pets for at least four hours before departing, and give them ample time to relieve themselves before putting them in the car. Take a container of water from home if possible, to lessen the chances of problems from strange water sources.

You and your pet will probably both be happier if they are crated. Your vet or pet supply dealer can provide you with the proper type of crate. Equip it with a blanket and a favorite toy or two, and your pet should take to it with a minimum of fuss—most pets actually love their crates for the feeling of security it gives them. If your pets are overly active, nervous, or prone to motion sickness, talk with your vet about tranquilizers or sedatives.

If your pets are not used to car travel, acclimate them with short trips prior to the moving. Also, don't let your dog hang his head out the window while you are driving. It can cause a number of problems, including eye and nose irritation.

Plan on rest stops at least every four hours so that your pets can stretch and relieve themselves. Also, avoid common rest stop "pet potty areas", since they are often a breeding ground for Parveau and other infectious diseases. Keep your pet on a leash—including cats—when outside the car. It is very easy for them to become disoriented in a strange environment and wander off, perhaps into traffic.

Whenever you stop and must leave your pets in the car, keep the stops brief. Park in the shade whenever possible and keep the windows partially open for ventilation. Don't ever forget that it takes a very short time for the temperature inside a closed car to reach deadly levels. Also, try not to leave your pet unattended in the car. If you must, be sure to remove his leash and collar. A pet can be strangled to death if his collar becomes entangled with the gearshift, window handle, or other protruding object in the car's interior.

If you plan to stop overnight, arrange your motel reservations in advance and make sure they allow pets. Automobile clubs and motel guidebooks usually have this information. Be prepared to pay a little extra—many motels charge a two to five dollar additional fee per pet.

Transporting By Air

Many airlines will allow small pets to accompany you on board the airplane. Typically, you will be required to house your pet in a carrier that will fit under the seat—21 by 18 × 8 inches is the standard size. These rules do not apply to seeing eye or hearing ear dogs, but the airline still must be notified in advance that the dog is to be brought on board.

Make your flight reservations well in advance and notify the airline that you wish to bring your pet on board. Pay strict attention to their rules. Remember, too, that you will be expected to check in at least one hour prior to departure.

Most pets travel unaccompanied on the airline. Once again, make your reservations well in advance, and plan on arriving at least two hours before flight time to check the pet through.

You will be responsible for providing an approved shipping container in which your pet must travel. The restrictions governing these containers are fairly strict, and often vary between airlines. You may be able to buy or rent a container directly from the airline, or check with your pet supply dealer or veterinarian.

If your flight involves transfers, be aware that you cannot check your pet through. At each transfer point, you will need to oversee the unloading and reloading of the pet, or arrange for someone to meet the flight and take care of the transferring for you. Also, if you are not traveling on the same plane with your pet, arrangements will need to be made for someone to meet the flight when it arrives to claim the animal. If not claimed within a reasonable time after arrival, the animal will be boarded in a local kennel at your expense. Be certain that whoever meets the flight has all the necessary paperwork from the airline, or they won't be able to claim your pet.

Smaller and Larger Pets

Small pets such as birds and fish can usually only be transported by car, although some airlines will allow them. For your birds, simply plan on transporting them in the same cage they normally use. Remove the water container to prevent spills, empty food dishes to only about 1/3 full, remove any toys that could move around during transit and possibly harm the birds, and keep the cage covered while driving to keep the birds warm and less anxious. Bring their water container and a small supply of water from home, and place it back in the cage each time you stop.

Fish should be removed from their normal glass aquarium and placed in a waterproof, unbreakable container. Fill the container about 1/3 to 1/2 full with water removed from the aquarium. Cover the container, and secure it with a strap or rubber band, then place the container in a sturdy outer box or foam cooler. Adding foam "peanuts" between the container and the outer box will lessen the vibration, and liquid healing compounds, available from most pet stores, can help with any bruising of the fish that may occur. Remember to open the container at each rest stop—a minimum of every 5 hours—to allow air to enter the container. Consult with your pet supply dealer or veterinarian for more specific instructions depending on the size and type of fish you are transporting.

If it is necessary to move the entire aquarium while filled, remember that it cannot be transported aboard a moving van. Lower the water level in the tank to only about 2/3 full, and remove the heater, aerator, large decorations, and anything else that might move around in transit and break the glass. Cover the aquarium with plastic to prevent spilling, or place the entire tank inside two or three plastic trash bags. Finally, place the tank inside a larger outer carton and pad it carefully with paper or foam. Store the heater and aerator in the same box—separately wrapped—so that you don't have to sort through boxes looking for them later, and replace and activate both of them as soon as you arrive in your new home. If suggested by your vet, you may even need to activate one or both of the units at night when you stop at a motel.

If you have a horse to transport, there are several options available to you. You can rent a horse trailer from the same agency where you rented your moving truck, and tow the trailer behind the truck or your car. Check with the rental yard to determine if your car is of sufficient size and properly equipped for towing that much weight. If your horse has never been trailered before, get him used to the trailer gradually, and consult with your vet to determine if tranquilizers will be necessary.

If you would rather not tow a trailer, you can employ the services of an I.C.C.-approved horse mover. They have the proper trucks and trailers, and are experienced with the care and safe transporting of horses, ponies, llamas, and similar animals. Check with your regular feed supplier for recommendations, or look in the Yellow Pages under "Horse Transporting" or "Livestock Transporting". A company such as this is also your best bet for transporting goats, sheep, and other livestock.

A third possibility is to transport the horse by air. Consult with your travel agent or airline representative well in advance to book the flight and arrange the details. Most airlines will require that a handler or attendant accompany the horse, and you will be responsible for providing a shipping stall and any other equipment the airline requires. Also, due to the labor involved in loading and unloading the horse on the plane, most airlines will only allow them on nonstop flights. If you cannot make suitable arrangements with an airline, or if you have several horses to move at once, you might want to check with a private air freight hauler. Check the Yellow Pages under "Air Freight Services".

Moving Your Plants

Plants are one of the more difficult things in your house to move. They are relatively fragile, and often respond poorly to the shock of being transported. You might want to consider having a plant sale before you move, and save the proceeds to replace them when you get to your new home. Favorite plants can be transported, either in your car or in the moving van, with a little care and some special packing. Remember that the plants will take some time to adjust to the new levels of light and humidity in your new home and won't look their best for awhile. Some, now matter how careful you are, simply won't survive the trip.

Check On State And Federal Regulations

As with the transportation of animals, your first step is to know the laws. Most common houseplants can be moved from state to state with no problem, but be aware that some restrictions may apply. Some states require that plants be checked and certified free of any insects or disease. You may be required to show such certification at border agricultural inspection stations. Other states may not allow certain types of plants to be imported into the area at all.

Transporting Options

In most cases, you will have better luck with your plants if they are transported by car. This allows you total control over their environment—something you can't do if they are on a plane or in a moving van—and you can regulate the air temperature and ventilation in the car and adjust their positioning to prevent damage.

Your plants are best transported on the rear floor if

they're small enough, or on the back seat. Do not place them on the shelf under the rear window where they will be exposed to strong direct sunlight. To do so will also obscure your view. Avoid placing plants on the front seat or front floorboards. Since plants tend to be topheavy and unstable, they can tip over into you while you're driving.

Since you have no control over the environment there, do not place plants in the trunk. Julie discovered this the hard way. With her husband driving a rented moving truck, Julie followed behind in the family car with the dog, vacuum cleaner, and a variety of other items with her. Since the move was "short"—about five hours driving time—and the car was heavily loaded, her collection of favorite plants went into the truck. Temperatures on that snowy drive dropped to twenty five degrees. When the plants arrived at their new home, they looked fine. The first indication of trouble came when Julie moved them into the house. She bumped a particularly large plant against a doorway, and several branches snapped off—the plants looked great because they were frozen. As they warmed and thawed, most simply turned black, and, despite Julie's best efforts over the next few weeks to save them, couldn't be revived. Of twelve original plants, only one somewhat stunted survivor still adorns a windowsill.

Your plants can be transported aboard the moving van, within the guidelines set forth by the I.C.C. Standard regulations require that the trip be under 150 miles, or that the plants be unloaded within 24 hours. Also, those regulations usually prohibit storage of the plants by the moving company, watering, pruning, or other servicing. Consult with your moving company representative for more information. You can also move your plants in your rented moving truck, although careful packing and securing is required, and they are again at the mercy of the unheated, or in summer overheated, environment inside the back of the truck.

The final option, air transport, is actually not much of an option at all. Air transport is relatively expensive, you will be required to provide documentation pertaining to the species and condition of the plants. Since they are typically transported in the unheated, unpressurized cargo area of the plane, an air trip is a difficult thing for your plants to survive. If you have large and valuable plants that you would like to transport by air, consult with an airline representative for more information.

Preparing Your Plants For Transport

One commercial moving company offered the following tips for preparing and transporting your plants:

Beginning about four weeks before the move, consult with the proper agencies for information concerning moving the plants to a new state. Have the plants checked and certified as per their requirements. If there are no specific restrictions or guidelines, care for the plants yourself to rid them of any pests or disease.

About two weeks before the move, keep the plants a little drier than usual.

The day before the move, water the plants well, and wrap the pots in plastic or aluminum foil to prevent water leakage. Large or weak plants should have the branches bound against the main stem or against a sturdy stake. Bend the branches in the normal direction of growth, and use a soft, flexible binding material—old nylon stockings work well. To protect the leaves, you can roll and tape light-weight cardboard into a funnel shape, then invert it over the plant.

On moving day, place the plants in sturdy shipping containers. Use moisture-proof waxed boxes, if possible. You can probably obtain a few of these by asking at your local grocery store, where they are often used to transport damp produce. Lining the inside of regular boxes with plastic sheeting or large plastic garbage bags also works well. Use foam packing material or crumpled paper between the plants, and pack them in such a manner that they are snug enough in the boxes to prevent tipping, but not crushed against each other. Be sure the plants are the last things to be loaded and the first to be removed.

Remember that temperature and moisture are the most important things to the survival of your plants. Don't over water them, and try to keep the temperature within the range of 45 to 80 degrees. You can also transport plant cuttings by placing them in sealed plastic bags. They will last several days if packed in a bed of damp peat moss or layers of damp paper towels. Once again, pack the bags of cuttings in sturdy boxes, and cushion them to prevent movement and damage.

Transporting Extra Vehicles

If you have additional vehicles that have to be moved to your new home but ones that you are not planning to drive, there are several options open to you for transporting them.

The safest and most secure option—and the most expensive—is to have the vehicle placed in an enclosed truck and driven to your new home. This eliminates the problems of towing, and the vehicle is safe from road damage and vandalism. On the other hand, since you are employing a truck and driver for this use, the costs will be, in most instances, prohibitive. A similarly secure and similarly expensive option is rail transport, where the vehicle is placed in a special auto-transport train car and delivered to the train station closest to your home.

Another possibility is hiring a driver. There are agencies that have insured and bonded professional drivers who will pick up your car or recreational vehicle at your home and deliver it to your new address within a guaranteed time period. As with the moving company, remember that you will need to have cash on hand to pay the driver upon arrival.

You can also take the cheaper, but riskier option, of

checking the classified newspaper advertisements—or placing an advertisement yourself—to find someone who needs transportation to a destination near your new home, and hiring someone to transport the car. Friends or family members, anxious to see your new home, might be willing to drive an extra vehicle. In this case, you will be responsible for their return air or rail fare.

Your final option is towing. If your moving company is utilizing a short van, as opposed to a large truck and trailer rig, they may be able to tow the vehicle for you. If you are moving yourself, you can rent a tow bar or flat bed, car transport trailer to tow behind the moving truck. The rental dealer can provide you with the necessary equipment. Boats and travel trailers must obviously be towed in this way, but remember that fifth-wheel trailers and larger recreational vehicles may need special towing arrangements. Once again, consult with your mover or truck rental agent for more specific information.

8

You Made It—Now What?

There are two things to aim at in life: first, to get what you want; and, after that, to enjoy it. Only the wisest of mankind achieve the second.

—Logan Pearsall Smith,
Afterthoughts

You have agonized over the decision to move for months, in many cases years. You have researched, worried, planned, sacrificed—and you have finally made it. But now that the plans and the decisions and the excitement of the quest are over, how do you truly enjoy it?

For most people, the first few weeks following relocation are a jumble of thoughts, emotions, and activities. The new house needs to be arranged, new stores to find, new places to discover. Then there are those great recreational activities you have always dreamed of doing; so you lose yourself for another few weeks in fishing, skiing, hiking, golfing and basking in the clean mountain air. It all seems heavenly—until the second thoughts start.

One day, you casually walk into a grocery store and, unlike the one where you had shopped for years, you suddenly realize that you don't know where anything is. On the drive back home, you get lost on an unfamiliar back street. You finally find your street again, and drive past neighbors who are total strangers to you. Suddenly, and with an amazing intensity, you become overwhelmed with a feeling of being lost and out of place.

Back in the house there are familiar things around you, but in different places and on different walls. Without thinking, you reach for the phone to call your best friend, but, at the last minute, you realize that asking a friend to drive 600 miles for coffee and commiseration is out of the question.

Finally, you sink into your favorite chair and moodily descend into a myriad of "Did I do the right thing?" thoughts.

For whatever comfort it might be, you are not alone. Virtually everyone who has made a major move such as this—an enormous uprooting of their lives is actually a more accurate description—has suffered from this "post-relocation depression" syndrome. It is natural and, for most people, unavoidable. It is also fairly easy to cope with, given a little time and some positive steps on your part.

The Story of Nick and Louise

For nine years, Nick B. owned his own company in San Francisco. It consisted of five employees and had a loyal clientele. Nick also had a healthy bank account. Louise enjoyed a high-paying accounting position with a law firm. Their story is familiar in many ways. Becoming tired of the crowds and the crime, and wanting a slower, saner way of life, they discovered a small town in northern Idaho while on a driving vacation one year. They returned two years later and the town became a yearly destination. Soon after that, it became a daily obsession.

The death of Nick's mother actually became the turning point for the couple. She dreamt all her life of retirement and of having a home in Connecticut. But she lost her five year battle with cancer at the early age of sixty-one. Shaken by the loss and haunted by the specter of her unfulfilled dreams, Nick and Louise decided the move was now or never. After seven years of visits, dreams, plans, and hesitations, their actual decision to move was made in less than a week.

The house went on the market, the business was liquidated, the movers were called, and within three short, hectic, whirlwind months after his mother's death, Nick and Louise were Idaho residents.

It felt wonderful at first, actually living where other people vacationed. They took long walks along the river with their dogs, stayed up late and slept late, and frugally used the proceeds from the sale of their house for living expenses. They looked into businesses to buy and businesses to start; Nick toyed with the idea of writing, and Louise thought of continuing her education.

Then boredom and the lack of outside interaction began to take its toll. Plans once enthusiastically discussed for hours were now dismissed after a few moments of desultory conversation. The self-indulgent luxury of a few extra hours of sleep in the morning turned into a way of avoiding having to deal with life. The money dwindled and the walls seemed to close in on them.

Nine months passed, and Christmas approached. There was no joy in shopping, because the stores suddenly seemed alien and unfamiliar. There was no one with whom to share the excitement of the season, and their sense of being outsiders in the community intensified. They even talked of moving back to their old neighborhood.

In the new year, faced with an increasingly desperate financial situation, Louise contacted a local employment agency. With her excellent skills and background, she had no trouble getting a new position. Their situation began almost immediately to turn around. Now there was a place to go each day, new things to discover and new people to meet. Nick enjoyed his wife's happiness and growing satisfaction and followed suit. He revived his construction company on a smaller scale, and quickly found himself involved in the enjoyment of working, living, and dreaming of the future.

Five years have passed, and Nick and Louise are thriving. Nick's business, while not at the income level of his previous one, is doing very well. He is also teaching part time. Louise is now the supervisor of her department, an officer on the board of directors of the Humane Society and is still pursuing her dream of going back to school. Their new home is under construction on twenty secluded acres, and a resident herd of deer has become a common evening sighting. Neither would return to their old life in San Francisco for anything in the world. They make that statement with obvious and sincere conviction.

Their story is not unusual, nor was it selected or adjusted to have the happy ending we all savor. It is merely indicative of the adjustment process through which everyone goes. They suffered some, they changed some, but they survived and prospered—and so will you. The main thing is, they did it. They made the move, and none of the joy and satisfaction they have in their lives today would have been possible without that first effort to try and make a change for the better.

What they learned, and what you can learn from their situation, is that the changes involved in making a major relocation require some honest effort and a realistic attitude about what to expect. There are adjustments to be made, and a new community with which to adapt. This means finding new ways of doing things, new places to find and with which to become familiar, new and different people to meet and deal with in the day-to-day living experience.

In the end, for them and for virtually everyone who has made the move, all the effort was worth it. Repeatedly and without reservation, dropouts respond to the simple questions "was it worth it?" and "would you do it again?" with a very resounding *YES.*

SETTLE YOURSELF IN

The first big step to adjusting to your new environment is to settle in, surround yourself with familiar objects and artifacts, and get yourself a comfortable base from which to work. Everyone in the family will be feeling a little disoriented in the beginning—a little lost and out of place—so concentrate on establishing your presence in your new home and in your new town.

Being able to see and touch all the everyday pieces of your life that were neatly packed away in those boxes will suddenly become an important anchor for you in your new town, as well as a dose of "I really do live here now" reality. Then, with your home established as a base and safe haven of refuge, you can begin forays into town and finally into the community structure itself.

Open a Bank Account

Unless you are traveling with a large amount of cash—which you shouldn't be—it is recommended that your first stop be at a bank of your choice to open a new checking account. That will make it more convenient for you to shop and pay for new services.

As far as selecting a bank is concerned, ask various

people for recommendations. Talk to your realtor, the local moving company or truck rental representative, or any other "local" with which you happen to strike up a conversation. Ask them where they bank, and whether or not they are pleased with the service. You should also take into consideration what your future dealings with a bank might be. If you will need mortgage or consumer loans, or perhaps business banking services, select a bank that can accommodate as many of these future needs as possible.

You may want to stay with the local branch of your old bank, assuming you were happy with their services and a branch is in your new town. On the other hand, don't overlook the possibility of using a locally-owned bank. They are usually much more committed to using local money for local economic improvement, and may be more flexible in the future with help for your business, construction, and other loan needs.

If you obtained a certified check when you closed out your old account, you will have no problem opening a new account using that check as an initial deposit. You can also open the account with cash, of course, or by depositing any traveler's checks you have. If your account at your previous bank is not yet closed, you can arrange to have funds wired from that bank to your new one, although there may be a slight charge for this service.

Establish Basic Services

One of the first things needed to be done upon arrival in your new town is to set up utilities and other basic services. This will quickly accomplish two things—you will get a taste of the town and learn where at least a few things are located, and, of course, get your new house ready for occupancy.

If you are using the services of a moving company, you can usually arrange to arrive in town a day or two ahead of the truck, which is an ideal time to take care of all these details. If you are moving yourself, you should make a trip to the town a few weeks before moving to take care of as many advance details as possible.

The first detail is a good city map. Ask your realtor for one in advance, or stop at the Chamber of Commerce for one. If you are not sufficiently acclimated to find the Chamber building, try a grocery store, gas station, or convenience store; they usually have local maps for sale.

Begin with the basic, more essential services—electricity, gas, water, sewer, garbage, telephone, and cable television. Names, addresses, and telephone numbers for all these services can easily be obtained from your realtor, the Chamber of Commerce, or the local telephone directory.

As a new resident, most utility companies require some form of proof of residency. There are a variety of forms of proof, including a rent receipt from your new landlord or escrow papers from the purchase of your new house. Even a letter or two in your name that you've received at your new address will suffice. Remember that whatever form of residency proof you submit, it must contain both your name and your new address. To save yourself steps and headaches, call the various utilities in advance to determine exactly what they require.

Also, be prepared to pay a deposit for new services. This is a typical requirement for new customers, especially ones new to the area, so don't be offended. Discuss the situation with the company representative. You may find that a letter or phone call from your old utility confirming your good credit may suffice in lieu of a deposit.

Getting Your Pets Settled

Don't overlook the needs of your pets during the stressful hours and days of unpacking and acclimating yourself. This move has been just as traumatic for them, and their health, comfort, and safety should be considered as soon as possible.

Dogs need to become acclimated to the house, yard, and neighborhood. Take your dog through the house, and let it explore its nooks and crannies. Walk around the yard, and let the dog get a feel of its new home. If the dog will not be staying inside with you, immediately provide it with a fenced or otherwise enclosed area so there is no opportunity for your pet to wander.

Remember that your dog will be somewhat disoriented, and that none of the neighborhood sights and smells will be familiar. Your new acreage and the wide open spaces will be wonderful for your dog, but they do not provide a reason to let your pet run free. You will be endangering your dog's health, as well as the safety of wildlife and livestock in the area.

Cats likewise need to become oriented and adjusted, and may need dietary supplements or other special care to help them adjust to the move and their new environment. For the protection of wildlife, and simply as a matter of courtesy to your neighbors, cats should also not be allowed to simply roam the neighborhood at will.

Be aware of how the new climate affects your pets. Provide them with shelter from the extremes of both heat and cold, and, in cold climates, remember to check that their water bowl is not frozen.

If you have fish, be sure and set up their tank and equipment right away. Use the water in which you moved the fish from home to start, and add additional water at the temperature and nutrient level recommended for your particular species of fish. Birds should be placed in a clean cage, located in a bright, draft-free area. Get them situated quickly so they are out of the cold and also out of the path of incoming furniture and people.

As soon as it's convenient, take your pet to a local veterinarian for a checkup. Have the vet explain how the new climate and altitude can affect your pet, and inquire about any local diseases, pests, or other potential problems that could affect your pet. Your new vet should be provided with a complete medical background on all your pets, so that he or she can suggest any medications or special attention necessary to help them adjust to their new environment.

Finally, take the time to acquaint yourself with the local laws pertaining to pet ownership. Many towns require that your pet be licensed. Local "leash laws" may require that your dog be on a leash and under your control when you take it out for a walk. Also be aware that the laws in many agricultural communities place severe penalties on you and your dog should the dog be proven guilty of injuring or even just chasing livestock.

Organize Your Home

The obvious place to start your settling in process is with your house, so begin the unpacking process as soon as possible. Empty the boxes, break out the coffee pot, and peel the stickers off everything. Surround yourself with your furniture and your clothes, your books and your music, your toys and your hobbies—it really makes a tremendous difference in your attitude. Nothing is worse than living in a clutter of packing boxes and open suitcases. All this does is add to the disorientation and the feeling of being rootless and transient.

First, unpack the car and bring in the cleaning supplies. Get the plants out of the car and into a warm, out of the way place until they can be arranged. Open your "load last, unload first box" on the kitchen counter, and get out your tools, coffee pot, and radio. Fix the kids a snack, feed your pets, and brew some coffee and perhaps turn on the radio or your stereo to some soothing music.

Begin the unpacking and settling in process by getting as many of the boxes as possible into their respective rooms. For the boxes of lesser importance that don't have specific rooms yet—for example, boxes of storage items that came from your old attic and will probably go back into your new one —stack them out of the way in the garage or a spare room. Reducing the general clutter and disorganization as quickly as possible is one of the keys to a more enjoyable unpacking process.

With the boxes out of the way, start placing your furniture where you want it. Initially, arrange the furniture in groupings that are similar to how it was in your old house. Your mind will "imprint" furniture arrangements (that's how you can walk through your living room in the dead of night without bumping into anything), so familiar settings will be seen in your "mind's eye." You can always rearrange things later if you like, which for many people seems to be yet another part of the adjustment process.

Equally important is putting things on the walls, so get out the hammer and nails and do this right away, even as you are placing the furniture. Hang your pictures and paintings, let the teenagers get the posters on their walls, and stick your four-year-old's art work back on the refrigerator. There is probably no more transient and impermanent feeling in life then being in a house with bare, impersonal walls.

Get the children started on their rooms, and let them help with the unpacking. They need to feel that they are part of the move and are included in the decision-making processes—no matter in what way. The sooner they can have their own toys and other belongings around, and sleep in their own beds and slip into old, comfortable clothes, the sooner the adjustment process to their new home will begin.

The next room to attack is the kitchen, truly the nerve center of any home. The kitchen is the room most sorely missed when it's out of commission—just ask anyone who has ever suffered through a three- or four-week kitchen remodeling project. Start by mapping out the cabinet layout and mentally arranging where everything will go; then methodically start unpacking, rinsing, and putting away—and you will feel good for having taken the time getting all the boxes properly organized when you packed.

If a moving company performed the move for you, be sure to keep track of any damage you encounter as you unpack. Save the broken pieces, save the packing container whether you did the packing or not, and note the inventory number of the damaged item, or the number of the box in which it was packed. You will need all this information in order to file a claim, and the local company representative will usually want to come out to the house to see the damage for himself.

Continue working your way through the entire house over the next couple of days. Concentrate on one room at a time, as much as possible, and get it finished before moving onto the next. Remove the packing clutter as you proceed and try to get the house settled and livable in as short a period of time as possible.

One final unpacking tip. If you used actual mover's packing boxes, as opposed to boxes from the grocery store, slit the tape holding the ends together, flatten them out, and store them in a corner of the garage. These boxes have a definite resale value, so when you are finished unpacking, contact your mover or truck rental agency, or place an advertisement in the paper about selling them. Approximately one half their original cost is a fair selling price.

GETTING CHILDREN SETTLED IN

Moving a long distance and into a new and different type of environment is difficult and exhausting for everyone, and it is not unusual for children to get a little lost in the confusion. There is so much to do and, since kids always seem so resilient and adaptable, they don't always get the after-move attention they need.

Psychologists offer a variety of suggestions to help orient and adjust after a major move such as this one. These are not difficult, but they do take a little time and understanding.

Take them on a complete guided tour of the new house as soon as you arrive, including the garage, basement, and any out buildings. This serves the dual purpose of letting them feel more involved in their new home, and gives you the opportunity to point out potential hazards in the house and yard. Once you are settled, it is always a good idea to map out escape routes with your children in case of fire, explain to them what the sound of the smoke alarm means, and then hold a family fire drill.

As mentioned earlier, let the kids unpack and decorate their own rooms. Give them the freedom to suggest where their bed and other furniture be placed. If you are buying curtains or wallpaper, get their input. Leave it up to them to put things on the shelves and in the closets. Let them arrange and hang pictures and posters on the walls with your help. This is their space, and it's important that it be personalized.

Make the move and the settling in an exciting adventure. Take some pictures of the new house and new neighborhood, then buy a scrapbook so they can start a journal. You might even want to help them compare the new photographs to pictures of their old neighborhood, and encourage them to chronicle the tale of the entire move.

Take a family walking tour of the new neighborhood. Point out the interesting sights, walk them by their new school if possible, and discuss safe routes home from school, the park, and other areas your children will be frequenting. Discuss and explain any potential hazards they should avoid. Later, take them on a driving tour of the town and the immediate surrounding area. Point out interesting sights and recreation areas, and emphasize the positive things about the new town.

Tell your kids all about the area, about its history, industry, and anything else that will pique their interest and give them a sense of pride and belonging. Bob C.'s son Jason, for example, was having a hard time adjusting to his new home in rural eastern Oregon, until Bob read an article in the local paper about the nearby ruins of an early western town. A Sunday picnic was arranged, and Jason came back with a camera—and his imagination—filled with visions of Indians and early settlers. Jason has now become something of a local history buff, and his letters to old friends are filled with local lore.

Encourage them to make new friends, but don't cut them off from their old ones. Suggest writing letters and sending pictures to close friends in their old town, and occasionally give them long distance telephone privileges.

Contact the local parks and recreation department regarding programs for kids they might sponsor. This is especially important if you moved during the summer. That way, your kids won't have to wait until school starts in the fall to meet new friends and become involved in various activities. You can also check with the schools, museums, and the local library about other fun and educational things to keep them occupied during their free time.

If your kids were actively involved in a sport or other leisure activity in their old home, find out what's available in a similar vein in your new town. It shouldn't take long to locate a soccer or Little League team, a chess club, or a gymnastics school that will be an exciting diversion for them.

Arrange to go with your children to their new school to show them around and give them the opportunity to meet their teachers before their first day of classes. Ask the teachers about the school's dress code and how the other kids normally dress, so that your children won't feel out of place on the first day. You might ask the teachers for any other suggestions to help ease your children's transition to the new school. Depending on the ages of your children, you might also want to make arrangements to accompany them to school for the first few days.

As your children make new friends and become involved in new activities, it is important for you to also participate. Plan on attending school and club activities, and encourage your kids to bring their new friends home to visit and play.

Do anything you can to help build confidence in your children. Encourage and compliment them often, particularly in the period after the move. Increasing the child's self-confidence will make it that much easier for them to make new friends, participate in school and community activities, and adjust to their new and still unfamiliar environment.

Finally, psychologists agree that you should give your children's old memories ample time to fade. Be supportive, and also be tolerant of unusual behavior. Only in the event of such obvious symptoms as sleeplessness, loss of weight, or continued withdrawal should you consult a physician. Let your child know that the only thing that has changed is the house and the town in which they live. The family and its foundation of warmth and security has not changed at all.

GETTING ACCLIMATED, ACQUAINTED AND ADJUSTED

Every newcomer faces the need to acclimate himself. Quite often, many thoughts of "did I do the right thing" that newly transplanted people experience can be traced to simply not knowing their way around. There is, in most people, an instinctive need to explore, to make contact with other people, and to become a part of their environment. Knowing your way around is often synonymous to belonging, and it is a good way to make you feel like you are an active member of the community.

Newcomer Services

A very pleasant and informative way to be introduced to your new community is through the newcomer services offered by many cities. There are different services in different areas, from home visits to social gatherings to guided tours. Check with the Chamber of Commerce or visitors information bureau if there are any such services available in your area.

James C., for example, was a widower who left his home in Sacramento, California after the death of his wife. He wanted safer and less crowded surroundings and a new start in life. He decided on a small town in Washington state, and arranged and executed the move quickly, almost on a whim.

While the immediate change proved stimulating, it was also lonely. Then the local moving company representative mentioned a community-service group called "Welcome To Town." The club met once a month expressly to welcome newcomers to the area and show them around. James signed up immediately to attend the next meeting.

The group met at a local restaurant, where complimentary rolls and coffee were served while "old-timers" from the town gave colorful talks about the history of the area. Then the tour guide passed out information packets containing maps, informative booklets covering a wide range of topics—recreational activities, educational opportunities, even winter driving tips—and special discount coupons from local businesses. The morning culminated with a 90-minute bus tour of the area, where the guide pointed out everything from the schools and utility offices to pizza parlors and ski rental outlets. It was a marvelous introduction, and, four years later, James still counts some of the people he met on that bus among his closest friends. And as a long-time volunteer for the "Welcome To Town" group, new friends come his way every day.

Local Television and Newspapers

At an early point in your unpacking process, set up a television set in a central location, connect the antenna or cable, and tune it to a local station. Even if you do not watch much television, leave the set on while you unpack.

As you work, you'll find yourself being introduced to a large part of your community: the loud car salesman and the twang of the guy at the feed store; local models from local clothing stores; the latest deals in everything from groceries to furniture. Names will begin to register, as will addresses and locations. Without realizing it, you have started the acclimation process.

Many local business owners do their own television commercials. Suddenly the faces you see on television are the same ones you see at the grocery store. It is a fun way to help you acclimate and also helps you find stores you'd like to patronize—or avoid.

Pay particular attention to the local news broadcasts. You will hear about the issues that affect the town and important state-wide issues. You'll learn the area's political slant, and begin hearing the names of local business people, politicians, and the "movers and shakers" of the area. A growing familiarity with the names and issues that affect and influence your new home will help you feel more a part of what is happening in your town, as well as help you become better informed in conversation and be a more more knowledgeable participant in your new community.

You should subscribe to the local newspaper. It makes fun and interesting reading while taking breaks from unpacking, and it can be a tremendous help in familiarizing yourself with the community. Once again you'll learn about the issues, large and small; the political slant of the area—or at least of the paper; the important and not-so-important names in the news;

the stores and what they sell; and the local sports, recreation and entertainment possibilities.

Shopping

As you unpack and settle in, you will find a variety of things that you need, from a carton of milk to light bulbs to hooks for hanging the paintings. You need to go shopping—exciting for some people, intimidating for others—but it is a great way to discover things about the town.

The grocery store is usually first, and if you are like most people, knowing your way around a grocery store is tantamount to being a "local." Being able to dash into the store and unerringly find exactly what you need seems to generate a self-satisfied feeling of belonging. You may have never thought of it, but it's very true for many people. In fact, a large number of dropouts tell similar stories about first feeling like "an outsider" when confronted with the intricacies of a new and strange grocery store. Many discovered—certainly to their surprise—that when you disrupt the grocery shopping routine you tend to get a little disoriented. On subsequent shopping trips when the store began to feel comfortably familiar, the whole town seemed to become a friendlier and easier place with which to deal.

Try a leisurely tour of the neighborhood grocery store. It is not meant to be the high point of your first week, but it is a surprisingly enjoyable and comforting ritual.

Visit other stores as you have the time and the need arises. As you enter a store, slow down and browse. You are not in Manhattan, so adjust your pace, your breathing, and your aggressiveness accordingly. Take the time to smile and say a friendly word. In all seriousness, this is a habit that may take a little cultivating. See what each store has to offer, chat with the owner, and ease yourself into a new style of shopping.

Touring

Among the most truly pleasurable aspects of moving to a more rural environment are the slow and leisurely voyages of discovery. Taking walks around the neighborhood, admiring the lines of an old Victorian-era farmhouse, pausing under a 200-year-old oak that stands like a proud old friend in front of the house on the corner can be joyous experiences. A Saturday bicycle tour, coasting along sun-dappled country lanes in near-silence, or a weekend with the family, driving the back roads into the mountains, culminating in a two-hour picnic spent basking in the pristine solitude of a high-mountain lake can both bring moments of breathless beauty to your new way of life.

Touring is a purely marvelous pastime, and it allows you the chance to become acclimated to the area while indulging in the time to see and experience the serenity that drew you out of the city. Walk and window shop. Find a quaint cafe. Buy an old milk can for the front porch. Take an hour or an entire weekend to explore your backyard or half of the entire state.

Restaurants

Eating out is one of the nice rewards you can give yourself. It's a relaxing treat, and gives you the opportunity for a little more exploring and to meet a few more people.

Ted and Emily M., for example, made a habit of eating out at least once each week when they first moved to town, and each time at a different restaurant. They discovered some surprisingly excellent cooking, and had the opportunity to visit virtually every part of town. By making it a weekly ritual, they were "forced" to get out of the house and become more involved, all in a pleasant, non-threatening manner.

Climate and Altitude

Another adjustment that you may be faced with is the change in weather or altitude at your new home. It's something that few people stop to consider, unless they are making the move for health-related reasons.

A few dropouts report problems with high altitude after moving to high-mountain communities. A few also mentioned having to struggle a little with colder winters than had been anticipated. One dropout mentioned a problem with hotter summers and higher humidity. Most of these problems are relatively minor, and the remarkably-adaptable human body will adjust to the changes in climate and altitude in a fairly short time. If physical problems persist however, especially shortness of breath, dizziness, or aching in the joints, consult with a physician.

If you are moving to an area where the winters are more severe than what you've previously been used to, here are a few adjustments to consider:

Winter driving: Driving in the snow and ice requires some special skills. Probably the most important to remember is to simply slow down and allow more time for each maneuver. The Chamber of Commerce, police department, or Department of Motor Vehicles can provide you with a pamphlet of simple and safe driving tips.

You may also need to take some protective measures for your car, including snow tires and higher levels of antifreeze, as well as having a few basic emergency supplies in the trunk. Have your mechanic thoroughly check your car and suggest what it might need.

Home weatherization: If you have just bought a house, or if you're planning to build one, installing good levels of insulation and taking protective measures against air leakage can make the house more comfortable—and also help reduce the size of your utility bills. For specific suggestions on weatherizing your home, talk with the energy conservation specialist at your utility company, or with an experienced weatherization contractor. If you depend on wood for home heating, plan early. Prices and availability of good firewood can climb sharply during the winter months.

ESTABLISHING OTHER NEEDED SERVICES

You will need to locate a wide variety of other services, from doctors to gas stations, when you settle in your new town. Some you may need to know immediately; others can be sought out as the need arises, or simply "discovered" as you become more familiar with the town.

Personal recommendations are always the best way of finding good people and good businesses, so get in the habit of asking your neighbors, local residents and co-workers for recommendations. Your real estate agent might be able to suggest a barber, or your insurance agent can point out a good dry cleaner. One person can lead to another, so keep your eyes and ears open and don't be afraid to ask questions.

What follows is a list of suggestions for additional services you may need to establish:

Doctors and dentists: If you have a specific medical condition, check if your previous doctor can recommend someone in your new area who specializes in the type of treatment you need. You can also check the Yellow Pages under "Physicians" to see if a local physicians reference service is offered. Follow the same procedure for dentists.

Accountant: If you have moved from one state to another, remember that you will need to file state income tax forms in both states the first year. If you continue to receive income from your old state such as pensions or contract payments, you may need to continue filing dual state tax returns.

Also, if you moved your business to your new location, or moved because of a job transfer or in order to take a new job, your moving expenses may be tax deductible. If you sold a home or business prior to moving, you should be aware of how capital gains taxes affect you, and what needs to be done to defer them. It's a good idea to consult with a local accountant soon after moving to your new town to get all your questions answered.

Lawyer: It may be important to seek out a lawyer if your are buying, moving, or starting a business, or if you have complicated real estate dealings.

Department of Motor Vehicles: Remember that if you moved from out of state, you have a set period of time in which to transfer your car registration and obtain a new driver's license. If you have changed addresses within the same state, it's a good idea to apply for a new driver's license with the updated information on it. This is required in some states. The laws vary widely from state to state, as do the time limits and testing procedures, so check with the local Department of Motor Vehicles office for information pertaining to your state.

Pharmacy: Your new doctor can probably recommend a good pharmacy, or ask for recommendations. Your new pharmacy can usually arrange for the transfer of all your prescription records with just a phone call.

Insurance: If you were satisfied with your insurance company at your old location, chances are there is an agent for the same company in your new town. Check the Yellow Pages. You might also consider the services of an independent agent, who can place your insurance with a variety of different companies based on price and your specific needs. Also, check with your previous employer about extending or transferring your medical insurance, and ask your current employer for details on insuring your spouse and children under any policy you have at work.

Service Stations and Garages: You may again want to show loyalty to a service station company you've been happy with in the past. Or you may want to try the station closest to your home or job. Most people go where it is most convenient, and let the station earn their repeat business. For a garage, try to get a word-of-mouth recommendation, or ask at the local Better Business Bureau office. If you have a car that's under warranty, check the Yellow Pages for local dealerships that sell the same make of automobile, or ask your previous dealer for the name of the closest representative who will honor the warranty.

Liquor Stores: Laws in your new state or county pertaining to the sale of alcoholic beverages may be different from where you used to live. Some states allow the sale of liquor just about anywhere, while others will allow the sale only through state-run outlets. Still other states or counties are "dry", and may limit or completely prohibit the sale of some or all types of alcohol. Check with the local Chamber of Commerce for more information.

GETTING INVOLVED

Moving to a new community means more than just unpacking boxes from a rental truck—it means getting involved. Humans are social animals, needing interaction and positive encounters. They need to feel helpful and important, recognized and accepted.

Getting involved in the community meets those needs, and is a big part of the fun and satisfaction of dropping out of the urban rat race. There are tremendous varieties of activities available to you, and an equally diverse variety of people with which to do them.

Small towns and rural communities are great for getting involved. There is more openness, more time and space to step in and do something. While it's true that one person can make a difference no matter where he or she lives, the small town environment seems to cultivate and nurture the outgoing and altruistic side of us all.

Volunteer

A truly excellent way to become involved in the community is to volunteer some of your free time. You will have the opportunity to meet people with similar interests, and be doing something worthwhile to improve your community and your world. Many ex-urbanites, sequestered for years behind multiple padlocks on their apartment doors at the end of the work day, have cited their volunteer work as being the single most important aspect of relocation. They have rediscovered people and community-centered activities, and have once again found it is possible to trust and care for others.

Volunteering can take as much or as little of your time as you choose, and most organizations are more than willing to offer whatever training is necessary. It's an ideal opportunity for you to share what you know with others.

The two most typical questions are "Volunteer for what?" and "How do I do it?" The possibilities are virtually endless. Inquire at any agency or business where you think you might have an interest. If you like children, try a day care center. If you like animals, try the Humane Society. If you like acting, try the local theater.

You can also check the local paper. Many newspapers publish "Volunteers Wanted" columns, or there may be listings in the classified ads. Here, for inspiration, are fifteen examples from the "Volunteer Search" listing in one community newspaper. This small paper had *fifty three different listings* of organizations seeking volunteers, and each listing contained a description of the organization, the type of volunteers they were seeking, and a phone number for more information. No matter what your interests and abilities, there are always organizations which would greatly appreciate having you join their volunteer team:

Outdoor guide service: looking for volunteer board members and people to help the handicapped with outdoor activities;

American Cancer Society: needs people to transport cancer patients to the doctor;

American Red Cross: looking for nurses and technicians to volunteer time on blood drives;

Community theater: needs actors, set builders, lighting people, makeup people, bartenders, and more;

Community center: needs people to mend clothes and cook meals for the poor;

Girl Scouts and Boy Scouts: need volunteers to teach crafts and lead a variety of activities;

Council on Aging: looking for a wide variety of volunteers—escorts to help elderly people with shopping and other appointments, drivers for Meals On Wheels program, carpenters and other tradespeople to do minor repairs, and even a calligrapher to write certificates for fund raising projects;

Special education program: needs people to teach job skills to mildly handicapped workers;

Humane Society: looking for people to walk and groom dogs, and to help out at community informational fairs and events;

Thrift stores: a variety of different thrift stores looking for people to pick up donations, sort and repair donated items, staff the sales counters, and various other tasks;

Pregnancy counseling center: needs sympathetic volunteers to counsel teenagers on pregnancy, birth control, abortion, and adoption—they even offer training for the volunteer counselors;

The library: looking for people to take books to

homebound people, and to help at book sales and other community events;

Community arts council: needs volunteers to give art and craft demonstrations, writing classes, and to help out at community art shows and fund raisers in a variety of capacities;

Recycling center: needs people to help collect and sort recycled materials;

Area museums: always looking for tour guides, people to lead nature walks or work with animals, people to staff information and sales booths, and much more.

School Activities

Another excellent way to get yourself into the community is through your children's schools. Whether you volunteer to help with after-school projects, assist a teacher, join the P.T.A., or simply attend school activities, you will meet other parents and learn about your town. You'll be helping to enrich your child's life tremendously.

Even if your children are already out of school—or you don't have children but would like to work with them—many schools would welcome your participation. There are also schools for the handicapped and for troubled youths, all of whom need help at a variety of levels and with a variety of tasks.

Church Activities

Again, the church is a great place to meet people with interests similar to yours. Whatever your particular religious denomination, you are almost sure to find a church or synagogue in your community. Whether you simply attend services or choose to become involved with church-sponsored activities, you will be easing into the community in a comfortable, nonthreatening manner.

Adult Education Classes—Teaching and Taking

Many communities sponsor a wonderful and entertaining variety of educational opportunities for adults. Community colleges, parks and recreation departments, and even private "learning exchange" programs offer adult education classes in virtually every imaginable subject. Pick up a catalog or program newsletter, and you are likely to find classes in writing, painting, weight lifting, wine tasting, star gazing, opera appreciation, horse care, cross country skiing, French and Italian language, upholstery, engine repair, judo, real estate financing, beginning piano, juggling, estate planning, and hula dancing.

Adult education classes offer terrific possibilities from both ends of the spectrum from taking a class to teaching one. Taking classes is inexpensive, interesting, and fun—no matter how long it has been since you attended school. There is no homework, no tests, no grades, and no pressure; just the opportunity to expose yourself to new ideas and activities, and to meet a variety of interesting people.

If you have a skill or a hobby you would like to share, teach a class. You don't need to be a certified teacher or even a college graduate. No matter what your vocation or avocation, you probably have something you do well enough that you could share it with someone else who would like to know about it. It is also a good way to earn a few extra dollars.

Another purely wonderful way to help yourself and those around you is to join your community's illiteracy program. They provide you with thorough training, so you don't need any special skills. With just a few hours of your time each week, you can give someone in your community one of the most precious gifts of all—the ability to read.

Some Other Possibilities

The possibilities open to you for meeting people and getting involved in your community are limited only by your imagination. Here are a few more ideas from other successful dropouts:

Write for the local paper: If you like to write, talk to the local paper about doing some freelance work for them. The editors are always looking for people with community-oriented ideas, and it's a great way to get out and explore what is occurring in your town. If you're an avid photographer, there may be a market for your pictures.

Work at a preschool: Many dropouts have found tremendous satisfaction helping out at preschools and day care centers, either in paid or volunteer positions.

Farm work: One dropout likes to help out on area farms at harvest time. He likes the outdoors, the physical activity, and he picks up some extra money working on the farms.

Singles groups: Some of the single people who have moved to a smaller community mentioned the difficulty meeting other single people, especially single parents. Many have joined singles groups—one person even started one—as a way to meet new people and to share activities. For friendship or even the possibility of a romance, a singles group may be the ideal answer.

Classified ads: A surprising number of people have had great success with placing an advertisement in the "Personals" or "Want To Meet" section of the local paper, or just by answering the advertisements placed by others. Whether you are looking for a wife or husband or just someone to jog with, don't overlook this interesting approach.

Get a job: Many people who don't necessarily need to work have taken a job just for the enjoyment of it. Jim F. is retired and on a comfortable pension, but works winters at a local ski resort. The extra money he earns is an added bonus, and goes toward a vacation each summer; Laura B. dabbles in real estate, buying and selling properties for her own enjoyment and as a means of adding to her husband's future retirement fund; Ted F. and his girlfriend Sally, both comfortable enough from investment dividends to not really need more income, opened a small used book store for the sheer pleasure of it.

Consult: Many urban dropouts with skills to share said they had become consultants. Some opened actual consulting companies, and are doing it for a living. Others volunteer their time with such organizations as the Small Business Administration to help advise business owners.

ATTITUDE ADJUSTMENTS

According to a large percentage of urban dropouts, moving is just half the battle. For a surprisingly large number of people, leaving the big city attitude behind is more difficult than suspected.

Neil S.'s case is typical, and mirrors the experiences of many dropouts. As a stock broker, he had spent virtually all his adult life since college graduation in a fast-paced, high-pressure life style. He had a huge number of nodding acquaintances, but few trusted friends. He conditioned himself not to trust anyone since being the victim of a burglary by the employee of a firm he'd hired to work on his apartment. Constantly wary of the plotting of ambitious co-workers, he learned to take no one at face value and to suspect the motives behind every gesture, no matter how innocent or well-meaning.

In stores and restaurants, he perfected the art of aggressive communication—push your way to the front and demand attention or you'll be forever lost at the end of the line. On the streets and subways, he instinctively retreated behind the glass-eyed stare found only on big-city avenues, cultivating the essential ability to look past thousands of passing faces and never see a single human feature. He kept his steps purposeful and direct, his destination well defined and carefully plotted for the most direct route. Casual strolling was the mark of the tourist, easy prey for the beggars, the muggers, and the con artists with their nefarious schemes who inhabit the city streets.

He created a wall around himself, making his own personal space amid the constant press of the jostling crowds. He found, later, that he had also walled off a part of himself in the process.

Neil's rural relocation came as a rather drastic shock. He had dreamed of the slow pace, the friendly people, and the absence of crowds and crime. What he discovered was that the reality of that dream took time and acclimation.

Slow Down

The simplest and most difficult advice you will receive is to slow down. Small towns operate at a pace that is slower than that of a large city, and you will have to adjust your own internal pacing mechanisms to accommodate this slower lifestyle. The bank teller may take a little longer with a customer because she's showing him a picture of her new puppy. The butcher keeps you waiting a moment while he checks the back freezer to find a special cut of beef for a customer's dinner party.

In many parts of the rural United States, such as Oregon or Pennsylvania, you will probably find a business closed or a serviceperson unavailable at the start of hunting season. Stores in a small Vermont town may not open after a heavy snow if the owner simply doesn't feel like getting out early with a snow shovel.

As you travel around town, stop and relax. Pay attention to what is around you—really see the mountains and the trees. Feel what it is that gives your chosen town its particular ambiance, You will start slowing down on your own accord. This is, after all, one of the main reasons you moved in the first place.

Avoid Aggressive Behavior

Part of the slowing down process also involves the avoidance of aggressive behavior. Yelling at the teller with the puppy portrait won't get you faster service, but it will earn you a disdainful look and a none-too-softly muttered "damned Californian" or "damned New Yorker" or "damned foreigner." It is not that small town people are not aggressive or impatient. Their pace allows them the luxury of refining their aggressiveness into a less overt—some might say less obnoxious—form of expression. It may be a sigh, a tapping of the fingers, even an impatient look, but rarely much more.

Remember that this was their town before it was yours. It's up to you to adjust to the local pace and customs. Coming on too strong is simply going to offend people, and that is certainly the last thing you want to do in a new and smaller community where your actions may be subject to a little more scrutiny than they were in a large city.

While a certain amount of aggressive behavior is sometimes necessary in life, it has its place. The pressures and fast pace of a big city existence can bring aggressiveness to the forefront of your behavior and may even be necessary to be able to compete and survive in that environment. If, after you have removed yourself from the city and have chosen a slower, more bucolic way of life, your aggressiveness persists, this may indicate other stresses at work in your life.

Avoid "Small-Town Stereotyping"

One of the worst behavioral mistakes you can make is assuming that you, the former big-city dweller, are on a higher evolutionary plane than your small-town neighbors. In surveying a variety of dropouts, some took the attitude of having to overcome the "small-town mentality" or the "rural ignorance." They talked of "uneducated locals," and complained that "for really good products or services, you have to go to a big city."

There are uneducated people in small towns, and there are people who are ignorant of all the social graces. There are bigots, racists and arrogant know-it-alls of all shapes and sizes, as well as plenty of basic, plain fools. Not surprisingly, it's just like the big city in that respect.

Every city and town the world over, regardless of size, has its share of misfits and undesirables and those with whom, for whatever reason, you would just as soon not associate. To assume that ignorance and lack of sophistication is something you have to automatically accept in a small town is to sell that town and its people short.

Every small town, like every big city, has a purely wonderful cross-section of warm and witty people, of artisans and craftsman, of just plain good folks. There are great restaurants and meticulous builders, professors and Ph.D.s, good music and terrific live theater. These people are your equals, and you are theirs. There is no reason to be condescending or arrogant. These are two common complaints voiced over and over by locals in towns that have seen an influx of urban dropouts.

A Different Perspective On Money

Money is no yardstick of a person's worth, either. If you come from a world of six-figure incomes, so what? You will find that most people in smaller towns are much more willing to judge you for yourself rather than for your wealth.

Money is necessary, and the ruralite appreciates, respects, and desires it just as much as anyone. They are not as likely to center their entire life around it, however. You will not be considered a more worthwhile person just because you happen to possess more money than they do.

If you have a bank account when you move, it is certainly to your advantage. Money makes the move easier, and allows you more options for how you choose to live your life. There is no need to hide your money or to give it away; simply avoid thinking that having it and flaunting it will give you instant respect, acceptance, and credibility. That—like your money—will have to be earned.

Accentuate the Positive

As discussed in Chapter Two, there are some personality traits that, while not assuring a successful relocation, can help you prepare for and execute the move. It will be advantageous to list a few of those again, to help smooth the after-move adjustment.

During surveys and interviews successful and non-successful urban dropouts, certain key words and phrases kept recurring as traits that they felt were important and even essential in making a successful move. These traits comprise three basic aspects that we all possess to some degree, but may not always fully exercise.

Take a few insightful moments to explore your own thinking. Discover how and where your attitude and your way of doing things might reflect these three important traits. Ask yourself how you might accentuate these traits even further to make your relocation adjustment easier:

1) Flexibility: This word comes up over and over again when talking with any urban dropout—the need to be flexible in what you want to do and what you want to achieve. If you demand and fully expect your new town be Utopia, it will most assuredly disappoint you. If you have rigid guidelines how you expect to establish a new business or exactly the type of employment you will accept, you probably will find these strict guidelines troublesome.

Start with the simple premise that your new town is not your old one—and don't lose sight that you really don't want it to be. With that elementary thought, it is a short and logical next step to realize that some adjustments will have to be made to accommodate the altered conditions present after the move, and to continue this in future developments. Your new business may need to make adjustments in inventory to accommodate local tastes and trends. You may need to change the way you build houses to allow for climate, soil conditions, or the availability of lumber. How you cater a dinner party will reflect local foods and lifestyles. You may not find employment in an aerospace company in your new town, but your engineering background may be just what a local agricultural research firm is seeking.

A number of dropouts are now working in jobs they had long dreamt about—and in some cases had never even heard. Some now own businesses even though they never had any intention to do so, while others—long-time shop owners—are consultants. Be flexible about what you want and what you can do, and be open to the opportunities and possibilities that surround you.

2) Realism: As important as being flexible is the need to be realistic. Don't look for things that simply don't exist, and don't try to make things what they aren't. Nick and Louise's situation offered earlier in the chapter gave a perfect example of how unrealistically-high expectations about the relocation or the new town can lead to disappointment and even bitterness.

Moving to a small town and escaping the rat race of fast-track city living is a positive thing, a change you have consciously made to improve your life. Early acceptance that some aspects of your new town won't be perfect—nothing ever is and no place ever will be—is realistic. Expect good things, a good life, and a change for the better, but don't expect perfection. That one simple attitude adjustment will make the relocation considerably easier, and allow you to accept all the wondrous aspects of your new home that *are* real.

3) Optimism: A positive, optimistic attitude is the third trait to work. You will find that positive thinking can make positive things happen.

9

Quality of Life

If one advances confidently in the direction of his dreams, and endeavors to live the life which he has imagined, he will meet with a success unexpected in common hours.

—Henry David Thoreau
Walden

Many things about relocation can be calculated, priced out, and studied with an objective and analytical eye—the cost of a new home or land, the difference in wages at a new job, the cost of buying or starting a business, the savings each month in not having to commute or pay for parking. But what of those more elusive, subjective things that do not have a price tag, that can not be quantified, or fit into neat categories on a balance sheet? What is the real value to be placed on that often-mentioned, often-misunderstood or underestimated intangible called "Quality of Life?"

Ask ten different dropouts about quality of life, and you

will probably get ten different answers. What constitutes an improvement in lifestyle for one person may be unimportant, or even a move in the wrong direction, for someone else. But talk with those ten people long enough, and you will find a number of similarities, goals which they were all seeking to accomplish when they moved, things that virtually all have discovered.

In the final analysis, the hope of a better-quality life has prompted every dropout to finally make the commitment, give up a modicum of security and move toward the rural countryside. This amorphous value called quality of life is so important that we decided to pose that question to a number of established dropouts and dropouts-to-be. They told us what they were seeking and what they had found. Their answers are presented on the following pages.

What you are ultimately seeking may well be different, as may be what you eventually find. And while we can not always tell you what to expect, we can tell you what others have found. We can also tell you, with the enthusiastic agreement of dropouts everywhere, that a better life really *is* out there.

LESS STRESS

Given the extremely fast pace of today's typical lifestyle, it is not surprising that the need to get away from the stress and pressure of city life was the most frequently-cited reason for moving. Over and over again, we heard terms and descriptions such as "I was suffocating," "It was like living inside a pressure cooker," "I had to force myself to find time to relax and, even then, I never really could," or "My doctor said to do something about my high blood pressure—now—or a heart attack was simply a matter of time."

Reducing the stress of a fast-track city lifestyle is all well and good, but is just making the move enough? Dropping out is not necessarily a magic cure-all for every form of stress or stressful situation. You need to look first at your lifestyle to ascertain what constitutes stress in your life today. How would the move change that? Here are the most frequently cited *causes* of stress among people with whom we have spoken:

Lack of Time: It does not matter who you are, where you live, or how much money you have in the bank. There are still only twenty four hours in the day. Fill that space with twenty *five* hours worth of activities, and you have the most commonly-cited cause of constant, killing stress—not enough time.

This is a composite of a typical week among our survey respondents, before dropping out:

Monday: Rise at 5:00 a.m. Gather papers worked on last night. Shower, breakfast consisting of two cups of coffee. In car by 6:00 a.m. for ninety-minute drive to office. At work by 7:30 a.m. Meetings scheduled until noon. Working lunch at desk. Meetings and phone calls constant all afternoon. leave work at 6:00 p.m. Ninety-minute commute home. Stop at grocery shop. Home by 8:00 p.m. Quick dinner alone (kids have already eaten). Help kids with homework until 9:30 p.m. Review contracts for morning meeting. In bed by 11:30 p.m.

Tuesday—Friday: Variations on the same theme.

Saturday: Up at 6:00 a.m., hurried breakfast. At gym by 7:30 a.m., in line behind several others to use equipment. Stop at hardware store, cleaners, mechanic, library, and vet. Home by 3:30 p.m. Repair kitchen faucet, mow lawn. Fast-food dinner at 6:30 p.m., then to elementary school play at 7:30 p.m. Home by 9:00 p.m., asleep in front of television set by 10:00 p.m.

Sunday: Breakfast with family planned, but kids already

gone for various activities. Drive to office to pick up papers, work on computer for two hours while office is quiet. Home by 3:00 p.m. Dress for barbecue at co-workers house at 4:00 p.m. Home by 9:00 p.m. More paperwork for Monday breakfast meeting. Asleep at midnight.

A composite—yes. Unrealistic—not at all. Weeks like this are very typical, as today's couples fight to find time for work, time for home, time for family, time for each other and time for themselves.

Time is that most precious of commodities. We each have a finite amount, and we each need to make the decision for ourselves as to how we will spend it. For most people it is here, in this decision-making process and in the realization that a change definitely needs to be made, that relocation becomes so important.

A rural environment allows you many more options about how to spend your time because, quite simply, it allows you more time to spend. Driving times to and from work are much shorter. Just think what it would mean to you if you suddenly were given back two or three hours out of each work day. Stores are more centrally located, and grouped within a smaller traveling distance. Lines, if they exist at all, are shorter, and you'll find yourself running five or six errands in the time you used to spend trying to accomplish one.

Just as you will find yourself with more time for others; you will find others having more time for you. You doctor will be more willing to talk with you about non-specific aches and pains; the contractor will have the time to discuss your remodeling plans in more detail; the waitress will be around more frequently to refill your coffee cup.

Slower Pace of Life: A slower pace leads naturally to a less stressful existence. The rural environment is not one of fighting for a taxi or rushing to a store before it is crowded with other shoppers. There is time to chat with people and to do a little window shopping. Simply put, there are less people competing for available services; whether it be parking places, seats in a theatre, tables in a restaurant, or just space on the sidewalk. In a small town, you can go to dinner and a movie on a whim—and you will actually find a table at the restaurant and have plenty of time remaining to get to the theatre.

Reduced competition is also apparent in the workplace. Most offices are more relaxed and casual. There is still ambition, drive and the desire to succeed, but the small-town has discovered that money isn't everything. The result is a different attitude, where you do not feel the need to protect your position from an ambitious colleague in your office.

NATURE AND THE ENVIRONMENT

Second on virtually every dropout's wish list is the desire for clean air and clean water. While all of us, hopefully, are becoming more aware of the damage we are doing to the world's ecosystem, it is not everyday conversation for most people, particularly in the city. Surprisingly, many people are bothered by their environmental surroundings. They may not talk much about it, preferring to adopt a pseudo-humorous attitude about liking to breathe air they can see, but, over and over again, dropouts cited the need for a cleaner environment as a major factor in their moving plans.

Smaller towns offer much lower concentrations of industry and automobiles, the two worst air polluters. There are fewer buildings and more open land in and around the town, which allows for cool, fresh winds to circulate. There are more trees, supplying more oxygen and more shade.

Small towns have lower summer temperatures than their big city neighbors, simply because there are less heat-absorbing masses such as concrete and asphalt, resulting in more sunlight reflected rather than absorbed. A ninety degree day in the woods or in a grassy pasture feels vastly different from ninety degrees of sun-baked concrete amid swirling truck exhaust.

There is also a greater *awareness* of the environment in a rural area. People are closer to the land and are much more in tune with its cycles. This is especially true in agricultural areas, where a feel for the land and the environmental forces affecting it can mean the difference between profit and loss. This is a pervasive feeling in almost all rural and semi-rural areas. People in smaller communities know what they have, and take steps to preserve their environment.

In states with heavily timber-based economics, there are strong laws protecting the forests. This is especially true for states whose economic base relies heavily on tourism. While the root of these laws are monetary, and were initially placed on the books for economic protection, they benefit us all by limiting growth and preserving scenic areas and the natural beauty of the regions involved.

Recreation: Part of the attraction in many rural and semi-rural areas is the abundance of recreational activities. No longer do you need to force yourself to relax, to try and schedule fifteen minutes into your day for a hobby, or to find temporary solace on an exercise bike or in a crowded downtown gym or health club. Relaxation and recreation simply become a part of your life.

No matter what you enjoy doing, a community exists where it abounds. If you settle in a mountain resort where skiing is twenty minutes away, you can squeeze a few runs into a leisurely half-day instead of having to plan an entire weekend outing. When the snow melts, fishing is excellent in clear, cold, high-mountain lakes, or perhaps hiking among the fresh scent of the thick pines will fulfill your recreational needs.

How about horseback riding along deserted country trails, or a walk along a beach that isn't knee-deep in people, or golf on a clean, quiet course, or being able to spend more time actually playing tennis instead of just waiting for a court?

For those of us with more sedentary tastes, there is quiet and solitude and the time for these pursuits as well. A spring afternoon under a tree reading a book, having time to write or play the piano, lazy winter evenings working on a model train layout or playing cribbage in front of the fireplace become joyous occasions of peaceful solace.

Wildlife: Rural areas allow a unique opportunity to experience the natural beauty of birds and animals. What can compare with watching a herd of deer graze just outside your windows, or seeing a flock of snow geese flying overhead in noisy formation? A fresh overnight snowfall can reveal an amazing collection of tracks the next morning.

Being in touch with the wild, natural surroundings of our world is important to our understanding of how delicate this balance is; but we still continue to tip the scales in an unfavorable direction. There is a tremendous sense of tranquility in being an observer and to better understand our place in the world's natural order.

SAFETY

Safety is the third reason most dropouts give as their need or desire to move. They are disgusted with the high crime rates in the cities, and decide that living behind triple-locked doors is no way to enjoy life.

Crime is an unfortunate part of life everywhere, even in the smallest of communities, and most likely always will be. But, truthfully, most rural areas average *one third* less crime per capita as do the big cities. And the more isolated the community is from the city—a small mountain or farming town, for example, as opposed to a suburban community—the more those crime figures improve.

Few things compare with the feeling of security in your home and in your town. Dropouts talk about how pleasant it is to take an evening walk around the neighborhood, or to leave the bedroom windows open at night to catch the breeze. Store owners report far fewer incidences of shoplifting and vandalism than they experienced in cities, and talk about how their own employees are much more honest.

A secure community has other benefits as well. Insurance on your home and car is lower because the chance of theft or vandalism is much lower. There are far fewer security cameras, one-way mirrors and store detectives in stores and malls. Shopping becomes a pleasant experience, and each customer granted a little more trust by the store owner tends to show that trust is justified—a sort of self-fulfilling cycle from which everyone benefits.

But crime is only one aspect of the overall safety picture. Smaller communities mean fewer cars and a decrease in traffic congestion. This results in a drop in the percentage of auto accidents per miles driven in small towns as opposed to larger cities. Along with the obvious peace of mind this brings, there is the added benefit of lower auto insurance rates.

Rural communities and small towns typically maintain excellent police and fire departments. There is a sense of pride in these organizations that is much more apparent in small communities than in large cities. There are also fewer calls to which to respond, resulting in faster response times, and crews that are willing and able to spend more time at the scene.

A SENSE OF COMMUNITY

If you grew up in the insular isolation of the city, alone in huge crowds, you will be very pleasantly surprised to discover what makes a true community. For those of you with small-town roots, the loss of that feeling of community pride and involvement during your years in the city may shock you.

Few people with whom we spoke over the years would list a "sense of community" as a motivating pre-move factor in their decision to relocate. This never enters most people's minds because they never had a community sense, so they don't know what they have missed. But those same people a few years *after* the move will talk in glowing phrases about the wonderful feeling being involved in a community and being a part of something as familiar and as wonderful as a town about which one truly cares.

Comments heard quite frequently are "I felt like I had finally come home" and "Now I know what it's like to finally have a 'home town'." True, it may seem a little corny, but many dropouts feel more attached to their new community and more at home there after six months or a year than they ever felt about the city where they had lived for twenty years.

What exactly is a "sense of community?" Here again, like "quality of life" in general, it is a feeling that is unique to each individual and, at the same time, common to everyone; it is a question we have posed on a number of occasions to a diverse group of dropouts in small towns and cities in different parts of the country. Here are some of the comments:

> "After living in New York and San Francisco, we found small town living just great! We liked the feeling of belonging to a community and running into people you know. We liked the friendliness and the helpfulness. We also found it easier to socialize—everyone is close by. Also, our business flourished in an environment where we could attract the right type of employee and our expenses were considerably less."
>
> —*Terry Dwyer*

"The people here are warm and friendly, and there's always someone nearby willing to lend a hand."

—*Hope Stevenson*

"What's a community? It's honesty, integrity, inner peace, clear air, and a sense of responsibility. At least, that's what it's been for me."

—*Jeff Atkinson*

"I love walking down the street and saying Hi to people you know. I like to walk into a store and be recognized and remembered. I like the feeling that I can be myself here and be accepted for that."

—*Steve Manina*

"The people are just friendlier in a small town. Most of them are here because they want to be here, and so they care about the community and each other. There's a much more positive feeling in the air."

—*Rose Long*

"Coming from Los Angeles, I can't believe the difference here. I walk places—at night, even—and it seems like there's always someone to say hi to. And you always feel that no matter what the situation, there's a neighbor—or even a complete stranger—that's willing to help."

—*Joy Ewing*

"The town is so much more real, very few superficial people. I don't feel the need to compete—as long as I'm honest with people, I'm accepted."

—*Bill Coyster*

"It's easier to be a part of things here, to feel like you make a difference and have a positive impact on the town and the people in your life. A small town has a sense of 'human scale' to it."

—*Wes Kyley*

For most people, a sense of community is best equated with a sense of belonging—perhaps for the first time in their lives. Small communities are simply easier in which to get around and easier to know. Together with the slower pace, more free time, and friendlier people, becoming accepted and known in the community is much easier to attain than in a city.

There is a greater feeling of civic pride and knowing that your efforts make a difference. The streets are cleaner, the shops a little brighter, the parks more tranquil and inviting. A small community is also simply easier to manage, so community-wide events are easier to plan and execute. You will find more county fairs, more parades, more Fourth of July celebrations, more Christmas spirit and holiday festivities scheduled in your new town.

A community is about people: individuals with individual tastes and dreams who can come together and work as a whole. You walk into stores and see donation jars on the counters to raise money to help the victim of an accident or for a local citizen who needs an expensive operation. If your car stalls, you can always find someone who will stop and lend a hand. If the store you frequent doesn't have a particular item you require, the sales people won't hesitate to recommend a competitor.

All these examples go into the unique and satisfying feeling of what makes a community, and they tend to be self-perpetuating. A smile gets another in return; a kind gesture from a stranger makes you willing to return the favor to someone else.

RELATIONSHIPS

Among the other, more obvious improvements in lifestyle that are part of the relocation process—the clean air, lower crime rates, slower pace—there are other, more subtle changes happening. Here again, most people do not cite reasons such as more time with the kids or an improved sex life as major considerations for moving, but these reasons often accompany relocation as surely as do your boxes and suitcases.

Stress can kill a relationship just as it can kill a person. There are obvious symptoms, such as smoking or excessive drinking, or even drug dependency. And there are more subtle ones, like moodiness, depression, a shorter temper, and a lessened ability to be flexible and accommodating with one's spouse, children and co-workers. We do not prescribe relocation as a panacea for stress or relationship problems, but a change of surroundings and a slower pace of life have worked wonders for many of the couples and families we have interviewed.

Marriage: Every relationship, like the individuals at its core, is unique. It has its own rules, and functions—or doesn't function—according to its own special structure. Marriage, or any type of strongly-bonded relationship between two people, can suffer from lack of time, communication and intimacy.

Moving to a smaller, slower-paced community that results in changes in your lifestyle can have positive effects on a relationship. It can be a time of shared discovery about new surroundings and each other. There is time to talk and the opportunity to reestablish bonds. Many couples report that intimacy has become easier on different levels, because of the additional time they have for one another and the less hurried pace of their lives.

For couples who are retired, the positive effects of moving often offset the sense of loss that may accompany retirement. They have found new excitement and adventure, and opportunities to become involved in community activities.

Unfortunately, relocation can be tough on an already shaky relationship. Long hours at work and a busy lifestyle may be deliberate attempts to avoid intimacy and communication. Suddenly having more time and being moved closer to a spouse may spell death for the marriage. Only one survey respondent reported a divorce following relocation, and stated that the relationship was floundering well before the move.

On the brighter side, we spoke with numerous couples who reported that their marriages and relationships became stronger since the move. There is a feeling of shared adventure in a change of surroundings, and closer bonding that comes from the renewed need for one another in the face of a challenge.

Children: Relationships with children often benefit as well. More than one couple cited the need "to find a better environment to raise my children" as a prime reason for moving. None of these couples said they were disappointed with the move.

Time is probably the single most important factor of the other positive lifestyle changes that accompany the relocation. Children need time as they grow—time for your input and guidance, and time for your participation in their activities and accomplishments. Relocation can give you that needed time.

Children also benefit from healthier surroundings and positive peer influences. There are open spaces in which to roam, more opportunities to experience nature and to learn from these experiences. There is a greater sense of trust in a smaller community, and that trust becomes ingrained in many young people. Freely given, and freely accepted, children learn to make trust a part of their own makeup.

The influence and teaching of parents can only reach so far, and the moment the front door closes behind kids, the rest of the world takes control. It is a simple fact that the better the world is that your kids move about in, the better they will turn out. There are drugs in small communities to be sure, but there are far less available and far fewer kids using them than in a big city environment. The same is true for many other negative things to which children are exposed in the city.

Do not overlook the need for compassion and understanding with your kids when planning and executing the move. Make them aware of your plans from the beginning, and involve them in the planning and moving as soon as possible.

With infants, there are virtually no emotional problems associated with moving. Younger children are resilient, and, while leaving friends may be tough initially, they make new friends quickly. The move is often viewed as an adventure, and they bounce back fairly soon from the rigors of relocation. However, keep them reassured when they see things being packed that they are not being abandoned.

Older children, particularly teenagers, need to be handled differently. Since they identify more with their own social set than with the family, allow them to maintain relationships after the move. They should also be encouraged to seek out new friends and activities in their new town as soon as possible.

QUALITY IS IN THE EYE OF THE BEHOLDER

While we have touched on those changes that are most prevalent and most important to the people with whom we have spoken, there are, of course, a myriad of others that constitute "quality of life."

During our surveys and interviews, we always encouraged people to tell us why they moved. Their comments, diverse and light-hearted, tell the story best:

> "I've seen more of old friends since moving than I did when we lived in the same town."

"The hardest part of moving was just making the decision. We don't regret any of it—except that we should have done it sooner."

"We've found that while we make less money, we definitely spend less. Money also just doesn't seem as important now as it used to."

"I've found that getting involved in a small community is a lot easier than I had anticipated. The people are open and friendly, and I was able to volunteer with several local groups that really seemed to appreciate my input."

"Friends and family said we'd never make it in a small town—they're too closed and clannish. We found the opposite to be true—that small town people are less suspicious and judgmental than people in the city are. Now my sister and brother-in-law are moving, as well as an old neighbor of ours."

" 'Are you nuts! You're going to raise alfalfa? Isn't that the stuff they put in sandwiches?' That's what our friends said, and I probably would have made the same comment a few years back."

"I live on a farm, have a horse, and make a difference by showing others that it can be done. I am content!"

"I like living where other people vacation."

"Friends said, 'There won't be enough of a challenge for you.' Ha—try farming, I tell them."

"At first, we missed some of the 'city activities.' But you quickly realize that while they're nice to have, they don't constitute the day-to-day living of a life."

"We would definitely make the move again. It was hard to get started, but now that we're settled in and established, I know most people would kill for our lifestyle."

"I never realized how a small community would affect me. It's so much calmer and more serene here, and I've rediscovered how much the land means to me. I mean, after all, you can't plant tomatoes in Central Park."

10

Self-Satisfaction—The Ultimate Test

There is only one success—to be able to spend your life in your own way.

—Christopher Morley,
Where the Blue Begins

There is such simple truth and wisdom in the above words by Christopher Morley. To be a true success in life depends on doing and achieving what you want, and not what someone else might think is best for you. To live and act in your own way, to follow the directions that you set for yourself, despite the doubts of friends or relatives, is often a difficult undertaking, but becomes very important and worthwhile in the overall scheme of life.

No major relocation such as that discussed in this book

is ever undertaken and accomplished without some doubts and some problems. Perhaps because of these doubts and problems, your achievements in your newly-adopted home become all the sweeter. As the months and years after the move pass, there may remain the twinge of doubt or the inner question of "What would life have been like had I stayed in the city".

Perhaps you learn that friends or former co-workers are achieving money or fame far beyond your own. Could that have been you? Perhaps the occasional long-distance telephone call to close friends and relatives is not satisfying enough to overcome their absence.

All of these post-relocation feelings are perfectly natural and were expressed to some degree by virtually every dropout with which we spoke. As the survey results in Chapter Two concluded, however, rare indeed is the person who makes the relocation and later regrets it.

Essentially, the way to handle the occasional fleeting moments of doubt or regret is to revel in the self-satisfaction of having made the relocation, and the knowledge that it truly is a better way to live. There are other things you can do to help you feel better if and when the "rural blues" set in. During the first few months following the move, these points will help keep things in their proper perspective for you. A list of suggestions that have worked well for us and for other dropouts we've interviewed follows.

YOUR WANTS AND NEEDS LIST REVISITED

Remember the hours you spent agonizing over creating a "Wants and Needs" list, trying to grasp all your mixed feeling about moving and bringing them into order and focus? Now is a good time to go back into the file folders and review that list.

First, take a look back at what you were so dissatisfied with about your life in the city. Once a problem has been recognized and removed and we have had time away from it, quite often we tend to forget its original severity, and downplay or trivialize how important the problem was to us in the first place. Look at your notes. Allow yourself to remember a few of those problems and relive how bad some of them really were.

Picture yourself back in the five o'clock rush hour traffic, sitting on the steaming asphalt at a dead stop, surrounded by other scowling drivers as the heat and the noxious exhaust fumes envelope your car. Feel the frustration of standing in line behind fifteen people at the bank, or waiting almost three hours to be seated in a restaurant. Remember the mornings when you looked out your office window, and the buildings just a block or two away were indistinct in the shimmering brown haze of the sky.

Remember how you wanted to change all that? Remember how angry and stressed out you were, and how you felt that "there's got to be a better way" came out when you analyzed your feelings and your priorities for the move? Well, there is a better way, and you found it—revel in it—and give yourself a hearty pat on the back for having had the guts and the intelligence to make the move before it was too late.

DROPPING BACK IN

Would you like a better dose of the reality you left behind than what you can get from just your notes? Try dropping back in for a few days.

Dropping back in is a very frequent occurrence for people who have relocated, and it seems to follow a fairly common pattern. Within the first six months of having left the city, most people have already returned at least once. It's perfectly natural. After all, that was home for however many years, and it is still very familiar. These drop-ins talk about driving around the old neighborhoods, going by the beloved house they sold, and having dinner in a longtime favorite restaurant.

That first visit back can be tough for three underlying reasons. Being forewarned about them and understanding them should help you tremendously to deal with your feelings.

Your Perspective Has Changed: As you drive through your old city, things probably won't look as bad as they did when you lived there. Familiarity is a strong attraction, and it will tend to overshadow any bad feelings you had about the place. The difference is all in your perspective.

Every city has wonderful things to offer. We've vacationed in Manhattan, Boston, Los Angeles and a number of other big cities, and have always had a terrific time—but that doesn't mean we'd want to deal with the city on a day-to-day basis as a full-time resident. The enjoyment of a vacation is far, far different from having to deal with commuter traffic, rude people and long lines as part of a daily routine.

It is very important that you not lose sight of that as you drive or walk around. You will see things from the perspective of an outsider and there is a big difference between your experience as a visitor to the city and what you went through when you lived there.

Your New Home Is Not Familiar:—If you have not lived in your new community very long, it is probably still not very familiar to you, and going back to your old haunts seems to make things worse. You know the streets like the back of your hand, every building is familiar, even the corner grocery store seems like an old friend.

Familiarity is a strong attraction and the result is that the old ways of the city seem pretty good compared with the new ways of your recently-adopted community. Just don't loose sight of the fact that traffic jams and smog are familiar, too.

You Haven't "Made It" Yet: The third set of feelings you

may be faced with is that you haven't yet made your mark in your new community. Your former neighbor just got a promotion, your sister-in-law got a big raise, a former co-worker got the associate partnership for which you might have been in line. "And you?" they ask, and you mumble something about the new business struggling to get off the ground, or the adjustments you are having to make to a new job in a new office.

Once again, you are equating success with money. Ask your friend or your neighbor about the extra hours that went with the promotion, or how much higher the stress level became when the partnership came through.

So much for that first visit back. In the next year, our surveys often showed that most people do at least one more visit. In several cases, there was another visit the following year. This assumes that the city in question is not one you are visiting for business reasons on a regular basis. After the initial visits, the recurrence of trips back drops off sharply, with most people staying away for three years or more before returning again.

With each return visit, the city's patina of attraction wears increasingly thin. This again is the result of your attitude adjustment and a further change in your own perspective. After a year or two, your new town has become familiar, and you are well settled in. Conversely, the city is constantly changing, and, with each passing season, becomes less and less of a familiar old acquaintance and more of the looming mass of unsympathetic buildings and people that it really is.

POSITIVE UNDERTAKINGS

Another good way of dealing with some of the doubts surrounding your relocation is to undertake some positive actions on your own behalf. Do things that make you feel good and keep you active and involved. If you purchased an older home, the time to jump right in on remodeling and renovation is now. The work is good therapy, and just going to the lumber yard or calling an electrician will get you in touch with new people and new situations.

If you have acreage, start clearing it and get it ready for planting. Put your garden in, or build a new barn. Get involved with the kids at school, or volunteer with your church or community action agency to help in any way you can.

Any positive steps you take will make you feel much better about yourself and your surroundings, and that goes a long, long way toward getting you settled into your new community.

STATUS IN YOUR NEW COMMUNITY

One of the real joys of living in a smaller community is being recognized when you enter a bank or a restaurant, and getting that little extra bit of service that comes with being "a regular". That, of course, takes time to achieve, but it will happen much faster in a small town than it will in the city. Within a relatively short period, you will have achieved these small but important levels of status in your community, and it is a very satisfying feeling.

Status and recognition in other areas takes a little time also, but it will happen almost before you realize it. You attend a business meeting and are introduced to someone for the first time. They'll mention that they had heard your name and were looking forward to meeting you. You run into someone at the market and they mention that they remember your name on a volunteer list and are happy to meet you. Community involvement and the recognition that comes with it will help dispel any feelings of displacement and isolation in a relatively short time.

VISITORS, VISITORS

It is not at all uncommon for you to have a steady stream of visitors if you live in a resort community where people normally go to vacation. One fellow we spoke with jokingly complained that since he and his wife moved to the ocean, they see more of their friends and relatives than they did when they only lived ten miles away. Another couple added a guest bedroom and extra bath on to their house for all the people who want to come and visit.

Friends from far away are always a wonderful treat, and they are a great cure for the post-move blues. You can play tour guide around your new community, and listen to their expressions of wonderment as they see the beautiful area in which you've settled. You can't help but bask in a little well-meaning envy from your friends.

Another great possibility is to plan a big holiday celebration, or perhaps a family reunion. Having everyone over at your new house, especially for a white Christmas, will certainly help drive away the relocation blues.

CORRESPONDENCE

Letter writing is a good way to stay in touch with your old neighbors, and a lot less expensive than phone calls. It's also great therapy. You can begin with all those address changes that you didn't get to in the hectic days before the move. Buy some "We've Moved" cards, and sit down and write a personal note to your friends. It will also encourage them to call or write back, which is also a nice bonus.

Take some pictures of you and the family and the pets in front of your new house or in some perfectly pastoral setting, and have duplicates made. It's nice to include photographs with your letters, and this helps you generate positive feelings of self-satisfaction with your new situation.

At Christmastime, consider photographs again for your Christmas cards. You can also write a nice Christmas letter that updates everyone on your new home and the progress of your new life. The letters and the pictures can become a tradition for each holiday season.

CITY VISITS

Visiting the city for pleasure is different from dropping back in. This is especially true if you moved some distance away, and the nearest major city that you'll be visiting is not the one in which you used to live.

Virtually everyone with whom we have talked looks forward to long weekends or mini-vacations in the city. They reserve a hotel room, see a show, do some shopping in stores not accessible back home, and generally just play. For most people, a city trip once or twice a year is sufficient. In addition, the crowds and the stoplights are enough to remind you why you don't live there anymore.

As one young couple summed it up, "It's a whole lot better to have to leave the country occasionally and travel to the city for shopping and entertainment, than it is to have to travel out to the country just to find a serenity. We can always find somewhere to go shopping—but we'd much rather live with the peace and quiet."

OUR CONCLUSIONS

We talked with literally hundreds of dropouts over the years, and we have made the transition ourselves. They struggled some, we struggled some, and so, probably, will you. But in the end, for virtually all of us, it's been more than worth it.

Success is much more than monetary wealth. Quality of life is an intangible thing—it's not measured in dollars or fame or social standing, but rather in peace of mind and your own personal yardstick of self-worth. Old friends in the city may scoff from their uptown condos, but listen closely and you might hear an undercurrent of wistfulness and envy.

You're the real success.

Urban Transplant Readiness Survey

(Please rate each item)

When I was growing up:	Not Important		Somewhat Important		Very Important
I wanted to:					
1. • Be financially successful	☐	☐	☐	☐	☐
2. • Own my own business	☐	☐	☐	☐	☐
3. • Be a performer, entertainer or executive	☐	☐	☐	☐	☐
4. • Work on the land	☐	☐	☐	☐	☐
5. • Be recognized distinctly as an individual in my career area	☐	☐	☐	☐	☐
6. • Live in a low-population density non-urban area.	☐	☐	☐	☐	☐
7. • I primarily enjoyed outdoor activities	☐	☐	☐	☐	☐
	No		Mixed		Yes
8. • I grew up in a small town (under 50,000) or low density population area and had pleasurable experiences there.	☐	☐	☐	☐	☐
Add the check marks in each column	☐	☐	☐	☐	☐

Multiply by:	x 0	x1	x2	x3	x4
TOTALS	☐	☐	☐	☐	☐

Add the numbers from each box (☐):

CHILDHOOD EXPERIENCE GRAND TOTAL ☐

I would describe myself as:

		Least		Sometimes		Most
9.	• Adventurous	☐	☐	☐	☐	☐
10.	• Speedy	☐	☐	☐	☐	☐
11.	• Bold	☐	☐	☐	☐	☐
12.	• Convincing	☐	☐	☐	☐	☐
13.	• Independent	☐	☐	☐	☐	☐
14.	• Unhurried	☐	☐	☐	☐	☐
		Most		Sometimes		Least
15.	• Fussy	☐	☐	☐	☐	☐
16.	• Shy	☐	☐	☐	☐	☐
	Add the check marks in each column	☐	☐	☐	☐	☐
	Multiply by:	x 0	x1	x2	x3	x4
	TOTALS	☐	☐	☐	☐	☐

Add the numbers from each box (☐):

PERSONALITY STYLE GRAND TOTAL ☐

Currently I:

		No		Somewhat		Yes
17.	• Enjoy doing outdoor activities.	☐	☐	☐	☐	☐
18.	• Am skilled and educated for a					

	variety of work opportunities.	☐	☐	☐	☐	☐
19.	• Have a specific non-urban spot identified where I'd really like to live.	☐	☐	☐	☐	☐
20.	• Visit my special non-urban spot frequently (at least 2 to 3 times per year).	☐	☐	☐	☐	☐
21.	• Have at easy access savings available to live for at least one year.	☐	☐	☐	☐	☐
22.	• Can drop scheduled activities to sit down and talk with a friend or interested acquaintance.	☐	☐	☐	☐	☐
23.	• I do not know of any significant allergies or climate problems that would be made worse in the new location.	☐	☐	☐	☐	☐
24.	• Have talked at length with other "urban transplants" in my prospective community and have discussed their recommendations.	☐	☐	☐	☐	☐

Add the check marks in each column	☐	☐	☐	☐	☐
Multiply by: x 0		x1	x2	x3	x4
TOTALS	☐	☐	☐	☐	☐
Add the numbers from each box (☐):					

CURRENT ADULT SITUATION GRAND TOTAL ☐

My current needs:

		No		Somewhat		Yes
25.	• For achieving basic economic and/or career goals have been satisfied.	☐	☐	☐	☐	☐
26.	• Strongly focus on pursuing my spiritual/ philosophical needs more than economic or career achievement.	☐	☐	☐	☐	☐
27.	• Perceive the urban lifestyle as being hassled and intolerable.	☐	☐	☐	☐	☐
28.	• For accomplishing my personal goals or dreams would best be achieved by moving to this new location.	☐	☐	☐	☐	☐
29.	• Tell me that this is a good time to					

	move to this location.	☐	☐	☐	☐	☐
30.	• Would be for a simpler lifestyle.	☐	☐	☐	☐	☐
		Yes		Somewhat		No
31.	• May not be met; I am doing this to please someone else.	☐	☐	☐	☐	☐
32.	• Tell me there is(are) another location(s) to which I should also consider before making a final moving decision.	☐	☐	☐	☐	☐
	Add the check marks in each column	☐	☐	☐	☐	☐
	Multiply by: x 0		x1	x2	x3	x4
	TOTALS	☐	☐	☐	☐	☐

Add the numbers from each box (☐):

CURRENT NEEDS GRAND TOTAL ☐

When approaching change:

		Never		Sometimes		Always
33.	• I see opportunity in the midst of chaos.	☐	☐	☐	☐	☐
34.	• I have a strong need to control the events that are happening around me.	☐	☐	☐	☐	☐

35.	• I will do whatever it takes to keep the commitments I have made to myself and others.	☐	☐	☐	☐	☐
36.	• I look at people's different attitudes and mannerisms as a chance to understand something new about them and me.	☐	☐	☐	☐	☐
37.	• I recognize my role in creating or attracting to myself the unpleasant events in my life.	☐	☐	☐	☐	☐
38.	• I see that I am responsible for the successes I achieve.	☐	☐	☐	☐	☐
	Add the check marks in each column	☐	☐	☐	☐	☐
	Multiply by: x 0		x1	x2	x3	x4
	TOTALS	☐	☐	☐	☐	☐

Add the numbers from each box (☐):

CHANGE HARDINESS GRAND TOTAL ☐ x 2 = ☐

Mentally I can:

		Never		Sometimes		Always
39.	• See myself being happy, successful and involved in a non-urban community.	☐	☐	☐	☐	☐
40.	• I am willing to work at something other than what I am doing currently or for which I am specifically trained.	☐	☐	☐	☐	☐
41.	• See myself enjoying the ways of the people and doing business in this special place.	☐	☐	☐	☐	☐
42.	• See that the special spot I want to live in "has room" for a good person of my skill/profession.	☐	☐	☐	☐	☐
43.	• Be happy getting my cultural "city fix" in 2 to 3 times per year.	☐	☐	☐	☐	☐
44.	• Have my needs for world and national news met in the new site.	☐	☐	☐	☐	☐
		No				Yes
45.	• Handle being initially black-balled from this new community	☐	☐	☐	☐	☐

46.	• Understand what kind of first impression I will make on the new community.	☐	☐	☐	☐	☐
47.	• Drop or modify my urban habits and status symbols, if necessary to "fit in."	☐	☐	☐	☐	☐
48.	• Cut back my lifestyle economically for 3–5 years if necessary.	☐	☐	☐	☐	☐
	Add the check marks in each column	☐	☐	☐	☐	☐
	Multiply by:	x 0	x1	x2	x3	x4
	TOTALS	☐	☐	☐	☐	☐

Add the numbers from each box (☐):

MENTAL PREPARATION GRAND TOTAL ☐

In my family:

		No or N/A				Yes
49.	• My spouse wants to move to a non-urban setting.	☐	☐	☐	☐	☐
50.	• My children want to move to a non-urban setting.	☐	☐	☐	☐	☐
51.	• My children would adapt and not feel					

	uprooted by moving at this time.	☐	☐	☐	☐	☐
52.	• My children are or will be in junior or senior high school at the time of the move	☐	☐	☐	☐	☐
53.	• My spouse would have a fulltime equivalent activity to occupy his/her time in the new location.	☐	☐	☐	☐	☐
54.	• I do not have children living at home	☐	☐	☐	☐	☐
		yes		somewhat		no
55.	• I am single, without a significant other	☐	☐	☐	☐	☐
56.	• I live alone and would live in the non-urban area by myself.	☐	☐	☐	☐	☐
	Add the check marks in each column	☐	☐	☐	☐	☐
	Multiply by:	x 0	x1	x2	x3	x4
	TOTALS	☐	☐	☐	☐	☐

Add the numbers from each box (☐):

FAMILY SUPPORT GRAND TOTAL ☐

URBAN TRANSPLANT READINESS SUMMARY:

Childhood Experiences	☐
Personality Style	☐
Current Adult Situation	☐
Current Needs	☐
Change Hardiness	☐
Mental Preparation	☐
Family Support	☐
TOTAL READINESS	☐

Scoring Interpretation:

200+	Do it!
170–199	Go for it!
150–169	Why not, it might be great!
130–149	Perhaps a bit premature . . .
100–129	Hmm . . . Have you really thought about it?!
60–99	Probably not a great idea . . .
under 60	Don't even think about contacting a moving company!

Basic Survey Demographics

95 Surveys mailed out January, 1990
42 Survey respondents January to March 1990
44 % return rate

From Metro Areas in:	
Southwest, So. Calif.	8
East Coast	3
Midwest	3
Rockies	6
Northern California & NW	16
Texas	2
Florida	1
Europe	1
Unknown	2

	42

MOVING DATES	
Pre 1975	5
1975 to 79	8
1980 to 84	15
1985 to 89	8

AGE AT TIME OF MOVE	
25 to 29	3
30 to 34	12
35 to 39	5
40 to 44	12
45 to 55	2
55 plus	5

Gender	
Males	27
Females	15

Pre-Move Careers			
Managers	10	Retired	2
Own business	5	Physician	1
Sales	3	Designer	1
Housewife	3	Graduate Student	1
Consultant	3	Contractor	1
Teacher	2	Accountant	1
Staff position with large corporation	2	Buyer	1
Unknown	6		

SUGGESTED CHARACTERISTICS TO BE SUCCESSFUL

Ability to adapt to change and roll with the punches.	20
Get along with all types of people, especially members and small town mind set and willingness to give to community.	16
Positive attitude: belief you can do anything, self-confidence, look to the future outlook and sense of wanting to control destiny and happiness	16
Diverse base of skills (already having experience and/or education needed to do a variety of income producing activities including running a business and love of hard work.	15
Be adventurous, enjoy risk-taking, be a self-starter, independent	13
Be outgoing and not shy, get involved quickly.	10
Prior familiarity with less urban lifestyles, have willingness to do with less or limit your expectations	9
Perspective, patience and a sense of humor, perseverance	8
Good marriage with supportive spouse, children grade school and younger.	5
Love of new area and associated activities of the community (sports, interests, etc.).	5
Substantial savings.	3
Good health.	2

PERSONALITY FACTORS

TRAIT SUMMARY N = 37 respondents

Natural Style Controlling 31/37 respondents 84%

Description:

. . . Are Known To Be:	. . In A Resistant State Can Be:
• Risk takers, take initiative	• Critical of others' inaction • Fighters, when they don't get own way

- Action and success oriented
- Ring leaders
- Forceful and often confronting
- Decisive, outcome oriented
- Self confident
- Resentful of close supervision
- Intolerant of incompetence

- Domineering, steamrollers

. . Want In Their Environment:

- Challenge and problems to solve
- Opportunity to succeed
- Control over important tasks
- Tangible rewards

Natural Style Outgoing 27/37 73%

Description:.

. . . Are Known To Be:

- Persuasive, good communicators
- Helpful, volunteer to help
- Socially well-adapted
- Expressive, dramatic, enthusiastic
- Good delegators
- Sensitive to people's feelings
- Crowd pleasers: need approval
- Team-oriented, like co-directing

. . .In A Resistant State Can Be:

- Indecisive, no direct answers
- Verbally abusive, exaggerating
- run away from difficulties

. . Want In The Environment:

- Opportunity to improve lifestyle
- To be friends with those admired
- Monetary/tangible rewards
- Praise and public acceptance

Natural Style Urgent 23/37 62%

Description:.

. . . Are Known To Be:

- Action-oriented
- Quick to react
- Eager to start projects
- Good at forcing decision making
- Overzealous in projecting completion times
- Involved with several activities at the same time

. . In A Resistant State Can Be:

- Abrupt
- Uncompassionate of feelings
- Wired or coilspring in reaction

. . Want In Their Environment:

- Frequent change of scenery and activity
- Instant results
- Freedom from waiting

Natural Style Generalizing 27/37 73%

Description:

. . . Are Known To Be:

- Concerned with the whole,
- not necessarily the parts
- Good at laughing at themselves
- Productive brainstormers
- Incorrigible, outspoken, inventive,
- not bound to past
- Independent
- Not bound by tradition or structure

. . In A Resistant State Can Be:

- Unable to document or prove
- original assumptions
- Prone to brush off seriousness
- of situations
- Flippant

. . .Want In Their Environment

- Freedom to do "own thing"
- Independence from structure
- Brief updates from others to scan activities

TRAIT COMBINATION ANALYSIS

Systematic Problem Solver	14	38%:	use step-by step, analytical linear logic
Innovative Problem Solver	15	41%:	use intuitive, big picture, non-linear logic
Balanced Problem Solvers	8	20%:	use a balance of intuition and analytical logic
Proactive **	30	81%:	self-starters, initiate projects well, growth and potential oriented
Responsive	3	8%:	follow established stystems, cautious, prefer to follow proven protocol
Balanced between initiating and finishing	4	11%:	are balanced between initiating and project and following directions given by others
Definite	11	30%:	outcome, end results oriented
Open-ended	1	11%:	process or means oriented and like to leave options open and have alternatives
Balanced definite/** open-ended***	22	59%:	are balanced between achieving an outcome and managing the process to get there; remaining flexible in how the end result is achieved

Objective Communicator	15	40%:	use factual, direct, to-the-point style of communicating
Personal Communicator	8	22%:	use an empathic, persuasive, feeling style of communicating
Balanced Communicator	14	38%:	use a balance of objectivity and personal sensitivity in communicating

AS CHILDREN

BORN IN TOWNS:

POPULATIONS		Number of Respondents
	Under 50 K	11
	Under 250 K	3
	Under 500 K	7
	1/2 to 1 million	7
	1 to 2 million	5
	2 to 5 million	3
	5 million plus	6
	unknown	*4*

HOBBIES:

Sports (team and individual)	27
Outdoors Activities	22
Performing Arts	5
Domestic Activities	4

WANTED TO BE:

Financially Successful	12
Own my own business	10
Performer / entertainer	9

Farmer / rancher		5
Top Executive		5
Teacher		4
Forest Ranger		3
Physician		3
Pro Athlete		3
Writer		2
Pilot		2
Fashion Designer		2
Engineer		1
Accountant		1
Scientist		1

AS CHILDREN

IDEAL LOCATION:

Low density populated special spot		27
Mountains	9	
Small Town or country living	5	
Ranch	5	
Beach/Ocean	4	
Resort	3	
Big City		5
Away! (California, Europe, Hawaii)		3
No response		7

POSITIVE EXPERIENCE IN HOME TOWN

YES	41
NO	1

AS ADULTS

CURRENT HOBBIES:

Sports: Golf/Skiing/etc	23

Outdoors: Hiking/ Fishing/Camping	15
Water sports	12
Photography	4
Reading	3
Music	2

Did the move help you to accomplish your dreams?	
YES	37
NO	5
N/A	1

DREAMS ACHIEVED BY MOVING	
Hobbies	22
Location	17
Opportunity for Success	12
Outdoor activities	12
Job	10
Own business	9
Miscellaneous Interests	5
Family	3
Goals changed	2

KEY CONSIDERATIONS IN MAKING THE MOVE

ITEM	NUMBER	COMMENTS	
Quality of Life	42	Less populated density	(4)
		Less traffic	(5)
		Less crime	(4)
		Slower pace	(3)
Environment	2	Air quality	(9)
		Outdoors	(4)
		Climate	(2)

Psychological	19	Less stress	(8)
		Inner peace	(2)
		Needed support during new phase of life (divorce, etc)	(3)
Family	18	Ability to spend time	(2)
		Quality place to raise family	(8)
Emotional	15	Feels good here	(2)
		Stability	
Financial	13	Lower cost of living (especially housing)	(5)
		New job opportunity	(3)
		Place to start business	(4)
		Dollars go further in new town	(2)
Friends	8	Real friendship	(2)
		Had friends already	(3)
		Friendlier communication	(2)
		Only 1 negative	
Education	2		
Travel Accessibility	2		

Living with children during the move	15/42	(36%)
under 5 years old 5		
5 to 12 years old 5		
13 to 19 years old 5		
No children at home during the move	27/42	(64%)
Living with children 3–5 years after move	19/42	(45%)
No children at home 3–5 years after move	23/42	(55%)

MARITAL STATUS

During the move		3 to 5 years after the move	
Married*	37	Married**	35
Divorced	2	Divorced***	6
Single	3	Single	1
* 3 noted as "shaky"		** 2 singles married	
		*** 2 of 3 "shaky" plus 2 others	

INCOME

	Prior to the move
$10,000 or less	3
10 to 20,000	6
20 to 50,000	10
50 to 100,000	12
100 to 150,000	4
150 to 250,000	1
250,000 plus	3

NOTE: "Dollars go further in smaller town."

PLANNING FOR MOVE

HOW LONG DID YOU PLAN PRIOR TO MOVE

Timeframe	Number		
Less than 3 months	6	less than 1 year	17
3 to 6 months	5		
6 to 12 months	6		
12 to 18 months	4	1 to 2 years	8
18 to 24 months	4		
2 to 3 years	4	2 to 7 years	12
3 to 5 years	3		
5 to 7 years	5		

REACTION OF FRIENDS TO MOVE

Mixed	16	"You'll be back within the year"	(9)
		"You're crazy	(7)
Skeptical	12	Not enough challenge	
		No money there	
Positive	11	Go for it	
		Envious	
		Didn't understand why or know area	

RELATIVES REACTIONS TO MOVE

Supportive	17	"We're coming too"	(2)
		"Go for it!"	(2)
		Envious	(1)
Mixed	13	Worried about professional opportunities and finances	(5)
		Hoped for the best	(2)
Skeptical	11	"You're crazy"	(4)
		One spouse's family positive, other negative	(4)

SAVINGS AVAILABLE FOR MOVE

Very limited	7	
3 to 12 months	8	
12 to 18 months	7	
Substantial (2 to 3 years)	6	63% more than one year
Significant savings back-up	4	
Didn't need to work or retired/pension	8	
Unknown	*2*	

PLANNING FOR THE MOVE

PROCESS USED IN DECIDING TO MOVE

Researched Livability 26 respondents
• Schools, taxes, people, population density, recreation, housing, cost of living, offering culture. Over half research area systematically, a few briefly or gut level decisions.

Personal Visits to Area 20 respondents
• Becoming more and more familiar with the area even buying property prior to move
• Most people mentioned recreating in area prior to move.
• Some discovered area by chance.

Researched Business Viability 8 respondents
• Market research for need of my business, airport accessibility, availability of qualified labor pool for my business, other employers should my work not go as planned.

Visited Several Areas Before Deciding on the One Selected	4
Job Offer	4
Family in New Location	4
Friends in New Location	4
No Choice, Business or Spouse's Job Required Relocation	4
Opportunity to make a difference in a community	3
Gut Level GO FOR IT	1

WHERE THEY MOVED	
Popular Small Towns in:	
W/Oregon, Washington	22
Colorado Rockies	7
Northern California	5
Idaho/UT/Rockies	3
Appalachia	1
New England	1
Unknown	*3*
	====
	42

CITY ACCESSIBILITY	
Less than 1 hour away	5
1 to 2 hours away	1
2 hours away	9
2 to 4 hours away	26
4 hours or more away	1
	====
	42

FAMILY MEMBERS IN THE SAME TOWN

	Before the move	3 to 5 years after the move
Parents	2	5
Siblings	3	5
Adult Children	0	1
Cousins	0	3
Grandparents	0	1

THE MOVE

EMPLOYMENT STATUS

Quit jobs	19
Sold business	4
Self employed	10
Retired	4
Married, not working	3
Finished school	1
Terminated	1

NEW LOCATION EMPLOYMENT STATUS

Started own business	16	Of those working, 76% were self employed
Continued self employment	10	
New Employer	9	
Bought new business	2	
Retired	5	

HOW DID YOU MOVE

		Comments
Self paid	41	Moving company (20) Self (21)
Company paid	1	

WERE YOU FRIGHTENED?

YES **18**

- Financial concerns (67 % of yes responses cited economic uncertainties)
- Change in general.
- Would have liked close family support.
- Job security and stability (not many employers).
- Social-cultural differences, wondered if they would fit in.
- Weather.

NO **17**

- We were young enough to start over if necessary.
- Never!

AFTER THE MOVE

FREQUENCY OF VISITS TO METROPOLITAN AREAS

1 time per week	3
2 times per month	4
1 time per month	10
1 time every 2 months	13
2 to 3 times per year	8
1 time per year	4

	42

Income Stability

	Prior to Move	1–2 years after	3–5 years after
$10,000 or less	3	3	0
10,000–20,000	6	11	2
20,000–50,000	10	12	11
50,000–100,000	12	8	12
100,000–150,000	4	0	9
150,000–250,000	1	1	5
250,000 or more	3	*2	2*
No response or n/a	*2*	*5*	*1*

Notes:* One retired

Number working 1–2 years after move:	34	
Drop in income during first 1–2 years	22	(65%)
(Experienced 50% or greater drop in income 11/22)		
No drop in income during first 1–2 years	12	(35%)
Retired or not working	8	
Number working 3–5 years after move	30	
Back at pre-move income within 3–5 years	26	(87%)

(Experienced 50% or greater increase in income 15/26)		
Continued drop in income	4	*(13%)
Retired or not working	8	
Insufficient data	3	

Notes:

* Two who experienced a continued drop in income even 3–5 years after the move were still making more than $100,000/year.

WOULD YOU DO IT AGAIN?

YES **40**

- Human scale when you get to know your neighbors.
- Risk is good for your soul.
- Sooner.
- Would have bought different business.
- It's great.
- Maybe different timing (recession hit right after move).

NO **2**

- Less than 1/2 income even 5 years after move.
- Would have moved to Oregon, not to Colorado.

AFTER THE MOVE

ADJUSTMENTS FOR FIRST YEAR

		Worse	Anticipated	Easier
Getting Home Settled				
	Yourself	3	29	10
	Spouse	7	15	9
	Children	4	9	5

NOTES:

- Tough move influenced future divorce, which was tough on kids
- Child care problem initially

- Junior high school age and older kids had tougher time with school adjustment.
- Missed living with my adult children.

Finding Employment			
Yourself	6	15	7
Spouse	6	11	4
Children	1	9	2

NOTES:

- Wife had to take "lesser" job; years later got right job.
- Good job market for minimum wage worker.
- Sales people can always find a way to make a living

Income Changes			
Yourself	11	17	9
Spouse	7	18	5
Children	1	7	

NOTE:

- Poor investments in new area initially (didn't know "terrritory").
- Money goes further in small town.
- Living on little growing up helped me prepare for income change.

Getting Involved in Community			
Yourself	3	12	27
Spouse	7	9	15
Children	2	6	7

NOTE:

- Husband's accent branded him as outsider.
- Job helped in community involvement.
- It's easier to get a handle on life blood in small community and make friends.

	Worse	Anticipated	Easier
Making New Friends			
Yourself	4	14	21
Spouse	3	9	22
Children	2	7	7

NOTE:
- Less to choose from.
- Single parents have tougher time.

ADJUSTMENTS FOR FIRST YEAR

	Worse	Anticipated	Easier
Pace			
Yourself	7	13	16
Spouse	8	12	12
Children	0	10	4

NOTE:
- Hard to unwind especially when starting a business.
- We worked harder initially, later smoothed out.
- No commuting is a time saver.

	Worse	Anticipated	Easier
Cultural Changes			
Yourself	5	21	12
Spouse	8	18	7
Children	0	12	4

NOTE:
- Occasionally missed intellectual stuff of Metromania.
- Different! Lack of convenience off set by beauty of nature and environment.

	Worse	Anticipated	Easier
Other Life Style			
Yourself	3	16	10
Spouse	4	15	3
Children	0	5	3

NOTE:
- Small town attitudes and negative thinking.
- Local people expect you to do business locally and will look down on being from outside.
- Living 7 miles outside of town hard on life.
- Male/female roles very conventional and defined.

Climate Changes

Yourself	4	16	19
Spouse	7	14	13
Children	1	10	5

NOTE:
- Cold is tougher to take.
- Altitude adjustment different.

Other Changes

Yourself	5	2	7
Spouse	2	3	3
Children	1		1

NOTE:
- Physical stress much tougher than anticipated, I was sick a lot.
- Business climate difficult to adjust to and understand.
- Tougher to adjust to socioeconomics as a single parent.
- Being home all day made it tough to fit in.
- Lived a more outdoor life, very enjoyable!
- It helps to be in an area where there are lots of other transplants.
- Made more <u>real</u> friends that I'd never anticipated.
- I feel I belong.
- People are so genuine and friendly.

RECOMMENDATIONS TO OTHERS

RECOMMENDATIONS

•Plan the pros and cons. Check employment, get chamber of commerce information	15
•Keep an open mind, stay positive and have fun in whatever you do. Volunteer or somehow get involved right away.	15
•Do it! And don't wait too long	9
•Know your needs.	7
•Visit location	6
•Understand the new areas mentality, economics, history, people and don't come across too strongly or as condescending.	5
•Bring your own job.	4
•Stay for the pay-off, have patience.	3
•Prepare to work hard if you need to support yourself.	2
•Make sure you're not running from something but moving towards something.	1